Cultural History and Modernity in Latin America

Technology and Culture in the Andes Region

CULTURAL *H*ISTORY AND MODERNITY IN *L*ATIN *A*MERICA

TECHNOLOGY AND CULTURE IN THE ANDES REGION

Constantin von Barloewen

Berghahn Books
Providence • Oxford

Published in 1995 by

Berghahn Books
Editorial offices:
165 Taber Avenue, Providence, RI 02906, USA
Bush House, Merewood Avenue, Oxford, OX3 8EF, UK

First published in German as
Kulturgeschichte und Modernität Lateinamerikas, 1992

Library of Congress Cataloging-in-Publication Data
Barloewen, Constantin von.
  [Kulturgeschichte und Modernität Lateinamerikas. English]
  History and modernity in Latin America: technology and culture
in the Andes Region/Constantin von Barloewen.
      p.   cm.
  Translation of: Kulturgeschichte und Modernität Lateinamerikas.
  Includes bibliographical references and index.
  ISBN 1-57181-012-9
  1. Latin America–Civilization–10th century. 2. Latin America–
Civilization–Philosophy. 3. Civilization, Modern–Philosophy.
4. Science–Social aspects–Andes Region. 5. Technology–Social
aspects–Andes Region. 6. Economic development–Social aspects.
I. Title.
F1414.2.B31513   1994   94-27020
980.03—dc20   CIP

British Library Cataloguing in Publication Data
A CIP catalogue record for this book is available from
the British Library.

Printed in the United States by
Princeton Academic Press, Princeton, NJ on permanent paper.

Contents

— ONE —

CULTURE IN THEORETICAL PERSPECTIVE

The Meaning of the Concept of Culture

The objective of this study is to show that the cultural identity of the Andes Pact states and the evolution of their cultural values must be reinforced to coincide with economic and technological factors. Only then can the states meet the prerequisites for long-term cooperative development. *These factors are decisive for the indigenous growth of a state, economy, society and culture, and for a necessary, holistic understanding of the overall phenomenon of technology transfer.* This approach is nourished by a respect for the variety of cultures in human evolution, as seen from the global standpoint of world civilization.

People cannot live without an identity, whether as individuals or in a larger group, such as a nation or culture. Their identity helps them to form an authentic view of themselves and imparts their *raison d'etre.* Any state and any culture that is indigenous is perforce authentic.

The concept of culture can be understood to mean the totality of a society's material and nonmaterial wisdom and practices, those without which it would cease to exist. Culture transmits existential frames of reference for meaning and significance. Negation, too, can harbor cultural truths. Nor can an economy become socially viable unless it projects our existential frames of reference.

Reality comes into being only through activities, and there must be points of convergence between reality and our symbols. Culture transmits knowledge capable of imparting meaning and governing human behavior, even economic behavior. This imparting of meaning determines the cultural identity of a country. Culture is an essential factor in the integration of personality, society and economy. Even processes of economic growth and technology transfer, if they are to have a lasting effect, must be tailored so as to be integrative in or compatible with culture. Otherwise, they run the risk of destroying or suppressing the ultimate source of meaning: culture.

No country can afford to gamble with its cultural identity in the race for technological advantages without sacrificing its own essence. This applies in particular to Latin America. An individual's cultural identity determines how life is viewed, whether that life is one's own or someone else's. To protect itself from the dangers of disintegration, every society must have a culture that is sufficiently consolidated. Culture is what comes about when human beings adapt to their surroundings; technology is a means with which they change these surroundings and adapt them to meet their needs.

Seen in this light, individuals must be perceived in relation to their family ties, as a part of nature, in their attitude toward the supernatural, their work ethic and their stance toward death. These are basic anthropological categories which also have far-reaching implications for economic development. It is the universal quality of cultural development in the evolutionary progress of humanity that is the key issue.

Cultural values determine our evolutionary social identity. They are the tools with which we consciously create change from our interpretation of the past and our links with the future. This study will demonstrate that scientific and technological development is unintelligible outside the context of culture. The point is not to insert culture into the international exchange of technology, but to realize that within this process culture is paramount.

Culture, as English-speaking anthropologists such as Clifford Geertz and Mary Douglas have proved, is a whole which cannot be divided into parts. It embraces all forms of social organization, the meaning of history, birth and death, the way we perceive our surroundings, and even the way we use technologies. As a holistic phenomenon, culture is evolutionary; it changes dynamically with the problems it confronts.

This study attempts to go beyond a Eurocentric approach to reach a dialogue between continents and cultures existing on a par. To understand Latin America, it is imperative to realize that one does not belong to a life community simply because one is born into it, but rather because one sees the world and all its comings and goings through the interpretive frameworks that prevail within that life community: namely, through culture.

There is an inherently productive dimension to the word "culture." From prehistoric times to our own, cultures have always been systems of signs. We can take culture to mean not only the totality of our institutions and ideas, but also the way we deal with simple, everyday tools and implements. Thus, culture is not only material (things) and institutional (social structures), but can also be viewed semiotically as consisting of signs (ideas, concepts). Ideas and concepts are connected with special moral and ethical notions, with politics, religion and aesthetics, and, not least of all, with economic processes. Castoriadis was able to show that every culture is capable of distinguishing between a functional and an imaginary level. Imagination plays a cardinal role in human history: as a culture produces images, it also produces symbols which serve as vehicles for imparting meaning in all walks of life. A country is continually subject to change as culture unleashes its imaginative power and recreates itself anew. In this way, culture constitutes a dynamic process, a confrontation of conflicts within the march of history. Culture, then, is not just the privilege of a few; it is the common heritage of vast populations.

This explains why cultural alienation in urban centers and the rural population has become a phenomenon of global proportions. Cultural variety makes up the wealth of a country; it is a priceless storehouse of discoveries, wisdom and, of course, technological capacities. *Cultural values are the nucleus of a dynamic society and economy.*

The Cultural Dimension of Technology

This study is concerned in particular with overcoming any and all forms of Eurocentricity. In this way, it can avoid superimposing values taken from a Eurocentric cultural context onto a different cultural sphere where contrary values are valid and operative.

Our objective is to bridge the gap between cultures and, at the same time, to overcome the sense of strangeness that prevents us from reaching an understanding of them. The strangeness of things is always measured against one's own experience. It affects any attempt on our part to understand a culture to which we do not belong, but which we approach from the allegedly safe position of our own culture.

The status of an economy, taken by itself, is not the major issue. The key question has to do with what we shall call the cultural dimension. Science and technology must literally be "acculturated."

When technology collides with culture, we either find resistance (even to the point of aggression) or the desired integration. It happens far too often that technology transfer and scientific organization are expected to proceed along established Western lines. In fact, however, the decision-making bodies do not belong to the culture in which the object is meant to be applied.

The cultural dimension can take various forms. It can involve a capacity to be creative, to produce a viable and efficient industry, or an inability to do so. This is why industrial and urban projects in non-European countries and cultures often lead to such unexpected results. Their unpredictable consequences and frequent failure show once again that technology is not neutral, but derives from value systems that may conflict partially or completely with the givens of a local culture.

In agriculture, labor techniques have their own logic and rationality that may be at once dynamic and contradictory. This becomes particularly evident when we consider the natural ecosystem, the agrarian system and the socioeconomic system (i.e., the social relations of production and the institutional forms of decision making). The agriculture of the Andes states reveals that land cannot be reduced simply to its juristic value. Instead, land represents an ecosystem in its entirety, and combines questions of cultivation with those of social relations and the age-old sacredness of the soil—in other words, with a specific cultural and religious history. This culture expresses a rational view of agriculture which will be taken up later in this study.

For donor nations, the integration of the cultural dimension holds promise of new forms of efficiency, insofar as projects are tailored to the circumstances of a regional culture.

For receiver nations, the cultural dimension provides an opportunity to summon their national strengths and design a development policy which builds on the human, technological and natural resources existing within their borders. Culture always constitutes a superordinate potential within a country. To deny this dimension is to contribute to the failure of technological integration. To acknowledge culture is more than an honorable moralistic adjunct —a *supplement d'âme*, to use Henri Bergson's phrase. It also means thinking coolly and clearly about the logic of technology transfer and development projects. Culture is not an ornament or a conglomerate of prescientific superfluities, but a vital force in the lives of individuals and societies, granting a nexus of identity and a sense of belonging.

The way projects have been designed, decided upon and put into action in the past must be thought out anew. Even their failure can be foreseen and offset from the perspective of the populations involved.

Factors that specify and distinguish a culture—its language, cosmology and religion, its philosophical and practical modes of cognition, its social and political institutions, all of which impinge on the identity of a given culture—must be brought to bear on technology. Culture is the main surety for the preservation of a people's identity, and it would be an historical error to attribute universality to any one culture. Cultures are not universal, but rather "universalistic": they have formed the bedrock of social coexistence in all ages and in all nations throughout history.

Each culture places its own value on an object. The categories that determine the object—time, space, causality, relativity—differ from culture to culture. Since technology, simply put, represents the use of objects, it becomes relevant to culture. The same applies to technological training and its use to undergird the transfer of culture. This is why technical training always represents a transfer of values, and is therefore fraught with dangers. Consequently, science and technology must be adapted to the culture for which they are intended. This applies especially to the multifarious cultures of Latin America.

Biological reproduction is not enough to establish social, economic and political reality. On the contrary, it is cultural reproduction that forms the historical background which vouchsafes the survival of a society or country. Technological knowledge, scientific discoveries, organizational capacities, philosophical and religious values—in short, the whole of a culture—are handed down from generation to generation as surety for its identity.

The culture of the Andes states, having been vanquished militarily ever since the colonial period, has marshalled its material dimension for purposes of defense. Like any such culture, it defended itself by rejecting the values of its material and military conquerors. Every country attempts to develop by material means and by producing elements of culture. This is what accounts for the dynamism of any indigenous evolution (we will have more to say about this later) that is directed toward improved use of the resources available within the physical, political and economic boundaries of a country. This train of thought exemplifies the direct connection between material development and the dimension of culture, a connection which until now has been largely neglected in economic analyses.

A glance at a culture's understanding of time will, for example, reveal much about its standing in the world. In their traditionalistic regions, the Andes states have an awareness of time that differs fundamentally from that of the industrial countries. As Durkheim insisted long ago, concepts of time—or, preferably, work time—form an integral part of the genesis of a culture. Every type of culture develops its own notions about time, which in turn affect its work ethic and thus its economy. As Mircea Eliade pointed out, in the industrial countries people have extracted themselves from cyclic time, once a sacred and sacrosanct domain. Modern industrial society now finds itself abandoned, secularized, without the clearly outlined figure of a deity, at the mercy of a never-ending flux of time. This fall into "free time" goes hand in hand with the secularization of labor and the mechanization of life. Cultural change and economic change are inextricably bound together.

In many cases, the traditional culture of the Andes states has not experienced this fragmentation of time into work time, school time, free time and sacred time. Gurvitch was able to demonstrate that modern individuals are living in many different patterns of time which place different, perhaps even contrary demands upon them. The Andes states do not share the time strategies of the industrial countries for scheduling, designing and organizing time. This difference has had crucial repercussions on economic development and the capacity to create an indigenous technology. The Andes cultures lack a comparable tradition of long-term development strategies and scheduling along industrial lines. They also have a different notion of progress. The modern industrial cultures of the West set their sights less on the past than on the future. In this respect, too, they differ from Latin America.

The factor of time is important for understanding the link between technological purpose and cultural dynamism. History has proved that throughout the whole of human evolution those groups with the more advanced technology have dominated those whose technology was less advanced. This phenomenon has only intensified in the age of urbanization and industrialization, of nuclear energy, microelectronics and data processing. The computerization of society even affects the way people conduct their daily affairs.

From the standpoint of non-European nations and the plurality of cultures, one question continues to arise: how can the variety and multifariousness of our species withstand the impact of technology without sacrificing our human identity. The new technologies made possible by the progress of science have imposed an industrial organization, centralization and concentration upon the world, sharpening the divisions between city and countryside, between industrial nations and largely archaic cultures. Patterns of labor are being standardized; the economy is being channeled by increasingly bureaucratic forms of administration. Both of these factors are causing society to become more anonymous.

These processes are not likely to take hold in the Andes Pact states, since the major Quechua-speaking segment of the population belongs to active and creative cultural traditions with entirely different roots. The process of innovation in Andean culture follows laws fundamentally at odds with those of Western industrial culture. The Andes Pact states have multicultural societies. This alone permits us to see in them a richness and a potential for innovation all their own. Their line of development represents a holistic entity. It embraces the economic, social and cultural dimensions, with all of these factors interacting in a dialectical or even contradictory manner.

To the extent that a country is "lord of its own castle" and has an authentic culture rather than one imposed upon it, it can assign its creative potential and its system of education and training a significance that will ultimately benefit its economy. If these two areas of life are separated (e.g., by a purely mechanical transfer of technology), its development will become lopsided. Identity, indigenousness and authenticity are indispensable for the creative powers of a country. The cultural dimension in the Andes countries emerges as a certainty, a hope and a disappointment at one and the same time.

The colonial empires have been destroyed since the nineteenth century; the liberated people have regained a voice of their own. But an element of disappointment remains: they cannot look back in happiness and pride at their culture, as this culture has been fractured and obstructed by their own history. There is no cosmological congruity between the emerging industrial culture and their still archaic native traditions.

For this reason, the present study takes an integrative approach, one that calls for interdisciplinary reflection. The validity of any economic growth that ignores the balance of a culture is questionable. Any attempt at indigenous evolution cries out for the reassurance of cultural identity.

Indigenous groups continue to be a key feature in the cultural melting pot of Latin America. Carlos Fuentes, though recognizing the vitality of Latin America's cultural traditions, sees its political legacy in jeopardy because no successful integration of its culture, economy and politics has yet taken place. This explains a certain reservation within large parts of the population toward political institutions which do not fully represent the cultural dimension of their respective nations. Accordingly, unless justice is done to the dimension of culture, there is little assurance that Latin America will develop effectively in the future.

Culture As a Factor in Development

Economic development cannot be understood solely in mechanistic terms, such as the transfer of capital and industrial plant, or the upgrading of factories and modes of production. Economic development also arises through opinions and attitudes, through the creation of avenues of cooperation and organization among individuals and communities. It is a social process in that it involves every member of a society. Economy, society and technology cannot be kept separate: capital is anchored in institutions, moral values can at least deflect evolutionary trends, and changes in technology inevitably bring about new types of human organization. Economic planning should therefore not be viewed as an act of a relatively limited group within government and business, but rather as a consequence of the labor of millions of people trying to enter into contact with each other.

This also shifts attention to nonmaterial goods as a means of gaining acceptance for new attitudes of cooperation. Thus, factors from everyday surroundings become key issues in the formulation of economic policy. In the Andean countries especially, the process is a spiritual and cultural achievement.

It is impossible to distinguish arbitrarily between the economic and noneconomic aspects of human actions because this distinction, while plausible in theory, has no practical application and is not in accord with the reality of history. Herein lies a major problem: the states of the Andes Pact were often torn violently from their origins and now have to reconstruct their past in tedious processes of adaptation.

Until now, research on this subject has been dominated mainly by econometrics, which has proved unequal to the task of arriving at a deeper understanding of non-European countries and cultures. A linear, one-dimensional view of progress as practiced in the West gives too little consideration to sociocultural factors—that is, to the contexts of cultural and religious history.

Understanding the impact of modern science and technology is a process which, in the Andes Pact states, began only in the latter half of the twentieth century. The key question arises again and again: how is it possible to adopt science and technology without abandoning the central values of cultural identity. The Andes Pact states must find new ways of absorbing science and technology in order to stimulate economic innovation and creativity without declining into passive imitation and further dependence on the West.

Political stability is unthinkable without a successful convergence of tradition and modernity. Science and technology must be applied in such a way that economically weaker countries are not forced to abandon their roots.

Approaches based mainly on economic rationality can give rise to a rational nihilism in humanity's awareness of their identity. Cost-efficiency analyses derive from a belief that everything must be measurable and quantifiable, regardless of qualitative differences in humankind. Even factors which, at first glance, do not seem "productive" from a materialistic standpoint may have large-scale repercussions in the long run.

Each culture has its own style of development. What is needed, then, are appropriate models for indigenously structuring the state and the economy.

In the Andes states, it has happened again and again that technology and modernization seemed acceptable to the political ruling class, but not to broad strata of the population who still belonged to archaic traditions. In such cases, traditional cultures may appear to be obstacles to modernization, e.g., when sections of the population regard new technologies as tools of subjugation wielded by the dominant foreign culture and reject them to preserve their identity. Technology transfer should take place as a form of exchange, not of subjugation. *We must initiate a process to find the point at which two cultures intersect, a point that preserves their cultural identity and yet puts the economically weaker culture in a position to invent its own technology.*

Torn between its existing heritage and the new technologies, culture can be seen as a movement forward toward an active economy and a creative state. But there can be no fruitful development unless a culture is given an opportunity to express itself freely, and unless progress and modernization are designed to be self-defining and to have their own indigenous dynamism.

In the dynamics of development today, cultural values undergo a constant reevaluation of the objects, experiences and modes of behavior available in any given situation. Cultural values are unintelligible without their sustaining vehicles—individuals or social groups—and are always located within a force field. Values are crystallized reflections of the highly varied, often contradictory interests of groups that have emerged within a country in the course of its history.

The notion of technological self-security and indigenous development embraces two different aspects: first, the ability to choose and control areas of partial technological dependency; and second, the ability to create and adapt technological systems and to connect them with the social and cultural needs that will inevitably arise during the next few decades.

On this basis, the present study outlines an alternative to previous policies and formulates an integral plan for indigenous development within the Andes Pact states.

Compatibility: The Key Issue

Science and technology are phenomena which increasingly come to the fore in times of economic need. In our century, science became a global field of study in a world market: regardless of local or national variants, the gathering of resources took on planetary proportions, just as the world's population came to be seen as a global village.

The technological relations of a country are part of its economic and political ties to other nations. They assume commanding importance above all in the developing or industrializing countries outside Europe. In these countries, the dynamics of the sociocultural sphere follow different historical laws than those of the industrialized countries, whose economic development dates from the Industrial Revolution. Technology does no harm to a society with a developed infrastructure and adequate labor forces. It can even become part of a native tradition and exist in harmony with the ethos of culture, economy and society. But this state of affairs does not exist in Latin America, where greater advances are still required.

When an individual approaches science and technology, it is first and foremost a spiritual and cultural matter. A process must be traversed that extends from initial acquaintance with an innovation to the moment of acceptance. This process must be distinguished from that of diffusion, the object-related dissemination of a new idea from its source of innovation to its final acceptance. One major difference between diffusion and acceptance is that the former occurs among groups of people while the latter takes place within an individual. These considerations and distinctions are important for our later understanding of how to incorporate innovations into the culture of the Andes Pact states.

One paramount issue is the *compatibility of culture and technology*, specifically, the degree to which a given innovation is consistent with a culture's existing values and past history. Obviously, an idea that is incompatible with the established cultural norms and values of a country will not be accepted as quickly as an idea that is compatible with them. The many-sidedness of an innovation, as understood by the members of a culture, also affects its acceptance. Ultimately, the communicability of an innovation governs its degree of acceptance, the degree to which its results can be handed on to other people.

Compatibility, many-sidedness, communicability: this study will apply all three factors as basic tools for analyzing the characteristics of new ideas, taking the Andean cultures as our example. *Without social and cultural innovation there is no way that technological progress can bring benefits to Latin America. This is why the present study has chosen to advocate an indigenous technological policy.*

The Plurality of Cultures As Resources of Identity

Long ago, Ralph Linton pointed out that by knowing a culture we can predict whether the majority of its members will welcome an innovation or resist it. Cultural resistance to new ideas arises in many areas: rituals, ethical and moral traditions, religious values. Not only do cultural values influence the original acceptance of, or resistance to, innovation, they also influence whether and to what extent a new idea can be integrated into existing ways.

In cultures that are still archaic and autochthonous, people are considerably less ready to accept new ideas than in modern industrial cultures. We notice this specifically in the Andean cultures, with their high and widespread proportion of indios. Preference is given to local traditions; there is little interchange with people of other cultures; a cosmopolitan spirit is unknown. From a Eurocentric perspective, there is a striking lack of economic rationality in daily dealings among people, even in the world of business. Moreover, it is difficult for members of cultures that are still archaic to step into new social and economic roles that are determined from the outside by the economy and have no bearing on their historical traditions.

Unlike people in archaic cultures, individuals in modern industrial culture have the ability to see themselves through the eyes of others. This is a basic precondition for developing a sophisticated political and economic structure.

In the Andes Pact states, it is clear that technology entails a cultural impoverishment. Outside methods and products serve only to level age-old cultural and religious traditions. The major national alliances were a synthesis of various and often conflicting cultures. The secret of change and historical progression is to be found in a confrontation with things that are different and alien. Yet, technology, now spread throughout the world, is turning into one of the most powerful agents of historical entropy, overriding regional and national peculiarities and blurring the distinctions between cultures. By putting an end to the plurality of cultures, technology, in a *reductio ad absurdum,* is threatening the essence of future human evolution. Every time a culture, no matter how allegedly marginal, is destroyed, we lose an historical aspect of human existence, and therefore part of our own future.

To be sure, the Andes Pact states show that suppressed cultures are able to resist modernity, when artificially imposed. Peru's political violence, for example, thrives in large part on this rejection, which has now escalated to the point of terrorism. The political events in Iran since the fall of the Shah provide more proof that technology cannot be imposed on a country without regard for its cultural and religious history, lest it summon forth fundamentalist rage and violence.

Seen globally, then, it is obvious that technology produces uniformity, but not any real political unity. Latin America is locked in a continuing dualism: it proclaims its modernity in political statements, but it is clearly premodern in its social and economic fabric. Social progress and industrial development are not equivalent.

Still, history takes place in the plural, even in Latin America. The various forms assumed by culture and religion are anything but irrelevant. To maintain this variety is to secure the resources of human identity. Our task, in the global civilization of the outgoing twentieth century, is to preserve even the peculiar and idiosyncratic, to uphold the right to be individual. Herein lies human potential.

This demand is of central importance to the Andes states, as they have kept a plurality of cultures, some of them archaic, to the present day. Consequently, they have extraordinary difficulties in adapting modernity, with its high-powered technologies, to their own cultural roots, which are often still pre-Columbian. The question of cultural compatibility has not even been addressed.

Acknowledgments

This book is based upon a pilot research project of the European Community under the Director General for Foreign Policy with the support of the German Ministry of Foreign Affairs in Bonn. The author worked with the cooperation of many libraries in Latin America and made frequent visits to Latin America for the purpose of empirical field research, particularly in the region of the Andes. In addition, library work and several research stays took place at Princeton, Harvard and the University of Texas, in the large Latin America collection in Austin. While in Latin America, the author had extensive conversations with professor colleagues, writers, ministers of state, presidents of state and official representatives of the churches in the Catholic Church hierarchy, as well as in Protestant circles and within the liberation theology movement.

The author thanks the European Community and the Institute for Comparative Cultural Research in Munich, Germany for their financial and strategic support during the period of preparation and research.

Suggestions for Further Reading

Aceves, Joseph. *Social Change in Spanish Village*. Cambridge, MA: Schenkman, 1971.

Adamic, Louis. *The Native's Return*. New York: Harper & Row, 1934.

Adams, Richard N. "Personnel in Cultural Change: A Test of a Hypothesis." *Social Forces* 30 (1951): 185–189.

____. "Notes on the Application of Anthropology." *Human Organization* 12, No. 2 (1953): 10–14.

____. "A Nutritional Research Program in Guatemala." *Health, Culture and Community*. Ed. B.D. Paul. New York: Russell Sage Foundation, 1955. pp. 435–458.

Altamira, Rafael. *A History of Spain from the Beginnings to the Present Day*. New York: Van Nostrand Reinhold, 1949.

American Anthropological Association Fellows. "Statement on Problems of Anthropological Research and Ethics." *American Anthropologist* 69 (1967): 381–382.

Apodaca, Anacleto. "Corn and Custom: The Introduction of Hybrid Corn to Spanish American Farmers in New Mexico." *Human Problems in Technological Change*. Ed. E.H. Spicer. New York: Russell Sage Foundation, 1952. pp. 35–39.

Banfield, Edward C. *The Moral Basis of a Backward Society*. New York: Free Press, 1958.

Barnett, H.G. "Applied Anthropology in 1860." *Applied Anthropology* (now *Human Organization*) 1, No. 3 (1942): 19–32.

____. *Innovation: The Basis of Cultural Change*. New York: McGraw-Hill, 1953.

____. *Anthropology in Administration*. New York: Harper & Row, 1956.

Batten, T.R. *Communities and Their Development: An Introductory Study with Special Reference to the Tropics*. London: Oxford University Press, 1957.

Benedict, Ruth. *Race: Science and Politics*. New York: Modern Age, 1940.

Biesanz, John, and Mavis Biesanz. *Costa Rican Life*. New York: Columbia University Press, 1944.

Brokensha, David, and Peter Hodge. *Community Development: An Interpretation*. San Francisco: Chandler, 1969.

Browning, Harley L., and Waltraut Feindt. "The Social and Economic Context of Migration to Monterrey, Mexico." Eds. F.F. Rabinovitz and F.M. Trueblood. *Latin American Urban Research* 1 (1971): 45–70.

Buitrón, Aníbal. "La investigatión y el mejoramiento de las condiciones de vida." CREFAL, Pátzcuaro, Mexico, *Boletín Informativo* Nos. 26–27 (1959): 6–9.

_____. "Problemas económico-sociales de la educación en la América Latina." *América Indígena* 20 (1960): 167–172.

Butterworth, Douglas S. "A Study of the Urbanization Process among the Mixtec Migrants from Tilaltongo in Mexico City." *América Indígena* 22 (1962): 257–274.

Caldwell, John C. *African Rural-Urban Migration: The Movement to Ghana's Towns.* New York: Columbia University Press, 1969.

Clark, Grahame. *Archaeology and Society.* Rev. 2nd ed. London: Methuen, 1947.

Clark, Margret. *Health in the Mexican-American Culture.* Berkeley: University of California Press, 1959.

Cobarruvias [Covarrubias] Orozco, Sebastián de. *Tesoro de la lengua castellana, o Española.* Madrid, 1611. Reprinted by S.A. Horta, Barcelona, 1943.

Davis, Stanley M. "Management's Effects on Worker Organizations in a Developing Country." *Human Organization* 27 (1968): 21–29.

Díaz-Guerrero, Rogelio. "The Active and Passive Syndromes." *Interamerican Journal of Psychology* 1 (1967): 263-272.

Elkin, A.P. "The Reaction of Primitive Races to the White Man's Culture." *The Hibbert Journal* 35 (1936-37): 537–545.

Erasmus, Charles J. "Agricultural Changes in Haiti: Patterns of Resistance and Acceptance." *Human Organization* 11, No. 4 (1952): 20–26.

_____. "An Anthropologist Views Technical Assistance." *The Scientific Monthly* 78 (1954): 147–158.

_____. *Reciprocal Labor: A Study of Its Occurrence and Disappearance among Farming Peoples in Latin America.* Unpublished dissertation. University of California, Berkeley, 1955.

Firth, Raymond. *Elements of Social Organization.* London: Watts, 1956.

Flinn, William L. "Rural and Intra-urban Migration in Colombia: Two Case Studies in Bogotá." Eds. F.F. Rabinovitz and F.M. Trueblood. *Latin American Urban Research* 1 (1971): 83–93.

Foster, George M. "Some Implications of Modern Mexican Mold-made Pottery." *Southwestern Journal of Anthropology* 4 (1948): 356–470.

_____. "Relationships Between Theoretical and Applied Anthropology: A Public Health Program Analysis." *Human Organization* 11, No. 3 (1952): 5–16.

_____. "Peasant Society and the Image of Limited Good." *American Anthropologist* 67 (1965): 293–315.

______. *Tzintzuntzan: Mexican Peasants in a Changing World*. Boston: Little, Brown, 1967.

______. "The Institute of Social Anthropology of the Smithsonian Institution, 1943–1952." *Anuario Indigenista* 7 (1967): 173–192.

Friedmann, F.G. "The World of 'La Miseria'." (Reprinted from *Partisan Review*, 1953) International Cooperation Administration, Washington, DC, *Community Development Review* No. 10: 16–28, 1958.

García Manzanedo, Héctor, and Isabel Kelly. *Comentarios al proyecto de la campaña para la erradicación del paludismo en México*. Mimeographed. D.F.: Dirección de Estudios Experimentales en Salubridad Pública, Instituto de Asuntos Inter-americanos, Mexico, 1955.

Geertz, Clifford. "The Rotating Credit Association: A 'Middle Rung' in Development." *Economic Development and Cultural Change* 10 (1962): 241–263.

Germani, Gino. "Inquiry into the Social Effects of Urbanization in a Working-class Sector of Greater Buenos Aires." *Urbanization in Latin America*. Ed. P.M. Hauser. New York: International Documents Service, 1961. pp. 206–233.

Gittler, Joseph B. "Man and His Prejudices." *The Scientific Monthly* 69 (1949): 43–47.

Hailey, Lord. "The Role of Anthropology in Colonial Development." *Man* 44 (1944): 10–15.

Hamamsy, Laila Shukry. "The Role of Women in a Changing Navaho Society." *American Anthropologist* 59 (1957): 101–111.

Hereford, Philip, ed. *The Ecclesiastical History of the English People by the Venerable Bede*. Trans. Thomas Stapleton. London: Burns & Oates, 1935.

Hesiod. *Hesiod*. Trans. Richard Lattimore. Ann Arbor: University of Michigan Press, 1959.

Hill, W.W. "The Navaho Indians and the Ghost Dance of 1890." *American Anthropologist* 46 (1944): 523–527.

Hofer, Tamás. "Comparative Notes on the Professional Personality of Two Disciplines." *Current Anthropology* 9 (1968): 311–315.

Hogbin, H. Ian. *Social Change*. London: Watts, 1958.

Horowitz, Irving Louis. "The Rise and Fall of Project Camelot." *The Rise and Fall of Project Camelot: Studies in the Relationships between Social and Practical Politics*. Ed. I.L. Horowitz. Cambridge, MA: MIT Press, 1967.

Hoyt, Elizabeth E. "The Impact of a Money Economy on Consumption Patterns." The Annals of the American Academy of Political and Social Science. In B.F. Hoselitz, ed. *Agrarian Societies in Transition*, 305 (1956): 12–22.

Hunter, John M. "Reflections on the Administrative Aspects of a Technical Assistance Project." *Economic Development and Cultural Change* 7 (1959): 445–451.

Kelly, Isabel. "Informe preliminar del proyecto de habitación en La Laguna, Ejido de El Cujie, cercano a Torreón, Coahuila." Mimeographed. D.F.: Instituto de Asuntos Interamericanos, Mexico, 1953.

____. "Cambios en los patrones relacionados con la alimentación." *Boletín del Instituto Internacional Americano de Protección a la Infancia* 32 (1958, Montevideo): 205–208.

____. *La antropologia, la cultura y la salud pública*. Imprenta del SCISP (Ministry of Public Health and Social Welfare), Lima, 1960.

Kemper, Robert Van. *Migration and Adaptation of Tzintzuntzan Peasants in Mexico City*. Unpublished dissertation. University of California, Berkeley, 1971.

King, Clarence. *Working with People in Small Communities*. New York: Harper & Row, 1958.

Kroeber, A.L. *Anthropology*. New York: Harcourt Brace Jovanovich, 1948.

Lange, Charles H. "The Role of Economics in Cochiti Pueblo Culture Change." *American Anthropologist* 55 (1953): 674–694.

Lewis, Oscar. *Life in a Mexican Village: Tepoztlán Restudied*. Urbana: University of Illinois Press, 1951.

Linton, Ralph. *The Study of Man: An Introduction*. London: Appleton, 1936.

____. *The Cultural Background of Personality*. New York: Appleton, 1945.

Lowie, Robert H. *Robert H. Lowie, Ethnologist: A Personal Record*. Berkeley: University of California Press, 1959.

Maddox, James G. *United Nations Technical Assistance to Mexico*. D.F.: American Universities Field Staff, Mexico, 1956.

Mair, Lucy P. *Studies in Applied Anthropology*. London School of Economics. Monographs on Social Anthropology, No. 16. London: University of London, Athlone Press, 1957.

Mangin, William P. "The Role of Regional Associations in the Adaptation of Rural Populations in Peru." *Sociologus* 9 (1959): 23–35.

____. "Mental Health and Migration to Cities: A Peruvian Case." Annals of the New York Academy of Sciences. In Vera Rubin, ed. *Culture, Society and Health* 84 (1960): 911–917.

Matos Mar, José. "Migration and Urbanization. The 'barriadas' of Lima: An Example of Integration into Urban Life." *Urbanization in Latin America*. Ed. P.M. Hauser. New York: Columbia University Press, International Documents Service, 1961. pp. 170–190.

McDermott, W., K. Deuschle, J. Adair, H. Fulmer, and B. Loughlin. "Introducing Modern Medicine in a Navajo Community." *Science* 131 (1960): 197–205, 280–287.

Menéndez Pidal, Rámon. *The Spaniards in Their History*. Trans. Walter Starkie. London: Hollis & Carter, 1950.

von Moltke, Willo. "The Evolution of the Linear Form." *Planning Urban Growth and Regional Development: The Experience of the Guayana Program of Venezuela*. Eds. Lloyd Rodwin and Associates. Cambridge, MA: MIT Press, 1969. Chap. 6.

Mosher, Arthur T. *Interrelationships Between Agricultural Development, Social Organization and Personal Attitudes and Values.* Comparative Extension Publication No. 12, New York State College of Agriculture at Cornell University, Ithaca, 1960.

Murphy, Robert F., and Buell Quain. *The Trumai Indians of Central Brazil.* Monograph No. 24, American Ethnological Society, New York, 1955.

Oberg, Kalervo. *Culture Shock.* Bobbs-Merrill Reprint Series on the Social Sciences, A-329. Indianapolis: Bobbs-Merrill, 1954.

Oberg, Kalervo, and José Arthur Rios. "A Community Improvement Project in Brazil." *Health, Culture and Community.* Ed. B.D. Paul. New York: Russell Sage Foundation, 1955. pp. 349–376.

Pineda, Virginia Gutiérrez de. "Causas culturales de la mortalidad infantil." *Revista Colombiana de Antropologia* 4 (1955): 13–85.

Pitt-Rivers, J.A. *The People of the Sierra.* London: Weidenfeld and Nicolson, 1954.

Read, Margret. *Education and Social Change in Tropical Areas.* Camden, NJ: T. Nelson, 1955.

Redfield, Robert. *Tepoztlán: A Mexican Village.* Chicago: University of Chicago Press, 1930.

_____. "The Folk Society." *The American Journal of Sociology* 52 (1947): 293–308.

Reichard. "The Navaho and Christianity." *American Anthropologist* 51 (1949): 66–71.

Simmons, Ozzie G. "The Clinical Team in a Chilean Health Center." *Health, Culture and Community.* Ed. B.D. Paul. New York: Russell Sage Foundation. pp. 325–348.

_____. "Drinking Patterns and Interpersonal Performances in a Peruvian Mestizo Community." *Quarterly Journal of Studies on Alcohol* 20 (1959): 103–111.

Soustelle, Georgette. *Tequila: un village nahuatl du Mexique oriental.* Travaux et Mémoires de l'Institut d'Ethnologie, No. 62. Université de Paris, Paris, 1958.

Spector, Paul, Augusto Torres, Stanley Lichtenstein, Harley O. Preston, Johnette B. Clark, and Susan B. Silverman. "Communication Media and Motivation in the Adoption of New Practices: An Experiment in Rural Ecuador." *Human Organization* 30 (1971): 39–46.

Staley, Eugene. *The Future of Underdeveloped Countries: Political Implications of Economic Development.* New York: Harper & Row, 1954.

Thompson, Wallace. *The Mexican Mind: A Study of National Psychology.* Boston: Little, Brown, 1922.

Wellin, Edward. "Water Boiling in a Peruvian Town." *Health, Culture and Community.* Ed. B.D. Paul. New York: Russell Sage Foundation, 1955. pp. 71–103.

Two

Science and Technology in Theoretical Perspective

Summary

When technology is used to solve problems, steps must be taken to ensure that the entire community is actively involved and that science and technology are used flexibly and responsively to meet the culture's actual needs. Ultimately, analyses must proceed from a culture's own problems rather than from abstract scientific positions. New indicators must be defined for a fresh alignment of science and technology in Latin America; the question of quality of life must be addressed. Even though these indicators cannot be captured in economic terms and are therefore not quantifiable, they nevertheless determine the performance capacity of a country as part of its intellectual and cultural history. Not until science and technology have been united in this overriding sense can they become a driving force in the productive capacity of a nation.

In tandem with these new indicators, new ideas and methods of training must be developed in the areas of science and technology. There must be an integrated system of education for children, young people and adults, the goal being to train those with talent and ability for scientific research and thus increase the acceptance of technological innovation. Politicians must be able to make long-term plans in order to expand the market for new goods and services and to integrate the capacity for technological innovation productively in the middle classes and in heavy industry. The ultimate objective is gradually to replace imports in the various fields of engineering, in the use of state purchasing power, in specific strategic programs, as well as in capital goods, computer sciences and telecommunications. Indigenous capacity for research and development must be enhanced in critical areas of higher education. Educational steps must take precedence over economic and financial measures. The capabilities of the Andes states for technological innovation must be promoted, especially in the sectors of telecommunications, metallurgy, civil engineering, computer sciences, microelectronics and biological engineering.

The Interaction of Cosmology, Rationality and Technology

Isaac Newton's thought derives from the central notion that the universe follows a number of laws that, in the final analysis, embody God in their perfection. Since then, the natural sciences have conveyed a completely different image of the universe: material bodies now have to be perceived in accordance with deterministic laws. In the centuries that followed Newton's death, pictures of the universe were reduced to mechanistic models. The human dimension seemed too insignificant to be inserted into them.

It is against this background that the rivalry emerged between the natural sciences and the humanities. This rivalry has continued to the present day on the highly contested level of ontology. Yet, it is often overlooked that technological rationality and science are both embedded in culture.

Neither science nor technology appears with the inevitability of natural phenomena. At the moment, they are a development specific to the West. The secular view of history that emerged at the end of the Renaissance, with its promise to redeem humankind from their earthly existence, played a special part in this development, as did the revolt against church dogma. The result was a new cosmology which viewed the cosmos as being essentially a combination of physical laws and natural resources, of which the latter were to be exploited for science and technology. This new view of the world was materialist and mechanistic. There was nothing remotely like it in the pre-Columbian cultures of the present-day Andes Pact states. This constitutes a fundamental problem for the adaptation of science and technology in Latin America.

In this study, too, science is understood as a conditional form of human knowledge, one that is connected at the moment with a

Western cosmology and that goes hand in hand with rationality—a rationality, moreover, which is thought to express an inherent superiority to non-European cultures.

In fact, every form of rationality is bound to a specific culture and must be distinguished from pure logic. Things which seem rational in one culture may be irrational in another. The historical cultures of the Andes, with their concepts of space and time, provide a useful example of this point, for these concepts differ fundamentally from their Western counterparts. *Rationality is the cultural essence of a cosmology.* In a particular culture, such as that of the Andes, rationality may be congruent with myth—something that would be unthinkable in modern Western civilization.

Every cosmology has a specific rationality with which to justify actions in the day-to-day practice of politics and economics. The global power of Western science and technology resides not only in the strength of its technology, but also, and especially, in the power of its form of rationality, which paralyzes thought in other cultures. From the Andean standpoint, this has summoned forth a revolt against the West's monopoly of the concept of rationality.

The point, then, is to aim for a universal element which runs like Ariadne's thread through the different cultures of the world. In this way we can locate transcultural aspects of human rationality and derive economic benefits from them for the Andes states.

Until now, industrial culture and Andean culture have been unable to understand each other. This is because science and technology can be introduced into Andean culture only through a process of osmosis lasting for generations. By the same token, there is no way to introduce Andean culture in one fell swoop into technology. If technology is a part of culture, it follows that Western technology does not have the right to advance claims of universality. It can only speak for modern Western culture, not for the cultural faculties of humanity as a whole.

Today, the technological culture dominating the world is based on features which emerged in the industrialized countries during the Industrial Revolution. These features included maximizing earnings, expanding productivity, enhancing vocational training (which likewise coincided with maximizing earnings) and increasing specialization. No comparable development ever took place in the peripheral nations, including the Andes Pact states.

The exchange of technology over national and cultural boundaries is as old as history itself. At all stages of culture, technological discoveries have been transported to areas where this particular knowledge was unknown. From medieval history, we know of skilled laborers who migrated from southern Europe to northern Europe, where cathedrals today bear witness to their skills. The classical process of industrialization, initiated in England, went through stages in which skilled laborers from Flanders, for example, emigrated and brought the art of weaving to England. In this way, the textile industry settled in a country which until then had been capable only of exporting its wool. Later, a veritable profusion of technology transfer arose through the transport of goods and equipment from England, where the export of machinery was not officially sanctioned until 1828. Finally, through economic and financial transactions, this profusion reached Germany and the rest of continental Europe.

At no time in the history of Latin America did this form of technology transfer, with a mutual exchange among cultures, ever take place. The transfer of technology between the nations of the First World and the industrializing and Third World nations took on a completely different character.

Defining Technology in Light of Cultural History

At this point, we must now examine more closely what we mean by the word "technology." Technology can be defined as the amount of industrial implements, tools, material, knowledge and skills necessary to meet the needs of the cultural community of a nation and to deal effectively with the geographical and ecological preconditions of its surroundings. In this light, technology is the ordered measure of skills applied in the production and marketing of services and goods. It is not limited to knowledge from the natural, social and humanist sciences, but also includes empirical knowledge made up of observations, experiences and traditions. Technology always determines the manner in which a culture makes use of nature and its resources. In short, *technology is the organized knowledge of production.*

Technology can also be taken to mean the totality of cultural practices employed in the transformation of natural resources to adapt them for immediate human use.

As seen from the productive sector, technology is a commodity with two principal characteristics:

1) Like every other commodity, technology has a utility value and an exchange value. These two must not be confused.

2) Technology consists of material and nonmaterial elements. The United Nations Conference on Trade and Development views technology on three levels:

1) As *capital goods,* including machinery and systems of production.

2) As *human labor power,* organizational capacity (management) and the application of specialized skills.

3) As *information* of both a technical and a commercial nature. The Andes states must import the bulk of all three of these forms of technology.

Scientific knowledge is unquestionably a major stimulant to technological development, given an empirical capability for innovation and adaptation. The problem for the Andes Pact states is that it is extremely difficult to export capital-intensive technologies from countries where capital is abundant and labor is in short supply, to countries where laborers are in abundance, but capital is seldom, if ever, available. Unless local culture is taken into account, technology transfer of this sort will not produce the desired results.

The world economy is not a homogeneous domain, a monolithic organization that continually replicates one and the same structure. Differences are built into it from the outset. Thus, to transfer technology linearly, without reflection, is to court uniformity. The countries of Latin America illustrate the extent to which the diffusion of technology from the industrial states can eradicate the cultural and religious distinctions that form the identity and originality of any culture.

The underdeveloped countries reveal an imitative behavior with three defining features. The first of these is political, and results from the pressure of economic nationalism exerted by the governing classes. The second results from the importation of international technology. The third is a pretense to ecological superiority which, in fact, does not exist in this form.

The various concepts of technology have several points in common:

1) Technology is made up of many different parameters: human beings, management, machinery, knowledge.

2) Technology is linked with scientific activity.

3) Technology cannot become productive until it is efficiently organized.

In the case of industrial production, technology includes the following basic elements:

1) "Feasibility" studies, market overviews and other services which precede investment.

2) Industrial planning and the staking out of available latitude.

3) The building of factories and the installation of industrial plant and machinery.

4) The training of technical and organizational personnel.

5) Management of production options.

6) Information on sales and marketing.

7) Improvement of production design.

Because it links material tools and abstract theory, technology determines what a society must do as well as how to do it. Thus, it is an expression of that society's history and culture in a comprehensive anthropological sense.

By technology we mean not only the means of production, the "hardware," but also the manufacturing process, marketing methods and product specification. Technology includes administrative and marketing techniques directly related to production. It includes services no less than administration and education, banking and the judiciary, manufacturing and agriculture. In short, we are dealing not merely with the "hardware" of technology, but also with a more comprehensive definition of this concept, one which relates hardware to "software." We must thus view technology as an "n"-dimensional vector that encompasses the nature of the product, the utilization of resources, equipment, skilled and unskilled labor, management, material, energy and the complementary products currently available. Factors such as currency exchange, technical skills, shortages of raw materials and the availability and cultivation of land also come into play.

In archaic cultures, technology has two key characteristics. First, there is a comparatively simple basis of labor spread throughout the entire culture. In this sense, technology is an integral part of individual and collective culture. Second, though technology does find empirical expression, the corpus of explanatory knowledge unfolds largely against a backdrop of myth and magic. This made the adoption of Western technology during the colonial period and, later, in the industrialization phase extremely difficult, as the mythic-magical backdrop obstructed the introduction of empirical and pragmatic technology.

Today, then, it is essential that we make technology an integral part of culture in the Andes states. Our task is not to reinvent the whole of technology, but rather to develop a capability for making social decisions regarding the employment, orientation and purpose of technology. And what this calls for is the creation of an integral technological capacity. Three items are necessary in order to accomplish this: the entire community must be involved in the solution of technological problems; science and technology must be reoriented so as to be more flexible with regard to the actual needs of the culture; finally, analyses must proceed from the culture's own problems, not from theoretical, scientific positions.

Precedence must be given here to adequate technological education. Technology, education and the overall evolution of a society are interrelated; together, they form the constitutive factors of the state. The need for "educative technology" in the Andes states is obvious. In this regard, technology resembles genetic material: it represents the code of the society that produced it, and its objective, given a favorable environment, is to reproduce this society.

The crucial point is that *educative technology must conform to the society's cultural and historical background.*

True, technology is a commodity that, at first glance, can be obtained anywhere. But this view is deceptive. It ignores the fact that technology is embedded in culture. Technology cannot simply be transferred over geographical and cultural boundaries. Seen in anthropological terms, technology embodies one of the defining entities of culture. So long as we refuse to view it as an expression of culture, there is no way we can erect a state and an economy on a long-term basis.

During the conquest of Latin America, the Spanish conquistadors imposed their technological implements on the native cultures without bothering to consider whether or not these implements were appropriate. The importation of technology from the leading industrial countries must encounter greater latitude for adaptability in the target country. This latitude must be created by educative technology.

To understand the historic synthesis of Andean technology and trace its evolution, we must first explain the factors that used to prevail in these cultures (see Chapter 4).

When Andean culture left its vernacular and autonomous pre-Columbian phase, it entered an era of dependence. Elements from magic and myth came into contact with empirical and rational elements to form a combination which even today constitutes a tinderbox of potential conflict in this area.

One major obstacle to the emergence of indigenous technology in the Andean region is the shallowness of its technological market, which has taken on the appearance of an incomplete market outlet dominated by arms dealers and foreign consultants. Transfer of technology from abroad is the usual practice.

A policy toward technology is invariably the final outgrowth of development policy. An increasing awareness of this fact can be seen in current attempts on the part of the Andes states to work out political guidelines for technological research. But up to now, these attempts have generally failed, except in Venezuela during the years of the oil boom. The Andes states consider the achievements of foreign technology to be harmful and disruptive, since they were tailored to serve the interests of the industrialized nations. This, however, works against Latin America's economic development. Most outside technologies do not meet the needs of the Andes states because they presuppose methods of production which apply to capital-intensive businesses rather than the unskilled laborers increasingly found in these countries. Predictably, this results in monopoly-like industrial conglomerates in the private and public sectors.

Since these countries are beholden to the imitative transfer of outside technology, they are increasingly restricted in their internal freedom to choose their own development strategies. What is needed instead is an adaptation of these strategies to the prerequisites and needs of Andean culture to obtain maximum benefit from their available resources, both human and natural. Only in this way is a future-oriented policy of alternative technologies possible.

The developed countries must suffer the reproach that they far too often employ industrial technology as a substitute for a comprehensive internal development strategy. The extent of technological change, however, will determine the pace of modernization as a whole in the Andes Pact states. Technology becomes the secular arm of science. The widespread application of technology in its present-day scope has already brought out internal contradictions in the Andean cultures.

When speaking of the Andean countries, we must distinguish between prescientific society, "colonial" science and the struggle to attain an independent scientific tradition. In the colonial period, European scientists traveled to the Andes region, explored its flora and fauna, studied its geographic and physical characteristics and its uncharted territories and returned to their starting point to bring their scientific work to completion. In colonial science, the principal object of interest and attention was natural history, although the scope for scientific activities began to expand in proportion to the rise of the colonial power. Colonial scientists were dependent in the sense that the roots and sources of the scientific tradition they upheld, the orientation of their activities and the forms of recognition granted to their work all came from a foreign metropolis, not from the country or region where they lived and did their work, namely, the Andes.

Colonial science anticipated aspects of the modern age in embryo. During a transitional period, colonial scientists, while receiving support from abroad, attempted to create institutions and traditions ultimately intended to form the basis of an independent scientific culture. These attempts were fatally flawed, however, for even to the present day it has proved impossible to establish a scientific tradition capable of supplanting colonial science with scholars whose interests actually and exclusively reside in the territory where they do their work.

The diffusion of Western science retained the upper hand. Andean science was governed by the dictates of a Eurocentric perspective whose forms of theoretical and empirical reasoning came into conflict with speculative modes of cognition deriving from traditions of magic and myth in Andean culture. Up to now, there has been little interaction between the science imported from the West and traditional forms of speculative thought. One valuable task of educative technology would be to reach a synthesis between them

The principal goal of the Andes states must be to bring forth an integral form of science and, most importantly, to give thought to an alternative indigenous technology in order to avoid having its creativity and knowledge completely subjected to Western logic. This new cultural setting must allow ample room for independent activity as an expression of human evolution.

In 1964, Frazer outlined concepts regarding the transition from magic to religion and science. His purpose was to observe the transition from passive contemplation and acceptance to a certain amount of action and interaction between human beings and the phenomena in the world about them. Joseph Needham, in his studies of Chinese culture of 1977, analyzed the manner in which China produced major achievements in the evolution of speculative thought about nature, and also, unlike Latin America, in logic and mathematics. Consequently, China was able to produce technologies based on abstract and systematic conceptions and developed an efficient social organization of production. At the time of the Renaissance, the philosophical and intellectual tradition in China was far more attuned to modern science than the Christian conception of the universe. Nonetheless, there were a number of social, economic and political factors in conflict with modern science that hindered the emergence of a native Chinese tradition of science and technology. Similar observations apply to India, the Islamic world and, above all, to Latin America.

Technological progress has dramatically changed the cultural fabric of the world, as its methods and contents are able to transcend national boundaries. Theoretical reasoning must always be transformed afresh into economic, social and political reality. For this reason, we must be aware of the cultural postulates of our knowledge and technology. Joseph Needham speaks of the need for "scientific ecumenism," meaning a confluence of many-sided traditions of technology and science under various cultural prerequisites. Cardinal problems, such as the relation between human beings and the biosphere, or patterns of production in industry and agriculture, all bear earmarks of the impact of science and technology.

As the example of the Andean countries clearly shows, technology always implies a loss of social cohesion and of individual identity. For this reason, we need to redefine development indicators which until now have not been sufficiently appreciated. We must account for dimensions of a country's quality of life. As these dimensions are not expressed in economic terms, they cannot be quantified. Nevertheless, they determine a country's potential for achievement within the framework of its intellectual and cultural history. Only the union of science and technology, understood in this encompassing sense, can serve as the driving force for the productive activity of a country. This in turn determines the country's technology, the social scope within which it is applied, the nature of its labor force and the distribution of labor within society. All spheres of social life are touched upon, as are all conditions of life, including education. *The point is to conjoin progress in science and technology with progress in society and culture.*

Not until we have subjected the development of science and technology to a control involving a country's social and cultural needs can we be sure that the productive capacity of the country will be genuine.

Science and Technology in Relation to Social Rationality and Educational Policy

This study deals with the conflict between different conceptions of science and technology. It does so by analyzing the cultural dynamics that unfolded from pre-Columbian culture through the colonial period and the era of the young republics up to the present day.

Because technological development is historical, its characteristics are largely determined by time and by the local circumstances within which any technology must develop. Hence, scientific and technological knowledge always changes in relation to a given location and a given time. Technologies can be introduced only if they are granted validity within the economy where they are meant to be employed. By the same token, economic and historical circumstances are a product of the technology utilized in a country or culture. Technical innovation and economic change are thus closely linked in a relation of cause and effect, forming a dynamic circle.

Technology gives a society significant points of reference for making economic decisions. Developments take shape in the form of new products, new methods of production and new commodities in which new materials can be utilized. These factors govern the activities of production.

This situation can be observed in the beginning of the twentieth century in Peru, when an attempt was made to expand and modernize the mining industry and coastal agriculture. Both of these activities were intended to increase exports. Particularly in the case of Peru, it is clear where the misconception lies: although the state can choose and introduce technology, its own technological options are limited to the extent that it is unable to generate indigenous capabilities for creating technology.

Peru's case is symptomatic. The Andes Pact states work largely with technologies they did not create themselves, but purchased in the industrial countries, usually at unfavorable terms—particularly with regard to licenses and equipment. The question arises as to whether newly purchased technologies can be adequately developed at home. In the Andes states, the dynamics of technology are not continuous but irregular, and bypass sustaining elements of the productive process. These dynamics are purely defensive, being designed to ward off economic challenges and to obviate the need for domestic production.

When commentators face the problem of how technology and culture can best interact in different countries, they often place an emphasis on the dynamics of scientific creation and technology. But they give too little attention to the confrontation between the different approaches to technology and science that have arisen in different cultural traditions.

In its balance and sophistication, a sociocultural system is comparable to a biological organism or an ecological system. Each part is connected to every other part and is governed by an overriding functionality. This applies to language patterns, rites, mythologies, forms of religion and standards of jurisprudence in addition to the worlds of material goods, technology and the economy. There is no such thing as a static community. Instead, what we see is a system made up of various levels and elements changing at different speeds.

Thus, we must isolate and pinpoint those cultural patterns and traditions that can either hinder or stimulate dynamic development. It is important to recognize cultural and religious activities (for example, in rituals or social events) that allow us to identify these patterns and traditions. By the same token, practices of consumption and lively reasoning allow us to draw conclusions about the social makeup of a culture.

Every culture derives its vitality from an integrated logic of space and time. This logic, or the efforts to counteract it, account for the mechanisms with which technological achievements are resisted or defended and accepted. This is important, since science is increasingly tending to converge with technology. In turn, the state of technological research is strongly influenced by the needs of industry, particularly (as it is in many cases) the needs of the same companies who finance this research.

Just as developed countries devise national strategies, underdeveloped countries must set about transforming their technology imports into an economy that is aligned with the needs of their entire population, that is adapted to local culture and that will lead to technological independence. And they must give these efforts the means to achieve success. Emphasis must be placed on a new policy of development and technology designed to expand and consolidate the nation's scientific and technological capacity. A new, independent—and hence indigenous—pattern of technological development should arise that offers alternatives to transnational and oligopolitical or imported and imitative approaches and thus strengthens the country's internal structure. The possibilities and repercussions of technological change must find greater expression in educational programs and professional qualifications.

New programs and educational methods in the area of science and technology must be developed and coordinated within the socioeconomic and cultural dimensions. The goal of this integrated program for children, young people and adults should be to train talent and ability in scientific research and to inculcate an acceptance of technological innovation. An important prerequisite for this alternative approach is a policy of long-term industrial development and modernization which is grounded in an expanding market of new goods and services—a policy that productively integrates a nation's capacity for technological innovation among its middle classes and heavy industry.

One important step is the gradual replacement of imports in the various fields of engineering, in the use of state purchasing power, in specific strategic programs, as well as in capital goods, computer sciences and telecommunications. Indigenous capacity for research and development must be enhanced in critical areas of higher education.

A policy of educative technology of this sort should include a system for incorporating advanced technologies into new national strategies for industry, society and agriculture. This integrative capability presupposes a full understanding of the new technological capacity, as well as an ability to imitate, reproduce, improve and adapt technological innovations. In the case of the computer sciences, biological engineering and microelectronics, not only must the capacity for production and innovation be increased, it is also essential that these fields be adapted to market conditions. The policy to be drawn up must also answer questions regarding public administration, which plays a key role in how these measures will function. Major branches of a country's public sector must be integrated wherever technologies appropriate to a given company are applied within their radius of production. Educational offerings, whether traditional or experimental, must be shifted from theoretical knowledge to practical application.

For this reason, talent for technological innovation in the Andes states must be promoted by creating technological research centers and institutions in all sectors of production: telecommunications, metallurgy, civil engineering, computer sciences, microelectronics and biological engineering. Educational measures must take precedence over economic and financial steps.

To ensure indigenousness, the technology policy must include means by which to identify criteria, purposes, priorities and options in the economy or in institutions. By democratizing this information, a path can be opened up to economic and scientific-technological autonomy.

This requires that new priorities be set in the jobs offered on the labor market. Here the emphasis should lie on educational innovations of a long-term nature. The creation of courses of study which combine the processes of education and social adaptation with labor strategies and professional qualifications will require greater experimentation in the area of teacher training

The process outlined above for "indigenizing" technology is the central thesis of this study. It is guided by an awareness of the cultural dimension, i.e., those parameters of behavior evidenced by different ethnic groups when faced with technologies that unavoidably undermine their identifying features and initiate cultural change.

The basis for this process is a fresh, conceptual understanding of how technology relates to culture. What is needed is a holistic anthropological view encompassing not only the Latin American people's attitude toward nature and the supernatural, but also the relation between nature and the deities of pre-Columbian culture. This calls for the inclusion of myth and religion, always with an eye to their compatibility with technology. Nor can we afford to overlook the relation of the Latin American people to time and space and their position in the universe: these factors, too, have an impact on government, society and the economy.

Suggestions for Further Reading

Aaronovitch, S., and M.C. Sawyer. "The Concentration of British Manufacturing." *Lloyds Bank Review* No. 14, October 1974.

Ademan, I., and C.T. Morris. *Economic Growth and Social Equity in Developing Countries*. Stanford: Stanford University Press, 1973.

Antonorsi-Blanco, Marcel. "Las consequencias sociales del cambio tecnológico y la búsqueda de tecnologías alternativas." CONICIT Caracas, *Reto* 4, Fall 1975.

Arrow, K.J. *Social Choice and Individual Values*. New York, 1951.

Atkinson, A.B., and J.B. Stiglitz. "A New View of Technological Change." *Economic Journal* 79, June 1962.

Baer, W., and M. Hervé. "Employment and Industrialization in Developing Countries." *Quarterly Journal of Economics* 80, February 1966.

Bain, J.S. *Barriers to New Competition*. Cambridge, MA: Harvard University Press, 1956.

Barnet, Richard J., and Ronald F. Muller. *Global Reach: The Power of Multinational Corporations*. New York: Simon & Schuster, 1974.

Baumol, W.J. *Economic Theory and Operations Analysis*. New York: Prentice Hall, 1961.

Ben-David, Joseph. *The Scientist's Role in Society: A Comparative Study*. New Jersey: Prentice Hall, 1971.

Bernal, J. *Science in History*. Harmondsworth: Penguin, 1969.

Boyle, Godfrey, and Peter Harper. *Radical Technology*. London: Wildwood House, 1976.

Bruno, M. "Development Policy and Dynamic Comparative Advantage." *The Technology Factor in International Trade*. R. Vernond, ed. Oficina Nacional de Investgación Económica, n.p. 1970.

Bruton, H. "Economic Development and Labor Use: A Review." *World Development* I, December 1973.

Business Intelligence Program. *Biotechnology and Agriculture*, Report 707, Fall 1984.

Calder, Nigel. *Technopolis*. Paris: Flammarion, 1971.

Casas, Rosalba. *Algunos lineamentos de política de ciencia y tecnología para al sector agropecuario*. Institutode Investigaciones Sociales, UNAM, Mexico, 1986.

Chenery, H.B., M.S. Ahluwalia, C.L.G. Bell, J.H. Duloy and R. Jolly. *Redistribution with Growth*. Oxford: Oxford University Press, 1974.

Chipman, J., L. Harwicz, M. Richter and H. Sonnenschen, eds. *Preferences, Utility and Demand*, Harcourt Brace, n.p. 1971.

Clarke, Robin, ed. *Notes for the Future (An Alternative History of the Past Decade)*. New York: Universe Books, 1975.

Comisíon Económica para la América Latina (CEPAL). *Choice of Technique in the Latin American Textile Industry*. New York: UNO, 1966.

Cooper, C. "Science, Technology and Production in the Underdeveloped Countries: An Introduction." *Journal of Development Studies* 9, October 1972.

____. "Science Policy and Technological Change in Underdeveloped Economies." *World Development* 2, March 1974.

Cooper, C., and F. Sercovich. "The Channels and Mechanisms for the Transfer of Technology from Developed to Developing Countries." Geneva: UNCTAD, TD/D/AC 11/5, Geneva, 1970.

Denison, E. *Why Growth Rates Differ*. Washington, DC: Brookings Institution, 1967.

Departamento de Asuntos Económicos y Sociales de las Naciones Unidas. *Panel of Foreign Investment in Latin America*, Colombia, 1971.

Dickson, D. *Alternative Technology and the Politics of Technical Change*. Bloomington: Fontana, 1974.

Dobb, M.H. *Theories of Value and Distribution Since Adam Smith*. Cambridge, 1973.

Domar, E. *Essays in the Theory of Growth*. Oxford: Oxford University Press, 1957.

Eckaus, R.S. "The Factor Proportions Problem in Underdeveloped Areas." *American Economic Review* 45, September 1955.

Edel, Matthew. *Economies and the Environment*. n.p. 1973.

Edwards, E.O., ed. *Employment in Developing Countries*. New York: Columbia University Press, 1974.

Ehrlich, Paul and Anne. *Population, Resources, Environment*. Paris: Fayard, 1972.

Ehrlich, Paul, et al. *Human Ecology: Problems and Solutions*. San Francisco: W.R. Freeman and Co., 1973.

Emmanuel, A. *Unequal Exchange: A Study of the Imperialism of Trade*. Monthly Review Press, n.p. 1972.

Farvar, M.T., and J.P. Milton, eds. *The Careless Technology: Ecology and International Development*. New York: Natural History Press, Doubleday & Co., 1972.

Frank, A.G. *Capitalism and Underdevelopment in Latin America*. Monthly Review Press, London, 1967.

____. *Latin America: Underdevelopment or Revolution*. Monthly Review Press, London, 1969.

Freeman, C. "Research and Development: A Comparison between British and American Industry." *National Institute Economic and Social Review* 20, May 1962.

Furtado, C. *Development and Underdevelopment*. Berkeley: University of California Press, 1964.

Galbraith, J.K. *The New Industrial State*. Harmondsworth: Penguin, 1974.

Georgescu-Roegen, N. *The Entropy Law and the Economic Process*. Cambridge, MA: Harvard University Press, 1971.

Gerschenkron, A. *Economic Backwardness in Historical Perspective*. Cambridge, MA: Harvard University Press, 1962.

Griffin, Keith. *Underdevelopment in Spanish America*. London: Allen & Unwin, 1969.

Healey, J.M. "Industrialization, Capital Intensity and Efficiency." *Bulletin of the Oxford Institute of Economics and Statistics* 30, November 1968.

Helleiner, G.K. "Manufactured Exports from Less Developed Countries and Multinational Firms." *Economic Journal* 83, March 1973.

____. "The Role of Multinational Corporations in the Less Developed Countries' Trade in Technology." *World Development* 3, April 1975.

Herskovits, Melville J. *Les bases de l'anthropologie culturelle,*. Paris: Petite Bibliothèque Payot, 1967.

Hirsch, S. *Location of Industry and International Competitiveness*. Oxford: Clarendon Press,1967.

Hollis, M., and E.J. Nell. *Rational Economic Man: A Philosophical Critique of Neoclassical Economics*. Cambridge, 1975.

Hutchinson, T.W. *The Significance and Basic Postulates of Economic Theory*. London, 1960.

Johnson, H.G. *International Trade and Economic Growth*. London: Allen & Unwin, 1958.

____. *Comparative Cost and Commercial Policy: Theory for a Developing World Economy*. Conferencias Wicksell, n.p. 1968.

Kay, C. "Comparative Development of the European Manorial System and the Latin American Hacienda System." *Journal of Peasant Studies* 2, October 1974.

Landes, D.S. *The Unbound Prometheus*. Cambridge: Cambridge University Press, 1969.

Leff, N.H. *The Brazilian Capital Goods Industry, 1929-1964*. Cambridge, MA: Harvard University Press, 1968.

Lewis, W.A. *The Theory of Economic Growth*. London: Allen & Unwin, 1955.

Lowe, A. *On Economic Knowledge*. New York, 1965.

Maizels, A. *Industrial Growth on World Trade*. Cambridge: Cambridge University Press, 1963.

Mansfield, E. *The Economics of Technological Change*. New York: Longman, 1969.

Maritano, A. *A Latin American Common Market*. Notre Dame, Canada: University of Notre Dame Press, 1970.

McKinnon, R.L. *Money and Capital in Economic Development*. Washington, DC: Brookings Institution, 1973.

Meadows, D.H., et al. *The Limits of Growth*. New York: New American Library, 1972.

von Mises, L. *Epistemological Problems of Economics*. New Jersey: Princeton, 1960.

Morawetz, D. "Employment Implications of Industrialization in Developing Countries: A Survey." *Economic Journal* 84, September 1974.

____. "Elasticities of Substitution in Industry." *World Development* 4, No. 1, January 1976.

Müller-Plantenberg, Urs. "Technologie et dépendence." Critique de l'Economie Politique 3 (Spring 1971): 68–82.

Myrdal, G. *Economic Theory and Underdeveloped Regions*. London: Duckworth, 1957.

Office of Technology Assessment. *Technology, Public Policy, and the Changing Structure of American Agriculture*. Washington, DC: Congress of the United States, 1986.

Pickett, J., D. Forsyth and N. McBain. "The Choice of Technology, Economic Efficiency and Employment in Developing Countries." *World Development* 2, March 1986.

Prebisch, R. *Towards a New Trade Policy for Development*. New York: UNO, 1964.

Puiseux, Louis. *L'Energie et le désarroi post-industriel* (essai sur la croissance énergetique). Paris: Hachette, 1973.

Ranis, G., ed. *The Gap between Rich and Poor Nations*. New York: MacMillan, 1972.

Robinson, R., ed. *Industrialization in Developing Countries*. Cambridge: Cambridge Overseas Studies Committee, 1965.

Robson, P., ed. *International Economic Integration*. Harmondsworth: Penguin Readings, 1971.

Sachs, Ignacy. *Croissance et environnement: élements pour une stratégie d'harmonisation* (Estudio dirigido por Ignacy Sachs, para la Conferencia de Naciones Unidas para el Medio Ambiente Humano). New York, 1972.

____. "Développement, environnement et évaluation des techniques." *Revue Internationale des Sciences Sociales* 25 (1973): 301–312.

Salter, W.E.G. *Productivity and Technical Change*. Cambridge: Cambridge University Press, 1966.

Samuelson, P. "International Trade and the Equalization of Factor Prices." *Economic Journal* 58, June 1948.

____. "Some Notions of Causality and Teleology in Economics." *Cause and Effect*. P.D. Lerner, ed. New York, 1965.

Schumacher, E.F. *Small Is Beautiful: A Study of Economics As If People Mattered*. London: Blond & Briggs, 1973.

Sen, A.K. *Choice of Techniques: An Aspect of the Theory of Planned Economic Development*. Oxford: Basil Blackwell, 1972.

____. *Collective Choice and Social Welfare*. San Francisco, 1970.

_____. *On Economic Inequality*. Oxford, 1973.

Sercovich, F.C. *Foreign Technology and Control in the Argentinian Industry*. Dissertation. University of Sussex, London, 1974.

Smith, A., ed. *Wage Policy Issues in Economic Development*. New York: MacMillan, 1969.

Solow, R.M. *Growth Theory*. Oxford: Clarendon Press, 1970.

Staley, E., and R. Morse. *Modern Small Industry for Developing Countries*. New York: MacGraw Hill, 1965.

Strassman, W.P. *Technological Change and Economic Development*. Ithaca, NY: Cornell University Press, 1968.

_____. "Mass Production of Dwellings in Columbia: A Case Study." Mimeographed. OIT, Geneva, 1974.

Streeten, P.P. "Technology Gaps Between Rich and Poor Countries." *The Scottish Journal of Development Studies* 19, November 1972.

Sunkel, O. "National Development Policy and External Dependency in Latin America." *Journal of Development Studies* 6, October 1969.

_____. "Transnational Capital and National Disintegration in Latin America." *Social and Economic Studies* 22, March 1973.

Sylos-Labini, P. *Oligopoly and Technical Progress*. Trans. by E. Henderson. Cambridge, MA: Harvard University Press, 1969.

Szentes, T. *The Political Economy of Underdevelopment*. Budapest: Budapest Akademiai Kiado, 1971.

Tinbergen, Jan, et al. *RIO: Reshaping International Order*. A Report of the Club of Rome. New York: E.P. Dutton & Co., Inc., 1970.

Toffler, Alwin. *Future Shock*. New York: Bantam Books, 1970.

Turnham, D. *The Employment Problem in Less Developed Countries. A Review of the Evidence*. OCDE, 1971.

UN Conference on Trade and Development (UNCTAD). *Dominant Positions of Market Power of Transnational Corporations: Use of the Transfer Pricing Mechanism*. ST/MD/6. Geneva, 1977.

United Nations Industrial Development Organization (UNIDO). *Small Scale Industry in Latin America*. Vienna, 1969.

Varian, H.R. "Equity, Envy and Efficiency." *Journal of Economic Theory*, 1974.

_____. "Distributive Justice, Welfare, Economics and the Theory of Fairness." *Philosophy and Public Affairs*, 1975.

_____. "Two Problems in the Theory of Fairness." *Journal of Public Economics*, 1976.

Weisskopf, R. Levy, L. Nisonoff and E. Wolff. "A Multi-sector Simulation Model of Employment, Growth and Income Distribution in Puerto Rico: A Re-evaluation of 'Successful' Development Strategy." Mimeographed. New Haven: Yale, 1973.

Wilkinson, R.G. *Poverty and Progress*. London: Methuen, 1973.

Wong, S. "The 'F-Tuist' and the Methodology of Paul Samuelson." *American Economic Review*, 1973.

Wynne, Brian. "Technology Assessment." *Science for People* 24 (1974): 11–23.

Zevallos, M., et al. *Ciencia y tecnología para el desarrollo. Una bibliografía.* Centro de Investigaciones de la Universidad del Pacífico, Lima, 1980.

THREE

SCIENCE AND TECHNOLOGY IN LATIN AMERICA

Summary

The peripheral role forced upon the Andes Pact states by the colonial powers has made it essential for them to develop an integrated national plan for science and technology. Not until these countries have a scientific-technological system rooted in their own culture will it be possible to overcome their disadvantaged development. Outside technologies, when transferred, must be modified and adapted to local cultural circumstances. Industries that rely on foreign capital must also be encouraged to focus more strongly on local research. Various tasks are necessary to achieve this: first, feasibility studies and market overviews must be made before and after investment; second, the technological spectrum must be marked out and suitable technologies selected. An expanded concept of what constitutes a technological system is imperative.

Technology and Cultural Plurality

In the last few decades, Latin America's percentage of the world economy has noticeably declined. The reasons for this must be pointed out. Latin America has an ethnic and cultural variety which is particularly evident in the Andes Pact states. However, its ethnic variety is not matched by a comparable variety on the political and economic levels, one of the region's cardinal problems. On the contrary, the Andes Pact states are dominated by an unrealistic notion of a national society that merely pretends to be culturally homogeneous, in its political decisions above all.

Still, the need to recognize Latin America's cultural variety must be stressed. This is a mandatory prerequisite if the Latin American countries are to formulate new cultural and national identities. To do this, many conditions must be fulfilled. First, there must be an awareness that every culture is the result of an initially unique, nonreduplicative historical process that enriches the whole of human experience. Second, the crisis in the national economies must be seen as a crisis of national cultural models. Other cultures whose right to exist has been denied up to now can lead us to an important realization: once their right to exist has been granted and assured, they may help to solve problems at first considered insoluble. A greater interest in traditional technologies and forms of social organization can, after extensive study, produce alternative solutions for national economies. This argument is directed above all at those trends toward uniformity that negate cultural diversity. People must be encouraged to reorganize the social and economic order in different cultural traditions. Until now, the economic crisis has dangerously reduced cultural variety to a threatening uniformity. Yet, in the Andes Pact states in particular, it is essential to create a fruitful coexistence of different cultures in a national alliance. Only in this way will it be possible to address the crucial issue—how can culture develop autonomously against the background of native technology and cultural plurality.

This presupposes that all problems regarding the territorial organization of a country have been solved. Similarly, the judiciary, which has been split off from traditional authorities, must be restored to a national equilibrium. Another prerequisite is the study of linguistic dialects and linguistic families in order to recognize the role of formal and informal religious systems in the interplay of cultural activities. A methodology and system of interpretation must be worked out to establish an intercultural dialogue in the Andes Pact states to counteract ethnocentric prejudices, to produce appropriate legal regulations for administrative bodies and finally to anchor science and technology within the state and the economy. All development projects must be evaluated in this light.

The struggle for cultural pluralism presupposes a mental decolonialization devoid of any and all forms of dogma.

Science and Technology in Early Latin America: The Colonial Example

Latin America's economic development was marked by the following historical stages: the precolonial native cultures; the preindustrial colonial period; the period of integration into the world market on the basis of exports of raw materials; the period of industrialization with the goal of import substitution; and finally, the period of growing difficulties with import substitution and export diversification.

In the precolonial, pre-Columbian period (see Chapter 4), there were no points of contact with foreign cultural systems. The first stage of contact extended from the early sixteenth to the nineteenth centuries, and was dominated by the needs of the colonial power, Spain. The second period began in the middle of the nineteenth century and lasted into the first third of the twentieth century. The prevailing form of economy resided in the export of a few types of raw materials and the import of industrial and consumer goods. After attaining political independence in the first quarter of the nineteenth century, a few governments made efforts to adapt their scientific facilities to developments then taking place in northern and central Europe and the United States of America under the banner of enlightenment and industrialization. The next period brought about industrialization in the form of import substitution.

The Spaniards who colonized Latin America were not so much peasants or artisans as soldiers and, above all, merchants. This constitutes a major difference with the settlers of North America in the seventeenth century, who settled on large areas of land rather than in a few coastal enclaves, as in Latin America. Large numbers of people emigrated to North America with the aim of establishing permanent communities rather than making short-term conquests for material gain.

Moreover, the empire of the Incas, which reached a very high level of cultural attainment, was based on an agrarian culture which in turn had repercussions on the organization of society. In addition, the ecology of the Iberian peninsula at the time of the conquistadors was fundamentally different from that of the Andean highlands. The important point is that, compared to England, Germany and France, only a very small number of technological innovations issued from the Iberian peninsula to fuel the Industrial Revolution during the centuries that followed.

The only steps taken to set up a "partial" infrastructure served the needs of exploiting and transporting raw materials and expanding the administrative and mercantile towns. The only schools established were mining schools; the Andean elite always strove to link their scientific system to Europe.

Early science in Hispanic America had two points of culmination. The first occurred in the sixteenth century, primarily in Mexico and Peru, where there arose a distinctive type of scholarship largely under European influence. The second period of interest occurred during the second half of the eighteenth century, especially from 1759 to 1788 under Carlos III of Spain. Major expeditions were undertaken, ideas began to circulate and a limited local development took place.

One source of a certain continuity in Latin America was the founding of universities during the colonial era, as well as the installation of printing presses, whose productivity went hand in hand with the university policy then current in Spain. During the colonial period, the Spaniards founded no fewer than thirty universities in Hispanic America. The University of Lima was founded in 1535, the Colegio del Rosario in Columbia in 1551.

Experiments in the natural sciences were limited from the very beginning. Mention should be made of the amalgamation technique, an early industrial process in Central America developed by Bartolome de Medina, who originally came from Seville. Medina emigrated from Spain in 1533; in 1555, after two years of experiments, he initiated the process of amalgamation later undertaken in Peru in 1571. His work was improved on in Peru in the sixteenth and seventeenth centuries by the research of Alonso Barba.

In addition, there arose a lively transfer of agrarian technology from the Spanish homeland to the colonies. Despite a number of innovations, however, relatively little was accomplished in the cultivation of local grains. The Spaniards introduced a wide variety of plants and animals to Latin America, as we can see from a list compiled by Bernabe Cobos in the seventeenth century. This list includes wheat, rice, various types of fruits and vegetables, as well as horses, cows, sheep, mules, chickens and geese. It comes as no surprise, then, that the outstanding science of the colonial period was botany, not least of all for the practical purpose of obtaining medicines.

Despite its pragmatic leanings, research in colonial Latin America was not really put to practical use. At this point, a practice began that was to have grave consequences for Latin America in the following centuries: hardly any contributions were made to scientific theory on the basis of empirical experimentation. The result was a hesitant practical utilization of research without a parallel theoretical superstructure.

Moreover, compared to the other countries of Europe, Spain had a paucity of scientific theory. Menendez y Pelayo noted this when he spoke of it as the land of mystics and idealists. The same sense is conveyed in a remark by the contemporary mathematician Rey Pastor, who found Spanish culture weak in pure science, particularly in the abstractions of mathematics. Furthermore, he continued, Latin American scientists of the colonial period felt to a great extent that because of their peripheral location, they had too little contact with luminaries in North America and Europe. While it is true that from the sixteenth to eighteenth centuries the Spaniards and Portuguese made efforts to examine local questions and products scientifically, in the end these efforts achieved only a very modest success.

A certain native scientific tradition seemed about to emerge in the wealthier colonies, such as Mexico during its three centuries of Spanish domination, or Columbia in the eighteenth century. However, with very few exceptions, science took on a practical bent, without the theoretical abstraction necessary to establish a far-reaching indigenous technology. Latin America lacked the practical-minded intelligence of a Benjamin Franklin, or what one might call a practical theory of the sort that, in North America, led to an early consolidation of industry and, in combination with Darwin's theory of evolution and Herbert Spencer's doctrine of social Darwinism, to an outstanding national ascendancy in science and technology.

Later efforts to produce industrial goods on location instead of importing them from abroad were limited to products intended to meet the needs of affluent classes oriented toward the centers of the world economy. As a result, findings from science and technology were adopted from the industrial countries rather than developed locally. Even today, this remains a basic problem for the Andes Pact states. Against this backdrop, an indigenous technology was hardly likely to emerge.

The local scientific-technological infrastructure was seldom challenged with new tasks. Even industrial plant, which had so enriched knowledge in Europe and the United States in, for example, the communications sciences and the production of staple goods, was built primarily on knowledge copied from the West. Moreover, it was installed and monitored under the supervision of European and North American experts. From the very beginning, due to the way it was integrated into the world market, Latin America lacked the close connection between high-growth industries and a scientific-technological infrastructure so characteristic of the industrial countries, and so essential to an indigenous technology. Thus arose an image of Andean science and technology as being historically backward and isolated. Underdevelopment and international disequilibrium are unavoidable in a system that focuses the technological progress of the world market on such a small number of countries.

The Value of Technological Development in Latin America

It was obvious that science and technology would become a major topic in the North-South dialogue. Recently, the question of what value to place on science and technology in the development of Latin America has come increasingly to the fore. Since then, there has hardly been a national or even regional development program that does not bear witness to this new awareness. Admittedly, sufficient attention is not always given to the limiting conditions of culture, even though they have since become a basic component of development policy.

The crisis of development in the technologically peripheral nations has always been a crisis of development theory as well. Economic growth alone, no matter how rapid, cannot solve social problems or reduce cultural tensions. Until now, the importance of science and technology in the overall development of society has penetrated the minds of politicians and planning officials far more quickly and noticeably than the equally important factor of cultural change, which has yet to integrate scientific-technological progress in any lasting way.

Only an all-embracing and interdisciplinary approach to research will be able to form a link between science and technology on the one hand, and the overall evolution of society on the other, including the evolution of culture. This interaction could be used to dismantle the structural dependency of the peripheral countries, transforming dependent relations into independent ones. As far as science and technology are concerned, what Latin America lacks is a decisive process of consolidation.

Because they are technical procedures, the transfer of technology and even intermediary or adapted technology have a profound impact on industrial production. Technology in its entirety may be viewed as the technical procedure used by science to comprehend the processes of change and transformation in matter, energy and the human environment—in short, in the extrinsic conditions of existence in human society. Seen in this light, technology includes not only scientific knowledge, but also the practical experience gained in the exploitation of this knowledge by governments and societies. In this way, it is fundamentally linked with culture. While it is true that technology is always a constituent part of a product, it can also be found in knowledge of technical procedures, whether contained in documents or in acquired patterns of behavior.

We can speak of "applied technology" whenever there are close relations between social and cultural conditions on the one hand, and the process of research and development using scientific and technological methods on the other. In this case, we are referring to production techniques that take into account the given economic, social and cultural conditions of a nation.

Every state is forced to place certain emphases on its science and technology. In doing so, it must cross qualitative and quantitative thresholds, at the very least in order to master the language of international scientific-technological affairs. In many cases, the Andes Pact states have yet to reach this threshold. At first glance, what the Andes Pact states have in common is their peripheral role in the world economy, both past and present, and the intrinsic heterogeneity of their production structures and markets, partly caused by extrinsic factors. The end result is unequal internal processes of development, exacerbated by extreme contrasts in society.

Up to the present day, the rapid pace of technological change has enabled the wealthy nations to continue to develop with relative flexibility. It is the lack of technological change that has condemned the underdeveloped countries to a drastic decline in per capita income.

Technological change and a concomitant monopoly of the knowledge required to increase productivity and wages ensure that the developed nations will have a relatively high rate of profitability. Furthermore, their monopoly of top-level technology puts them in a position to extract higher profits from the underdeveloped nations through trade and direct investment. The contrasts are made more glaring by the fact that part of the economic surplus of the underdeveloped countries is channeled exclusively to the wealthy nations. This is mainly because private entrepreneurs can improve their balance sheets by shifting production to the industrializing countries, thereby depleting human and financial resources in the underdeveloped countries, whereas foreign aid investments usually come from state organizations. This scientific-technological imbalance on a global scale is a basic cause of international social and economic disintegration.

Seen realistically, the problems of the underdeveloped countries can be solved only by setting up, rather than dismantling, a high level of technology. All the same, any economy based on technology must be flanked by problem-solving expertise covering a broad spectrum of activities, from science to administration and management. Yet, setting up an indigenous body of experts means creating a capacity to carry out research and development, thus leading us back to our starting point: educative technology. We must promote institutions that make it possible for scientists and engineers to work efficiently (see Chapter 7).

Nevertheless, though research and development have contributed substantially to the economic success of the industrial nations, the underdeveloped countries will not solve their technological problems by simply importing the necessary technology from the developed countries.

A political economy must transcend mechanistic models and realize that a human being is more than *homo oeconomicus*. Planning is not a property of the economy; it merely has an economic dimension. *Political economy, as understood here, must cast off the yoke of pure economy and accommodate the ecological, social and cultural dimensions of growth.*

Expanding the Concept of Technology

In a global sense, there is no double standard between the technologically advanced nations and the underdeveloped countries. Technology is always viewed as the process by which knowledge is created and disseminated. But this does not mean that the person who creates a technology is the same as the one who puts it to use, or that applied technology is employed at the same place where it was invented. On the contrary, these are interactive factors. Without a full-fledged scientific system, innovative technological development in any country is impossible. What is required is a triangle consisting of the scientific-technological system, the government and the productive sector.

What makes up the scientific-technological system? Put simply, we can say it is made up of the political organs that determine a country's scientific policy and the scientific-technological infrastructure, i.e., the totality of educational and scientific institutions that supply a country with knowledge. The productive sector is the source of a country's demand for knowledge and technology, which it receives in the form of services and products.

One responsibility that the productive sector of a country must assume is the utilization of resources. Here scientific and technological innovation is called for. The key role in aligning technological development with the social and economic goals of a country is played by government. For these reasons, it is the government that takes financial, fiscal and legislative steps to revitalize the technological system.

It goes without saying that technology is applied in building factories and installing equipment. Knowledge of technology is also required at the execution stage, that is, when organizing production facilities, improving the efficiency of the innovations employed and importing and adapting material and know-how.

In the industrialization process undergone by Latin America since the nineteenth century, only a minimal amount of applied technology has come from internal institutions, i.e., from research and development efforts of the countries themselves. We should remember, however, that it is not only the industrial nations, but also the underdeveloped and industrializing countries that have the capacity to create technological know-how. Indeed, we can even imagine the situation being reversed with the industrial nations buying technological expertise from the developing countries.

In the expanded sense used in this study, technology includes information on the technological potential of nature, information necessary for manufacturing industrial products. Here we can see points of contact with native traditions, though an awareness of this fact still has to be nurtured. One illustration is the cosmological thought of the indios, which we will discuss in the next chapter.

Suggestions for Further Reading

Alberti, Giorgio, and Enrique Mayer, eds. *Reciprocidad e intercambio en los Andes peruanos.* Instituto de Estudios Peruanos, Perú Problema 12, Lima, 1974.

Altimir, Oscar. *Las búsquedas de nuevas alternativas para el desarrollo de América Latina.* Junte del Acuerdo Cartagena. Seminario sobre el Grupo Andino: Nuevos enfoques para el desarrollo y la integración subregional, Lima, 17–19 September 1985.

Amat y Leon, C., et al. *Realidad del campo peruano depues de la reforma agraria. 10 ensayos criticos.* Centro de Investigación y Capacitación (CIC). Editora Ital Perú S.A., Lima, 1980.

Aseniero, George. "A Reflection on Developmentalism: From Development to Transformation." *Development as Social Transformation.* London: Hodder and Stoughton and United Nations University, 1985.

Baer, Werner, and Isaac Kerstenitzky. *Inflation and Growth in Latin America.* New Haven: Yale University Press, 1964.

Barrenecha, Carlos L., ed. *El problema regional hoy.* Lima: Tarea, 1983.

Barry, Brian. *Power and Political Theory.* London and New York: John Wiley, 1976.

Bitar, Sergio. "La inserción de América Latina en la economía mundial. Riesgos y desafíos." Unpublished. Santiago, April 1986.

Brunner, José Joaquín. *Universidad y sociedad latinoamericana: un esquema de interpretación.* CRESALC/UNESCO, Caracas, 1985.

Caballero, José Maria. *Economía agraria de la sierra peruana. Antes de la reforma agraria de 1969.* Instituto de Estudios Peruanos, Lima, 1981.

Carbonetto, Daniel. "El sector informal urbano: estructura y evidencias." *Desafíos para la economía peruana 1985–1990.* Ed. Germán Alarco. Centro de Investigación de la Universidad del Pacífico, Lima, 1985.

Cardoso, F.H., and E. Faletto. *Dependencia y desarrollo en América Latina.* Siglo XXI. Mexico, 1969.

Carr, M. *Economically Appropriate Technologies for Developing Countries: An Annotated Bibliography.* Grupo de Desarrollo de Tecnología Intermedia, n.p. 1976.

Casas Gonzalez, Antonio. "El potencial de las fuentes convencionales en el abastecimiento energético de la América Latina." El Trimestre Económico 200, Mexico, December, 1983.

Centre d'Etudes Prospectives et d'Informations Internationales (CEPII). *Economie mondiale: la montée des tensions*. Paris: Economica, 1983.

Chavez Achong, Julio. *Introdución al problema agrario en el Perú*. Lima: Ideas, 1983.

Chonchol, Jacques. "Revalorización del espacio rural como uno de los ejes fundamentales del desarrollo futuro de América Latina." Paris, 1985.

Comisíon Económica para la América Latina (CEPAL). *Choice of Technique in the Latin American Textile Industry*. UNO, New York, 1966.

_____. *Crisis y desarrollo: presente y futuro de América Latina y el Caribe*. Reunión de expertos sobre crisis y desarrollo de América Latina y el Caribe, Santiago de Chile, 29 April–3 May 1983.

_____. *América Latina y el programa de acción de Viena: ciencia y tecnología para el desarrollo de los años ochenta*. Noveno período de sesiones del Comité des Expertos Gubernamentales de Alto Nivel (CEGAL), Montevideo, 23–24 January 1984.

Cotler, Julio. *Clases, estado y nación en el Perú*. Instituto de Estudios Peruanos, Perú Problema 17, Lima, 1978.

Crozier, Brian. *A Theory of Conflict*. London: Hamish Hamilton, 1974.

Dagnino, Renato P. *Aspectos tecnológicos e económicos do armamentismo*. Proyecto prospectiva tecnológica para América Latina, Universidad Estatal de Campinhas, São Paulo, July 1985.

_____. *Novo desenvolvimento e novas tocnologías: una equação a resolver*. Mimeographed, s.p.d.i., February 1986.

Degregori, Carlos Iván. *Ayacucho, raíces de una crisis*. IER José Maria Arguedas, Ayacucho, 1986.

Degregori, Carlos Iván, C. Urrutia and Edwige Balutansky. "Apuntes sobre el desarrollo del capitalismo y la destrucción del área cultural Pokra-Chanca." Investigaciones. Universidad Nacional de San Cristóbal de Huamanga, Ayacucho, 1979. pp. 243–252.

Departamento de Asuntos Económicos y Sociales de las Naciones Unidas. *Panel of Foreign Investment in Latin America*. Colombia, 1971.

_____. *Tendencias y políticas actuales en la economía mundial*. New York, 1985.

Diaz Martinez, Antonio. *Ayacucho: hambre y esperanza*. Ayacucho: Waman Puma, 1969.

Dollfus, Olivier. "Les Andes Centrales tropicales vues par deux géographes: Isaiah Bowman et Carl Troll." *Boletín del Instituto Francés de Estudios Andinos* 7 (1978, Lima): 7–21.

Ernst, Dieter. "Industrial Redeployment and Control Over Technology—Consequences for the Third World." *Vierteljahresberichte* 83, 1981.

Espinoza, Gustavo, and Carlos Malpica. *El problema de la tierra*. Lima: Empresa Editora Amauta S.A., Biblioteca Amauta, 1978.

Fajnzylber, Fernando. "La industrialización de América Latina: especificidades y perspectivas." Mimeographed. August 1985.

Frank, A.G. *Capitalism and Underdevelopment in Latin America*. Monthly Review Press, London, 1967.

______. *Latin America: Underdevelopment or Revolution*. Monthly Review Press, London, 1969.

Fuenzalida, F., T. Valente, J. L. Villaran, J. Golte, C. I. Degregori and J. Casaverde. *El desafío de Huayopampa. Comuneros y empresarios*. Instituto de Estudios Peruanos, Lima, 1982.

García, Norberto, and Víctor Tokman. "Transformación ocupación y crisis." *Revista de la CEPAL* 24, Naciones Unidas, Santiago de Chile, December 1984.

Goldhamer, Herbert. *The Foreign Powers in Latin America*. Princeton: Princeton University Press, 1972.

Gonzales de Olarte, Efraín. "Comunidades campesinas: economía y diferenciación campesina." Instituto de Estudios Sociales, *Crítica Andina* 2 (1978, Cuzco): 137–163.

Griffin, Keith. *Underdevelopment in Spanish America*. London: Allen & Unwin, 1969.

Henriquez, Narda, José Blanes and Sandra Callenas. *Migraciones internas, estructura urbana y estructura productiva*. PUCP, Departamento de Ciencias Sociales, Lima, 1979.

Herrera, Amílcar O. *América Latina y la nueva onda de innovaciones*. Proyecto prospectiva para América Latina, Universidad Estatal de Campinhas, São Paulo, 1985.

______. *Ciencia y política en América Latina*. Siglo XXI, Mexico, 1971.

Herrera, Amílcar O., et al. *América Latina: ciencia y tecnología en el desarrollo y las sociedad*. Editorial Universitaria, Santiago de Chile, 1970.

Hopkins, Raúl. *Desarrollo desigual y crisis en la agricultura peruana, 1944–1969*. Instituto de Estudios Peruanos, Lima, 1981.

Horowitz, Irving Louis. *Historia y elementos de la sociología del conocimiento. Tomo I. Contenido y contexto de las ideas sociales*. EUDEBA (Editorial Univ. de Buenos Aires), Buenos Aires, 1964.

______. *Historia y elementos de la sociología del conocimiento. Tomo II. Contenido y contexto de las ideas sociales*. EUDEBA, Buenos Aires, 1964.

Hurtado, Hugo. *Formación de las comunidades campesinas en el Perú*. Ed. Tercer Mundo. Lima, 1974.

Kaplinsky, Raphael. *Automation: The Technology and Society*. Harlow, Essex: Longman, 1984.

_____. *Electronics Based Automation Technologies and the Onset of Systemofacture: Some Implications for Third World Industrialization*. Institute of Development Studies, University of Sussex, London, June 1984.

Katz, Jorge, Ricardo Soifer and Angel Castaño. *Cambio tecnológico en la industria metalmecánica latinoamericana*. Oficina de la CEPAL, Buenos Aires, September 1985.

Lipset, Seymour Martin, ed. *Elites in Latin America*. New York: Oxford University Press, 1967.

Maldonado, Guillermo. "La América Latina y la integración: opciones frente a la crisis." *Revista de la CEPAL* 27, Santiago de Chile, December 1985.

Maletta, Héctor, and Jesús Foronda. *La acumulación de capital en la agricultura peruana*. Centro de Investigación de la Universidad del Pacífico, Lima, 1980.

Maritano, A. *A Latin American Common Market*. Notre Dame, Canada: University of Notre Dame Press, 1970.

Matos Mar, José, and José Manuel Mejia, eds. *La reforma agraria en el Perú*. Instituto de Estudios Peruanos, Perú Problema 3, Lima, 1980.

_____. *Reforma agraria: logros y contradiciones, 1969–1979*. Instituto de Estudios Peruanos, Lima, 1980.

Nayudamma, Y. *An Alternative Pathway for Industrialization: A Biomass-based Strategy*. Discussion paper. UNIDO, Vienna, 29 June 1984.

Montoya, Rodrigo. *Capitalismo y no capitalismo. Un esudio histórico de su articulación en un eje regional*. Lima: Mosca Azul, 1980.

Murra, John V. *Formaciones económicas y políticas del mundo andino*. Instituto de Estudios Peruanos, Lima, 1975.

Pérez, Carlota. *Microelectronics, Long-waves and World Structural Change: New Perspectives for Developing Countries*. Science Policy Research Unit (SPRU), University of Sussex, London, July 1984.

Prebisch, Raúl. "Renovar el pensamiento económico latinoamericano, un imperativo." *Comercio Exterior* 36, June 1986.

Quintero Ramírez, Rodolfo, and Rosa Luz González. *Agricultura y alimentos, perspectivas mexicanas*. Ponencia presentada als Seminario TEPLA, Universidade de Campinas, April 1986.

Reynolds, Lloyd G. *Economic Growth in the Third World, 1850–1980*. New Haven: Yale University Press, 1985.

Sagasti, Francisco. "Hacia la incorporación de la ciencia y la tecnología en la concepción del desarrollo." *El Trimestre Económico* I, No. 3, Summer 1983.

_____. *Ciencia, tecnología y desarrollo latinoamericano*. Fondo de Cultura Económica, Mexico, 1981.

Sagasti, Francisco, and Cecilia Cook. *Tiempos difíciles: ciencia y tecnología en América Latina durante el decenio de 1980*. GRADE, Lima, December 1985.

Sagasti, Francisco, and Fernando Garland. *Crisis, Knowledge and Development: A Review of Long-term Perspectives on Science and Technology for Development*. GRADE, Lima, January 1985.

Sagasti, Francisco, Fernando Chaparro, Carlos Paredes and Hernán Jaramillo. *Un decenio de transición: ciencia y tecnología en América Latina durante los 70*. GRADE, Lima, March 1983.

Salgado, Germánico. *El Grupo Andino: problemas y perspectivas*. Quito, n.d.

Samir, Amin. *Le développement inégal. Essai sur les formations sociales du capitalisme périphérique*. Paris: Editions de Minuit, 1983.

Sánchez, Vicente. *Modalidades de desarrollo, relaciones internacionales y políticas ambientales*. Programa Desarrollo y Medio Ambiente, El Colegio de México, Mexico, December 1985.

Sánchez Albavera, Fernando, et al. *Problema nacional. Cultura y clases sociales*. DESCO, Lima, 1981.

Schaff, Adam. *Qué futuro nos aguarda?: las consecuencias sociales de la segunda revolución industrial*. Barcelona: Editorial Crítica, 1985.

Schatan, Jacobo. "América Latina. Deuda externa y desarrollo: un enfoque heterodoxo." *Revista Investigaciones Económicas* 215, Mexico.

Sempat Assadourian, Carlos. *El sistema de la economía colonial. Mercado interno, regiones y espacio económico*. Instituto de Estudios Peruanos, Lima, 1982.

Solis, José Luis. "Industrialización, crisis y estrategias alternativas del desarrollo en Centroamérica." *Revista Economía de América Latina*, Mexico, December 1984.

Sunkel, Osvaldo. *América Latina y la crisis económica internacional: ocho tesis y una propuesta*. Grupo Editor Latinoamericano, Buenos Aires, 1985.

Tavares, Maria da Conçeicão. *A retomada da hegemonia Norte America—un aprofundamento do debate*. Universidad Federal do Rio de Janeiro, Instituto de Economía Industrial, ANPEC/PNPE, Rio de Janeiro, August 1985.

Tedesco, Juan Carlos. "Crisis económica, educación y futuro de América Latina." *Revista Nueva Sociedad* 84, Caracas, June 1986.

Tokman, Víctor. "El proceso de acumulación y la debilidad de los actores." *Revista de la CEPAL* 26, Naciones Unidas, August 1985.

______. "Monetarismo global y destrucción industrial." *Revista de la CEPAL* 23, Naciones Unidas, August 1984.

United Nations Conference of Trade and Development (UNCTAD). "Una visión panorámica de las tendencias de la economía mundial." *Cuadernos sobre Prospectiva Energética*, El Colegio de México, Mexico, November 1985.

United Nations Industrial Development Organization (UNIDO). *Industry 2000—New Perspectives*. Vienna, 1979.

____. "Report of the International Forum on Technological Advances and Development." Tbilisi, 12–16 April 1983.

____. *Small Scale Industry in Latin America*. Vienna, 1969.

Urquidi, Víctor, Vicente Sánchez and Eduardo Terrazas. *Perspectivas y alternativas de América Latina ante los problemas mundiales*. Centro de Tepoztlán, Mexico, May 1981.

Wiarda, Hoeard J. "The Future of Latin America: Any Cause for Optimism?" Ed. H. Wiarda. *The Alternative Futures of Latin America*, AEI Foreign Policy and Defensive Review, American Enterprise Institute for Public Policy Research 5, No. 3, Washington, DC, 1985.

Four

The *Pre*-Columbian Cultures

Summary

The cosmology of Latin America's pre-Columbian cultures derives from a magic-mythical proximity to nature and a sense of oneness with the earth. Even today, it continues to be influential, especially in the region's agriculture. When forming our views on future agrarian technology, we must pay attention to technological alternatives that take into account the special traditions of the Andean region. To this end, research centers could be set up in various agricultural and ecological zones. At the same time, a mutuality and balance must be struck between the importation and the indigenous creation of technology. The cultures of the Andean region show an ability to adopt new concepts, provided these concepts are in tune with their traditional ways of thinking. It is at this point that the policy of the European Community should begin, since until now these points of contact have not been sufficiently pinpointed by Western scientists.

There can be no assurance of success in the future unless the propositions of Western science are translated into a specifically Andean form. By the same token, if Andean logic is to work with Western science and technology, the latter must be brought to a point of compatibility with local culture. The goal of the European Community must be to elaborate and develop a new organization of technology in the Andean tradition that meets the preconditions of the region's cultural and religious history. Technological policies of the future must ensure gradual transitions in order to coordinate these two different forms of rationality. Because there is a tight interaction between a technological system and its political economy—an interaction that the Andes Pact states will not be able to escape—the policy of the European Community should be to support an Andean political economy of technological choice.

The Spanish Conquest and the Fractured Cultural Assimilation

The discovery of America was a millennial event that ushered in a new age of history. It is conceivable that Latin America, at the end of the fifteenth century, was about to create its own preindustrial forms of production. But following Columbus's mighty deed, only Europe and North America were given incentives to pursue scientific and technological inventions. In Latin America itself, this same impetus was nowhere to be seen. For while it is true that by opening itself up to the rest of the world the new continent seemed to hold out the promise of growing productivity, in reality only European and North American forces were able to take advantage of the new situation. As a result, Latin America found itself in a contradictory dilemma.

This same period also witnessed the growing strength of the experimental sciences. It was in the seventeenth century that the theory of inductive logic was elaborated by Francis Bacon; later it was put into practice by John Stuart Mill with his philosophy of utilitarianism. The concept of reality became more empirical, and in Spain thinkers such as Ramon Sibuida, or Juan Luis Vives (1492–1540) with his book *Las Disciplinas,* tried to work out a new level of reality.

The prescientific thought of native America could only reject these new European sciences. Travelogues and research notes by early explorers such as Amerigo Vespucci betray a special arrogance in favor of European thought. Indio cultures were viewed from a theoretical and philosophical perspective that was beholden to the legacy of scholasticism as represented by Spanish chroniclers and royal emissaries. It was on this legacy that the paradigm of Spanish thought was erected. *From the European vantage point, the native cultures of Latin America were inferior by definition.* The prescientific cognition found in the cosmology of these cultures was flatly denied by Europeans both of the Reformation and the Counter Reformation.

As noted by Lopez de Gomara, among others, pre-Columbian cognition was an indigenous form of materialism. The New World had witnessed initial attempts at causality and rudimentary stages of conceptual and systematic thought. They incorporated prelogical results of natural necessity in the organization of the state. The crucial point for later developments, however, was that they posited an intuitive understanding of reality.

Latin America's theogony was rooted in myths of nature. At the beginning of the sixteenth century, the supreme deities in the hierarchy were the two beings that created the world: the sun and the moon. They represented divinities who, in the earliest theogony, appeared as constitutive forces. During this period, mythic-magical thought reached a high degree of complexity in which deities were worked into a hierarchy and sat in judgment on economic questions, such as fertility, harvest and health.

With the Spanish conquest, there began a process of syncretism and amalgamation. As the chroniclers José de Acosta and Cieza de Leon noted, the same mythical and magic symbols were held to be logical and necessary items in the life of the spirit and the state. The religion and the cosmology of the indigenous Andean cultures were strikingly varied and multilayered. It was catastrophic for the course of Andean history that Europeans considered them inferior. Religion stood on an intimate footing not only with allegedly supernatural elements, such as lightning, thunder and rain, all of which were embedded in cosmologies, but also with the material foundations of production, trade and consumption. Constantly encountering obstacles, Western technology made slow progress in these areas.

One point is paramount: even in those aspects of Andean culture where the events of the universe were given mathematical and physical interpretations, these quantitative approaches were part of a larger world view dominated by magic and myth. Consequently, we must be very cautious in speaking of early mathematics or astronomy in Andean culture, since these terms convey a false impression that we are dealing with exact sciences.

This same realization can be sensed in Garcilasco de la Vega's description of the astrology and natural philosophy of the Incas. Because the native culture was illiterate, the thoughts of the *amautas* (or philosophers) were transmitted by oral tradition. Certain principles in their "sciences" were understood in terms of a sort of natural religion. Even their astronomy was closely linked to the world of magic and myth. The result was a form of "metaphysical mathematics" which was difficult to reconcile with the mathematics of scientific-technological civilization. In this connection, Garcilasco de la Vega observed that the native knowledge of medicinal plants and herbs was based on values and experiences dictated by what might be called "natural necessity," rather than an elaborate and well-defined natural philosophy. The Andean cultures did not have a high degree of intellectual reflection at their disposal, something that hindered them from accepting the abstractions of the impending industrial age.

The native cultures had a fundamental difficulty in keeping step with the understanding of the physical universe. Later, this robbed them of a necessary prerequisite for successfully adapting Western technology. They did not have a sufficient level of self-reflective thought that might eventually have given rise to productive forces. The eschatology of these vanquished people had consequences at least as far-reaching for their scientific and technological capabilities as did the world view of the Spaniards.

Various documents from the native cultures provide evidence of a certain amount of religious fear just before the arrival of the Spaniards. Even if we assume that these documents were interpretations after the fact, they still reveal the trauma which the Andean peoples were made to undergo. Prophesies proclaimed the end of the world, the appearance of four-legged monsters mounted and led by pale creatures with human features. Obviously, the prophetic magic-mythical vision of the Incas even before the conquest can only have led to the ultimate failure of any attempt to assimilate Spanish culture.

In Peru, for example, the final years of Huayna Capac were accompanied by a series of major earthquakes. Accounts reveal that the palace of the Inca was struck by lightning and comets appeared in the sky. Indigenous accounts refer to a condor chased by a falcon during the Festival of the Sun that fell to earth in the middle of the grand plaza of Cuzco. The bird was taken up and nursed, but died a short time later. This was interpreted as an omen of war. One bright night the heavens were tinged with the color of blood, after which a greenish black and then a smoky gray spread over the sky. The blood was taken to mean that a vicious war was about to divide the children of Huayna Capac. Black signalled the destruction of the Incan empire, which, as signified by the final color, would perish in smoke.

This clearly shows how deeply the Incan view of existence was steeped in magic and myth. Early Incan culture had an other-worldly, mystical character in its cosmology which seemed irreconcilable with the demands of Western pragmatism in science and technology.

Many Latin American cosmologies contain the myth of a deity who, having created civilization, turned away following a beneficent reign with a promise to return one day. In Mexico, this deity was Quetzalcoatl, who set out mysteriously toward the east; in the Andean cultures, it was Viracocha, who disappeared in the western sea. In Mexico, the Spaniards advanced from the east, and 1519 was proclaimed to be the year of "ce-acatl." In Peru, they came from the west, and Atahuallpa was proclaimed the twelfth Inca. Once again we note that the Incas understood their history in terms of myth and saw the arrival of the Spaniards, to a certain extent, as a return of their deities. It is remarkable that native accounts from Mexico to Peru emphasize the same fearsome characteristics when describing the strangeness and power of the intruders: their white skin, their beards, their horses, their fiery weapons and their ability to write.

Andean chroniclers such as Titu Cusi reported that the Spaniards were regarded on their arrival as Viracochas—sons of the divine creator—because it was thought that they communicated among themselves with the aid of a white "cloth." What was meant was their ability to read and write books and letters. Above all, it was the nature of their weapons and their ability to write that marked the technological superiority of the invading Spaniards. An even greater handicap of the indio population was their inability to form a true-to-life picture of their surroundings and to come to grips with empirical reality. It was precisely this partial inability to identify with reality that later became a severe obstacle to their acceptance of Western technology, which presupposes an equilibrium with the empirical world. The roots of Andean culture in magic and myth left it ill-equipped for acculturation with the mathematically exact technology of the West.

Even those elements which might have suggested a level of exactitude in Incan cosmology were enshrouded in a cultural history of magic and myth. In this respect, Incan culture was diametrically opposed to Western science and technology, and its successors were all the less willing or able to merge traditional Incan technology with that of the West. This consequently hampered all attempts in the nineteenth and twentieth centuries to form a basis of scientific and technological cooperation between the two traditions.

Beyond a doubt, the lasting impression of the conquest must have been the technological and military superiority of the Spaniards. This does much to explain how a relatively small number of Spanish soldiers could take possession of and then increasingly destroy the once mighty empire of the Incas. Obsidian lances were pitched against steel swords, bows and arrows against crossbows, foot soldiers against cavalry. Even so, this superiority does not entirely account for the rapid conquest of Incan culture. The firearms were limited in number; as with the Spaniards' horses, the advantage was less military than psychological. This, in turn, allows us to draw conclusions about the Incas' fractured understanding of reality. Moreover, the victory of the Spaniards was made easier by political and ethnic divisions existing within Andean culture.

The Incan empire was itself established through a series of conquests. A number of groups within the Incas saw in the arrival of the Spaniards an opportunity to shake off the oppressive yoke of rival tribes by entering into a strategic alliance with the Spaniards. In Peru, for example, the Huascar faction took up arms with Pizarro, who also secured the support of other groups opposed to the hegemony of the Incas, such as the Canaris.

In Andean culture, the Inca, being a "son of the sur," held a vacillating position midway between gods and men. But he was venerated as a god. To a certain extent, he embodied the center of the universe, vouchsafing its balance and harmony. The death of the Inca meant losing the vital midpoint of the universe, the complete collapse of the system of order. Thus, the entire natural world took part in the drama of annihilation.

But the trauma of conquest was not limited to the psychological impact of the Europeans' arrival and the extermination of ancient deities. The Spanish judiciary system led to a further disintegration, even though it made use of native institutions and retained aspects of traditional Andean jurisprudence. In the half-century following the conquest, however, the native cultures collapsed on every front: demographic, economical, social, religious, cultural and intellectual.

The demographic collapse was grotesque and cataclysmic, comparable to that in Central America. The eschatology of these vanquished peoples reveals just how closely their defeat must be understood in terms of their cosmology; indeed, it even has elements of transcendence. The Spanish invasion was essentially of sacred and cosmic proportions. To the indios, the massacres, firearms and military conflicts meant the end of their world. They interpreted their defeat to mean that their traditional gods had lost their natural powers. Earthly life lost its meaning, and since the gods were dead, the indios saw no other alternative but to die as well. The loss of population in the northern Andes from 1530 to 1560 amounted to ten million people (Nathan Wachtel: *La Vision des Vanicus*, Paris, 1971, pp. 135–40).

The causes of this decline were epidemics: smallpox, measles, the plague. Even before Pizarro's first expedition of 1524, these epidemics had taken thousands of lives, including that of the Inca Huayna Capac. The much-invoked disease *matlazahuatl* decimated the area occupied today by Peru.

The Spanish colonial reign bore a considerable responsibility for the demographic collapse. The first census after the conquest reveals a particularly high rate of mortality among males, due to war. Added to this were many single and mass suicides and abortions among females, signifying desperation and resistance. The demographic curve in the second half of the sixteenth century reveals a decline in birth rate, which might be seen as the obverse side of the trauma of conquest. All of this points to a complete disintegration of the economic, social and cultural-religious system that had once imparted a larger meaning to government and culture. The indigenous world witnessed a dissolution of its age-old unity.

In order to interpret this process of destruction, it is important to understand certain characteristics of pre-Columbian culture. This is also a prerequisite for understanding the fabric of post-Columbian technology and the compatibility of technology and culture in the Andes states.

Before the rise of the Inca state Tahuantinsuyu, this vast region had been settled by different groups of various sizes. The Chupachos, from the region of Huanuco, numbered only about 10,000, while the Lupacas on the western shore of Lake Titicaca erected a mighty kingdom with a population of more than 100,000. At first, the Incas from the Cuzco region were a relatively insignificant ethnic group that stood out from the others only by virtue of its unique place in history. Like the *calpulli* of the Mexicans, the basic unit of these various ethnic groups was the *ayllu*, a social nucleus joining a number of kinship groups living in a particular territory.

The Inca state represented an umbrella organization covering these interlinked units. It had a political and military apparatus respected by all ethnic tribes, while the hierarchy of local leaders, the *curacas*, remained intact. The spiritual and material basis for all social relations was mutual assistance, which pervaded the entire process of production. To understand the technology of the post-Columbian era, however, it is essential to examine the background of these processes in magic and myth.

The citizens of Tahuantinsuyu performed their services for local deities and the *curacas*. They joined together to cultivate the soil of the Incas and the sun in a spirit of sacred ritual, and were given foodstuffs in return (*chica* and *coca*). Alternatively, they manufactured articles of clothing and carried out the office of *mita*, i.e., public tasks or military service.

The conquest exposed the sense of community in the pre-Columbian world to a process of inner decay. The major factors in this process were the newly introduced forms of tribute: money and the market economy. These events had a greater impact on the Andes region than in Mexico because the Inca's subjects, unlike the *macehuales* of the Aztec empire, owed the state only labor, not payments. To exact their tributes, the Spaniards set up a new system of payment. The earliest *encomenderos* made their decisions arbitrarily and paid no attention to laws of taxation, then or later. The indios were collectively responsible for paying the taxes. However, as their numbers declined drastically and the taxes remained the same, the system of taxation became more and more unjust.

Spanish merchants quickly took control of the market. Though here and there native traditions were able to survive, they were detached from their original context and crudely integrated into a colonial world under the hegemony of Spain.

Andean religion illustrates with even greater clarity the difficulties of developing technology in this region. Unlike the Mexicans, who enthusiastically embraced Christianity until about 1570, the indios of Peru held more closely to their own creeds and rituals. Even if the official adoration of the sun and the Inca vanished after the Spanish conquest, the popular veneration of local deities, the *huacas*, remained. The indios continued to cultivate fields dedicated to their gods; they exhumed their dead from the cemeteries and laid them out in traditional burial sites. Although they often paid reluctant obeisance to the external demands of Christianity, there was a deep-seated desire to continue the observation of traditional rites. The Spaniards, in turn, tried to offset this ambivalence by setting up crucifixes and churches on ancient sacred sites. The indios countered by shamefacedly hiding their deities and producing clandestine crucifixes.

The Spaniards viewed the native deities as symbols of the devil; the indios considered Christianity a form of idolatry. If the indios conceded the existence of the Christian god, they saw His sphere of influence as limited and sought protection in their own deities. Andean religion mirrored the division between the worlds of indio and European. Even today, in certain tribes (e.g., the indios of Puquio), anthropologists have discovered precepts in which Jesus Christ remained isolated from native culture. It is not Christ who protects them from danger, but rather the mountains.

This separation found clear expression in a letter of 1579 from Antonio de Zuniga to Philip II. He complains that the indios only pretend to participate in Catholic ceremonies, but are in fact no more Christian than they were at the time of the conquest. This state of affairs, to a certain extent still in effect today, is extremely important regarding the compatibility of technology and culture. A large percentage of the indio population can be presumed to have values in opposition to the acceptance of Western technology with its empiricism and mathematics. In the interplay of continuity and change, tradition has held its own against acculturation.

The indios retained elements of their native culture and borrowed fragments of Western culture, which they used as a sort of veneer. Where European morals, rites and customs were adopted, they had to be accommodated to indio culture. It is with this anthropological reality that the Andes Pact states should begin to critique their lack of an indigenous policy of technology. It is here that the contradictions lie between traditional culture, which has persisted to the present day, and modern technology. For the continuity of the Andean tradition was no less flawed than its assimilation of modern technology.

This dichotomy is exemplified by Guzman Poma de Ayala, an outstanding Peruvian writer who never abandoned his original voice. Although he wrote in Spanish and practiced Christianity, he continued to view the colonial world in the categories of space and time that had undergirded the Incan empire. Poma once drew a map of Peru whose basic outline, broken down into contour lines, recalled Spanish cartography. Yet, these lines had no geographical reality. Poma's drawing of Peru turned on two diagonal axes that marked out the former boundaries of the Incan empire—Chinchaysuyu to the west, Antisuyu in the north, Collasuyu to the east, Cuntisuyu to the south—and were explicitly indicated on the map. The two diagonals intersect in Cuzco, putting the former Incan capital at the map's center. Though the seat of the viceroy of Peru had long been Lima, as far as Poma was concerned, the center of his universe remained Cuzco, the symbol of native culture. Nor was this situation altered by the fact that his map is flanked on either side by emblems of Western power: the Pope and the King of Spain. Poma's example symbolizes the flawed acculturation of Peru.

As the indigenous culture of the Andes shows, during the colonial period recourse was taken in antiquated structures and institutions that, isolated from their cultural context, had survived only in fragments. The traditional limiting conditions of religion retained their importance, and a rift emerged between the local world view, which was aligned with a holistic image of the universe, and the partial continuity of institutions that had given this world view its meaning and significance. A divergence prevailed between these surviving relics and the destructive changes that triggered the dissolution of the indio world immediately after the European invasion. This crisis has remained to the present day and is of paramount importance for understanding the relation between technology and indio culture.

The conflict between the ruling Spanish culture, which from the colonial period had attempted to impose its values on the Andes region, and the subservient native culture opened up deep chasms in the social and economic constitutions of the two cultural systems. Since then, this conflict has deepened and explains why an indigenous technological development still encounters resistance today.

The empire of the Incas, like the Spanish colonial power, was interested in accumulating valuable metals. But there was a crucial difference: the native cultures used gold and silver for ornamental purposes, not to fuel a market economy.

Space and Time in Andean Culture

In the world of myth, empirical reality often remains hidden and partially unaccounted for, producing what might be referred to as a veiled transcendence. In pre-Columbian cultures, we notice this immediately in a mythical vision of nature, parts of which have remained in effect beyond the colonial period to the present day. Nature, to an Andean indio, was indomitable. This belief persistently undermined the efforts of Spanish colonial rulers to introduce Western technology. The Spaniards wanted to dominate nature, to lessen the effects of wind, rain, cold and drought by taking appropriate steps. The balance between the indio society and nature was destroyed by the conquest, and even today it has not been sufficiently reinstated.

All commentators agree that the Andean indios never perceived nature as their enemy. Instead, they viewed nature as a protector, regarding it as the source of life. The hardships of their living conditions called forth an ability to put up with any sufferings that nature might impose upon them.

In pre-Columbian culture, an individual's relation to nature was so intimate that rain, dawn, wind or cold represented acts of beneficence, gifts of nature. Human beings were bound to nature because they saw themselves as part of nature. What nature demanded of them was courtship and respect: they were obligated to bring offerings, to obey the rituals, so that ultimately the earth would bring forth what they needed. The sacred realm of Pacha Mama, with its magical claims to world dominion, was omnipresent. How different this was from the Western view, in which humanity is not seen as part of nature and a beneficiary of its grace.

Accordingly, the descendants of the Andean cultures are not as interested in the scientific study of nature and the universe as, for example, people of the Calvinist tradition in North America might be. In pre-Columbian culture, an individual's link with nature was paramount. The earth was the final arbiter that granted human existence. As the very basis of life, nature was not to be quizzed and probed by science.

This explains why the indio and mestizo populations have such difficulty living in urban industrial settlements without sacrificing their identity, which is vouchsafed by age-old rites. All the harvest rituals and festivities in the life of a community betoken a different concept of nature. When young members of a native culture settle in a city, they retain close connections to their community, which forms the nucleus of their lives.

A direct relation to living nature, with animal symbols that revealed new facets of a rich, inner life, predominated in Andean agriculture. The conquistadors altered not only the physical and empirical scenario of this living environment, but also the symbols within it—something that would later pose a major obstacle to the development of an indigenous technology. So-called primitive traditions were broken down into basic components, and the symbols of the colonizers were superimposed upon them. As a result, all symbols, such as birds, reptiles, domestic animals and wild beasts, were given new meanings. Nonetheless, this did not alter the fact that magic and myth continued to dominate the indio cultures and stand in the way of the Western notion of progress.

Magic is peopled with a wide variety of deities and spirits. As Marcel Mauss correctly observed, magic can also be translated into action. The world of the supernatural is situated in a sacred realm that, in its empirical offshoots, is incompatible with Western technology.

The lives of plants and animals were considered to be continuations of one's own life. Here solutions were found to one's problems—ill-health, disgrace—as animals provided milk and meat, and even plants guaranteed a foundation for existence. Due to this view of nature, the indio had notions of truth and reality that differed radically from that of Western society. The indio's relation to nature embodied the art of "gentle survival."

Consequently, indio notions of passivity and activity necessarily differed as well from those of Western culture. The indio world had a profoundly mythical core that was made actual and manifest in all areas of everyday culture and economic life. Notions of the sacred stood side by side with the development of agriculture: the earth was situated at the midpoint of indio cosmology and could not be summarily subjugated or technologically exploited.

There was a tellurian aspect to indio sensibility. Human beings coexisted with the earth in a type of family, a living community of earth, flora, fauna and humankind. This family relation took the form of a special religious perspective. The earth ultimately shaped the living world, everyday culture, the economic fabric.

The indios did not turn to the earth in order to exploit and subjugate it and to dominate it with technology, but rather to receive the fruits of their labor as a bounteous gift. The earth cannot be extracted from its context in cosmology and religion, a fact that present-day agrarian policy in the Andes states cannot afford to ignore.

Despite five hundred years of Catholicism, the earth still remains the center and keystone of indio cosmology, the source of life and fertility, the sacred setting in which indio thought, existence and activity unfold.

Moreover, the rationality of the indios was closely connected with a different concept of time that, in turn, was correlated with their respect for the sacred. This concept, too, was linked with nature. In indio cosmology, time was joined with the earth. Indio cultures had no notion of organizing time to improve efficiency. This realization is of central importance in explaining their fractured assimilation of Western technology. For the indio, time was sacred and unfolded in rituals and everyday actions in communion with nature.

Thus, the beginning of each new year was also the beginning of a new life, even in the oral tradition of indio native literature. The indios did not have a concept of eternity in the Christian sense so much as a view of time as constantly growing. Their notions of time and space differed from those of Western philosophy. The Andean indio found sanctuary in the sacred earth, and thereby received redemption in the community.

Indio philosophy, then, proceeded from the premise of a sacred universe. Hence, it had no notion of reification or concretization as found in Western philosophy and economic practice. The indio notion of existence was not a science but a wisdom based on religion. Octavio Paz has impressively shown that in Latin America the three forms of time—past, present and future—are related differently than in Europe, Asia or North America. This applies not only to archaic Latin American culture but equally to colonial and modern Latin America.

For archaic cultures, the archetype of time is the past. A timeless past is posited that repeats itself at regular intervals. Present and future must take their bearings from this past as part of an immutable pattern. What is more, the past is ever present and impervious to change.

In the Western view, the future is teleological or goal-directed. It must perforce be an improvement on the past, since it stands closer to divine redemption than the present. To the modern Western mind, time is the agency of change, a precondition for the creation of technology. *In archaic cultures, time is the factor that suppresses change.*

Pre-Columbian religion is predicated on a notion of the future that presupposes the foreordained destruction of the world. It is therefore more closely linked with a fear of apocalypse than with fear of the present or future.

This further explains why Latin America is handicapped in its adaptation to technological civilization, which posits a different notion of time. Archaic cultures take a negative stance toward the vicissitudes of time, regarding them as ominous and harmful. What Westerners call history is to them an aberration, a step in the wrong direction. This applies to the classical Mediterranean and Asian cultures no less than to pre-Columbian America.

The ultimate ideal of archaic culture is the past, the time before time began, that blissful primordial age when concord reigned between heaven and earth. This already suggests the recurrence that awaits human beings at the other end of the cycle. The past is thus a future time as well. The future, on the other hand, is demoted, being both the end of time and a new beginning. At the end of the cycle, the original past is reinstated. Here we can see one important point of difference from modern Christianity, in which perfect time is embodied in eternity and perfection is found not in the past but in a future that bears no similarity either to past or present. For Christianity, the future represents a realm of the unforeseen. For archaic cultures, time takes on a semblance of temporal progression and congeals to form history, but it is always a form of recurrence which negates both history and time.

The cyclic concept of time was supplanted by the Christian notion of finite, irreversible time. An emphasis fell on the heterogeneity of time, which could now move forward and strike out on unwonted byways. Even Adam's fall represents a caesura in the eternal present of paradise, allowing us to speak of a beginning of time. Every moment is unique and different; a notion of finiteness is presupposed. At this point, the Western concept of progress was introduced, a concept unknown in pre-Columbian Latin America and familiar only in a highly modified, transcendental form in the Catholic scholasticism of the colonial period. The "real reality" of Calvinist North American culture stands opposed to the "utopian reality" of Latin America. The problem is that before Latin America could take control of its own historical destiny, it had already become a vanguard of the European universe of ideas, serving as a chapter in the history of European utopias. Alejo Carpentier, in his essay "The Kingdom of This World," refers to a special "miraculous reality" in Latin America. To this, Angel Asturias adds the fundamental concept of "magic realism," presupposing an "irrationally perceivable reality" in contradistinction to the "rational" understanding of everyday reality. These concepts can be derived from the animistic view of the world maintained by the major pre-Columbian cultures. They can even be found in the present, for example, in the Afro-Brazilian culture of Macumba and Candomblé, or in the melancholy, fatalistic irrationalism of Andean culture. Accordingly, as Carlos Fuentes realized, it is not so important for Latin America to acknowledge modernism as to recognize its own native traditions.

Andean Technology As a Special Unity of Theory and Practice

Pre-Columbian science and technology have not been sufficiently studied. The questions they pose hover between the history of science and technology on the one hand and comparative ethnology on the other. To bridge these two fields, ethnology must be viewed as the study of scientific and technological phenomena in direct relation to their social, economic and cultural context. In the early stages, there is little difference between technology and science, since both follow directly from the daily activities and myths of humankind. A similar relation holds between art and religion. In ancient Peru, for example, the traditional *quipu* (a bundle of colored strings used for purposes of counting) clearly contained an element of science which went hand in hand with the divine principle embodied in the Inca.

The crucial point in the subsequent evolution of technology in the Andes region is that the pre-Columbian cultures left no evidence of scientific experimentation of the sort that yielded such successful results in the industrialized countries. This is an early indication of a deficiency that was to lead to stultified industrialization and an incompatibility between technology and culture.

It is extremely difficult to locate within pre-Columbian culture signs of analysis and experimentation on the empirical level indicative of scientific activities. The cultures in the Andean region felt the paralyzing impact of the completely contrary Spanish culture, which was motivated by different principles altogether. When they arrived in Latin America, the Europeans found some cultures which were highly developed yet radically different from their own. At the time of the conquest, cultures at a very high level of civilization could be found the whole length of the Andes, from Mexico to Chile. Nonetheless, relatively little is known about the science of pre-Columbian cultures; indeed, the very concept of science in these cultures remains obscure.

There can be little doubt that the intellectual elite, who processed metals, textiles and ceramics or worked in agriculture, possessed some understanding of natural phenomena. The impressive accomplishments apparent in pre-Columbian architecture and urban design, its roads and bridges and coastal navigation, warrant the assumption that these people had at least a basic knowledge of mathematics, physics and mechanics. Further examples are the high level of artistic creativity and the development of astronomy for practical and religious purposes. Even so, we must conclude that the intellectual elite of the Andean cultures did not develop science like that of the West, that is, a body of theory set against a background of experimentation and empiricism.

The main reason for the lack of scientific activity in pre-Columbian cultures lay in their conception of what was meant by science. In order to understand the technology of the Andes Pact states, we must view it as a unity of theory and practice.

These thoughts are axiomatic for any examination of technology in traditional Andean culture and society. What some may fondly refer to as myth is, for the Andean peoples, the "theory" behind their practice of transforming nature. A theory of mythic thought can help one understand their technological practice and social organization.

The connection between mythical-theoretical thought and everyday practice can be seen, for example, in the dialectic relation between agrarian production and medicinal healing. For the Andean people, these two levels are intimately linked, since both bring forth life. For peasants, an agricultural product is not only a sign of affluence and the result of their labor, it is also an embodiment of life as a product of the earth. Indeed, the Quechua expression *kawsay* means both life and agricultural product. Pacha Mama, the fertile soil, is the true source of life. On the other hand,

Andean medicine likewise symbolized the struggle for life in opposition to the forces of death.

The moon and its position in the sky had deep significance for the agrarian technology of the Andes people. In traditional cultures, farmers observe the course of the stars and the phases of the moon in order to determine future weather conditions and hence to decide which plants to cultivate. The position of the stars functions as an indicator for particular technological procedures. The two levels are joined by the fact that these people use stars not only for their technological bearings, but also for their world view. The moon, for example, is always opposed to the sun. It is also customary to equate the sun with the principle of masculinity and patriarchy, and the moon with femininity and matriarchy.

The chronicler Juan de Santa Cruz Pachacuti Yamqui relates how the cosmos found its representative in the Coricancha in Cuzco. According to this time scheme, the world was clearly divided into two parts: the sun and the moon. On one side of the moon, the following beings appeared: a woman, Mama Cocha (mother, lake or sea), together with a spring, a tree (*mallqui*) and a cloud. Obviously, the moon was connected with woman and water. Water was considered fertile in the form of rain, and represented a source of life in the form of the irrigation system. In Quechua the word *quilla* means both moon and month. This analogy with the life cycle is necessary, if we are to understand how the Andean people related the moon to technology. The "green" or waxing moon was considered feeble and incapable of dispensing energy. Like the moon, plants commanded youthful strength, but were immature and unproductive. The full moon, on the other hand, was an expression of power, as opposed to the waning moon which was gradually nearing death. The fertility of one season determined which seeds to sow in the next. Thus, the Andean people's practical technological needs are mirrored in their relation to the moon, which is felt to be strong when located in the right position. It should also be emphasized that, in the Andean way of thinking, one's ancestors are capable of bringing the desired rainfall. Like the moon, they belong to the world of darkness, and since they are located under the earth, they control the primordial sources of water. Similarly, it is the new moon, which in Andean mythology inhabits the underworld, that brings forth clouds.

Obviously, then, Andean thought makes use of categories that relate to ordinary life, but is built on overriding myths to a point of great richness and variety. Nature, technology and culture are bound together by a common thread.

The traditional form of Andean thought must be evaluated in the context of social organization and myth. Andean rationality is founded on mutually exclusive antonyms, such as life and death, or day and night. Mythical thought takes the form of a hermetic system, and yet it must serve as the backdrop for any attempt at technological innovation. It is clearly irreconcilable with the Western rationality introduced at the time of the Spanish conquest. In Andean culture, mythical thought constitutes the theoretical basis for all efforts to transform nature. The term "theoretical" is used in a figurative sense to indicate that myth occupies and represents a hierarchically superior level of thought. And a "theory" of mythical thought is the correct one for a study of the technological capacity of pre-Columbian America.

To show the extent to which the technological capabilities of the Andean cultures were influenced by mythical thought, we have taken the example of the moon as applied to agriculture. But there was a general connection between the movement of the stars and the application of technology, a transition from mythological perspective to technological capacity. A cosmological vision became the basis of practical activity. The moon and the light of the nighttime sky were contrasted with the sun and daylight. In Ayacucho, the phases of the moon were referred to as *wanuquilla*, meaning "the death of the moon." The presence of the moon, as we know from the writings of Guzman Poma de Ayala, bore witness to the moisture that came with the year's first rainstorms.

Agricultural labor was sustained by the tension between life and death—a relation that becomes even more evident in the case of medicine. Medicine and naturopathy demonstrate the mythological character of the Andean approach, culminating in the practice of witchcraft. A wide range of animal products and plant extracts were used for health care: *guaicum* wood for blood diseases, *quinca* to cure fever, *chili* for hemorrhoids.

Medicines were administered as a form of magic by shamans or *amautas* whose behavior was decidedly telluric. As in agrarian technology, the opposition of dry and wet was fundamental; in medicine this was expressed by the classifications of fresh and cooked. There was also an intermediate state in the form of the full moon, which struck a balance between the drying rays of the sun and the rain brought by the new moon. The counterpart in medicine was warmth as a midpoint between cold and heat. Here, too, we note the tightly woven network of correlations in Andean thought between the conceptions of life, technological practice and cultural organization.

The same ties applied to the relation between life and death, as described by Lauro Hinostroza for the Ayacucho tradition. To heal a sick person, the disease had to be drawn out of the body and the soul had to be called back. Often, the disease was meant to be transferred to another body, for example, to a pig. For a cure, the sick person gave offerings to Apusuyu, the god of the mountains, or to a god who was meting out the punishment. Disease signified a flaw in the harmony of the universe, as well as a want of respect for the gods and the power of nature.

Mythical thought, as it turns out, intervened in the process of human innovation, making use of cognitive categories which clearly distinguish Andean cosmology from that of the West. Not only was there a high degree of irrationality, there was also, and especially, a lack of abstract thought of the sort that might have made it possible to come to grips with modern Western technology. *Andean thought, as handed down from the precolonial period, made no distinction between an object and its conception, and was rooted in a cosmological vision directed toward the past.*

Mythical thought in Andean culture was at once a theory, a form of applied technology and a socioeconomic structure. Its practical side arose from the transformation of nature; its theory also undergirded the structure of society and the economy. It was this triangular relationship that made the transition to Western technology so difficult.

When forming our views on future agrarian technology, we must pay attention to technological alternatives which take into account the special traditions of the Andean region. Research centers could be set up for this purpose in various Andean agricultural and ecological zones. At the same time, a mutuality and balance must be struck between the importation and the indigenous creation of technology.

Mythological Prerequisites of Technology in the Andes Region

Among other things, culture can be understood as the totality of solutions to problems that arise in the course of a society's evolution.

These solutions include not only technological responses to the challenges of history, but also the creation, comprehension and transmission of knowledge. In order to make more realistic estimates of the future technological development in the Andes region, three questions are especially relevant:

1) What image of humankind prevails within the culture's own historical background?

2) How are ethical norms transmuted into standards of social and economic behavior?

3) What is a person's relation to nature? to the supernatural? to society?

Mythical thought gave categories to Andean culture by which its people could place themselves both within nature and within society. In the Andean region, the balance between nature and human actions differs from that of Western society, and rationality consequently is signified in other ways. In the Andean cultures, mythical discourse is the true expression of reality.

The profound disruptions in everyday Andean culture and social organization that followed the Spanish conquest and colonization called forth cultural responses in which the ancient Andean traditions were reinterpreted by being placed in a new context. Still, mythical tales continued to express social reality, and in this respect Andean thought was especially rich and varied.

In the Andean region, the indio population rebelled throughout the entire colonial period. Nor did these uprisings end with the wars of independence. The rebellions of Tupac Amaru and Pumacugua were significant examples, and to a certain extent carried on the initial Inca rebellion in Cuzco. During the years of the republic, there were major revolts in Atusparia, Ancash, Puno and Ayacucho. Before then, the bureaucracy of the vice royalty had been compelled to reach a rapprochement with the configurations of the ancient empire. As a result, the traditional culture of Peru was ambivalent, if not inimical, toward the historical progress of Western culture.

Colonial Exploitation of the Andean Region

During the last few centuries, European and indio cultures have coexisted in constant interaction within the same territory. The evolution of Latin America is noted for its mixtures of cultural and ethnic traditions, varying from region to region. Iberian, Amerindian and African elements have coalesced over a period of more than five hundred years. This process was set in motion not only by the Spaniards and Portuguese, but also, and especially, by the autochthonous cultures. Unlike those in the United States, these groups did not form geographically isolated ethnic minorities, but were spread over the entire continent.

There arose a character type which was to assume an ever increasing influence: the mestizo. In the Andean cultures, however, the Western-oriented part of the population formed a minority, e.g., in Cuzco, Ayacucho, Arequipa, Huarez, Puno, Jauja, Tarma, Huancayo, Cerro de Pasco and Huancavelica. Even today, there are parts of the Andean region that form an exception to the general rule by having a clear, almost anachronistic segregation of cultures. The pure-blooded indio population has been declining for generations, despite its increasing efforts to survive and to adapt to technological change. This is revealed by a glance at historical sources, such as the Peruvian chronicles of Pedro Cieza de Leon.

When the Spaniards advanced into the Andes region, they found a powerful empire, parts of which had already been geographically and demographically developed. They were not able to subjugate nature completely in this area, least of all in the highlands. Instead, the colonial masters concentrated at first in the valleys, which seemed to them more fertile. The Spaniards constantly pushed forward into the cores of the ancient cultures, whether in fertile valleys, such as Vilcanota, Andahuaylas, Cajamarca or Jauja, or in remote regions, such as Chachapoyas and Huancayo. Spanish towns, however, remained enclaves within indio territory. New plants and domestic animals were introduced: horses, wheat, legumes. The imagination and creativity of the indio cultures were stimulated. The horse, with its delicate contours, was recreated in pottery, where the figure was given the face of a deity. Mythical personalities entered legends in the form of animist deities that, in earlier tradition, had once inhabited rivers, lakes and forests.

The diffusion of Western values was met by the resistance of indio culture. The intermixture of languages in the coastal regions was different than that of the Andean highlands, where colonial masters, merchants and Catholic priests were forced to learn Quechua. At the same time, these language barriers demarcated the diffusion of Western culture in the highlands.

Catholic religious celebrations were permeated with elements from precolonial times. This behavior extends to the present, for many adherents of indio cultures have retained their indigenous traditions in areas of cultural overlap, and have given them an external veneer of traits from the Spanish heritage. In the village-like temple cities, indios dressed in seventeenth-century Spanish garb solemnly play *pututos*. They sing Spanish sacred hymns which have been translated into Quechua and set to indio music played with violins and *quena* flutes.

Despite this active assimilation of Western culture, at no time was indio culture fundamentally abandoned. The changes in the nuclei of these cultures took place and continue to take place very slowly. Nor are they finished today.

It proved very difficult for the indio cultures to deal with money as an exchange value, since they had inherited patterns of consumption different than those of Western culture. These difficulties proved to be an obstacle to the attainment of a modern economy, for money has yet to become a positive factor of economic production.

Obstacles to Acculturation in Andean Cosmology

The Q'ero indios of the Peruvian highlands, the last descendants of the Incas, reveal a fractured relation to Western culture in their myths regarding the origins of their people. These myths, in Quechua, are usually an amalgam of precolonial and Catholic elements; the name of the redemption figure, Inkarri, is a cross between the Quechua word *Inka* and the Spanish word *rey* (king). Oscar Nuñez del Prado interprets Inkarri as the first deity (apart from those other deities, the mountains) to defend human beings. Inkarri was the child of a savage woman and the sun. He created everything on earth, and was thus a creator-god before he was taken prisoner by the Spaniards, tortured and beheaded. His head, however, continued to live, awaiting reunification with his body. The moment of this reunification will also become the hour of the Last Judgment. Here we note clear affinities to the Christian doctrine of the Resurrection. The Q'eros were descendants of Inkarri's first-born son. Inkarri himself, following his journey through humanity, disappeared in the great jungle, the region of death in Q'ero mythology. It should be remarked that the Andes region has various versions of the Inkarri myth.

One important consideration is that the oral literature of the Andes lacks a Christian concept of heaven that spans the earth like a dome. Instead, transcendence is brought down to earth, and there can be no concept of purgatory or hell of the sort found in the Last Judgement of Christianity.

Nor was there any notion of the afterlife in which humanity is redeemed or compensated for injustices suffered in this world. Instead, the afterlife is situated in this world; all punishments, rewards and compensations take place in the here and now. Only on the surface does this represent an absence of transcendence; in fact, the realm of the dead spreads over the earth. The Puquio indios lived with the notion that the dead erected a tower on the peak of Quropuna, a tower which was never completed. This incompleteness gave them a profound sense of satisfaction.

Obviously, by incorporating the afterlife in the here and now, the Q'eros imparted a considerable degree of magic and myth to their empirical world. Their everyday culture took on that transcendental aspect that had to be abandoned in the nascent industrial culture. From the indio perspective, sinners had to toil on earth and eke out a living as condemned spirits. How different this was from the Christian doctrine of redemption and from the work ethic associated with this doctrine in, for instance, North American Calvinism.

The crucial point is that in Andean culture, the empirical world was never empirical pure and simple, a place where technology could evolve unimpeded. Instead, it was always permeated with transcendence and magic which were firmly entrenched in the here and now, obstructing the productive process in terms of industrialization. Transcendence and empiricism were interlocked in a delicate balance.

Today, the inhabitants of the Andes region must face a challenge no less severe than the technological acculturation that failed in the aftermath of the conquest: namely, their integration into the market economy and the modern world. Above all, this affects their standing in world society and their traditional sense of community, which is in a process of disintegration—particularly in agriculture where new technologies are being employed.

The incorporation of Western technology and science by the indio culture is an irreversible process that entails social disruption.

Traditional mythic forms are breaking down. This does not mean, however, that mythical thought is becoming extinct. Instead, ancient forms of expression that have remained intact to the present day are being transformed into new formulae that retain their former meaning and significance. The ancient mythical traditions must be viewed from new vantage points within a modern frame of discourse. Modern agriculture, as a form of technology, cannot be introduced into Andean culture solely on the basis of Western scientific experimentation; even in the future it will have to unfold beneath a superstructure of myth. When indios cultivate the earth, Pacha Mama, they will be on the lookout for a new divinity. The native cultures of the Andes region reveal an ability to adopt new concepts in their ways of thinking, provided these concepts are in accord with traditional thought. It is at this point that development policy should begin, since up to now these points of contact have not been sufficiently located by the modern natural sciences of the West.

Again and again, this process leads to conflicts as Western rationality, the prerequisite for the functioning of Western science and technology, is fundamentally different than its Andean counterpart. Without Western science and technology, the Andes region will never be able to link up to Western civilization and the world economy. If Andean traditionalists are to attain an understanding of the processes of nature and society, they will have to overcome a two-fold difficulty: first, they will have to learn to deal with abstract conceptions, as opposed to mythical thought which recognizes spiritual concepts only with concrete objects; and second, this change of paradigm presupposes that, at least in part, they will have to adopt a different mode of cognition.

Andean thought can be freed of its mythical basis only in theory, not in practice. The Andes Pact states can contribute to the general evolution of scientific-technological thought by remaining in harmony with their latent pre-Columbian modes of cognition.

The fact that the Andean people have begun to integrate some aspects of Western science and technology into their forms of production does not imply that they have abandoned their traditional mythical thought processes. It merely means that their logic has withdrawn from some areas and has taken on a new appearance. This is all the more important as the Andean cultural traditions, for example, in Ecuador and Peru, are intimately connected with the quest for a cultural and, ultimately, a national identity.

What we are now witnessing in the Andes Pact states is a major dilemma as real as it is seemingly insoluble. Everyday culture is based on a totality of representative features from indio aesthetics and economic organization. Only with great difficulty can these elements be reconciled with the scientific-technological production of the West, for native culture and outside technology seem to inhabit mutually incompatible realms. Any future policy of energy and technology must take this very real dilemma into account, particularly with regard to the regional and local circumstances of production, the *sine qua non* of any large-scale diffusion of technology.

It is above all in their images of cosmological creation, beginning with the origins of the universe and the question of whether it has always existed, that traditional Andean myths differ fundamentally from those of the West. Traditional Andean culture had no forerunners to the doctrine of evolution. There was no notion that human civilization might have progressed stage by stage over millions of years. The idea that we evolved by a natural process is opposed to the Andean notion that human beings were created miraculously by a demiurge.

The myths and religious conceptions of Andean culture always took their starting point in animism, the belief that all elements of nature, even mountains and rivers, air and fire, are animate and were summoned to life. The figure of God, as it appears in the Andean cultures, had different predecessors than the divinity of post-Columbian Christianity, in which the universe was created by a god of fire, thunder and lightning, a god with the function of instilling fear and terror in humanity. The Andean cultures also had a universal belief in a divine being that created the universe and vouchsafes the fertility of the earth by sending rainfall. But to the archaic mind, nature was not exclusively "natural."

The main issue for our study is the view of the world and the cosmos that prevailed in Incan culture. It is here that we find the roots of an early body of indio wisdom that reveals how difficult it was in the post-Columbian cultures to form a connection to Western technology with its keynote of pragmatism.

The cosmology of the Incas posited conceptions of space and time that differ from the linear Aristotelian notions of the West. Horizontal space was divided into four quadrants with the aid of four cardinal points. The unity of the world appeared in the guise of a figure divided into four sections. Each of these sections was attributed vital significance, as though it were one of the four extremities of an alligator, turtle or human being. In the middle was the heart, from which vantage point the four cardinal points could be observed. In practical terms, this midpoint was the theocratic city: the city-god or city-state. Each of these cardinal points embodied at once a god and a season of the year.

The Incas then proceeded from the conception of space to a notion of time. Here, there were two distinct levels: the calendar with its days, moons and secular subdivisions; and the doctrine of the age of the world, which outlined a mythical cosmology. The Incas had a "cubic" conception of the world in which the earth formed a central plane with two tiers representing higher and lower rungs: heaven and hell. The animal and plant kingdoms were subsumed in this higher realm, where the heavenly, divine authority always had an influence on empirical reality.

Andean thought was remote from daily affairs in the Western sense of the term. Nor was it innovative in its approach to technology, for even observations of the motion of the sun and the phases of the moon were not interpreted in terms of technology. In the cosmology of the Incas, the sun (Inti), moon (Quilla) and Venus (Chasca) were given highest priority. The calendar of the year was created by observing the rotation of the sun. The Incan calendar was made up of twelve months and three hundred sixty days. Time was measured according to the alignment of the sun with the highest peaks in the Andes and with twelve poles pointing in its direction. These poles, called *succanga*, were used to separate the religious factions and the harvest time. Unlike the Aztecs and the Mayas, whose year began in March, the Incas in the central Andes started their year in January, and assigned each month a name that held ritual significance.

Knowledge, religion and the economy were interrelated. They bore a certain resemblance to the natural sciences due to their mathematical precision (the solar year of the Mayan calendar, for example, is more accurate in its astronomical measurements than the Gregorian calendar). Ultimately, however, this relation was grounded in myth. Even the agricultural calendar of the Inca's religious system, as we know from the *Nueva y Buen Gobierno* of Felipe Guzman Poma de Ayala (1560–1641), was ultimately mythical. Economic symbols were interpreted qualitatively and intuitively, even if in historical memory they seemed to be quantitative. Andean culture was irrational and intuitive. In this respect, it provided the poorest soil imaginable for a compatibility with the objective and empirical foundations of Western technology.

The prime agents of astronomical, calendrical and climatic phenomena were mythological deities, not rational causes. Upon this basis, the components of the Incan conception of reality were erected, as can be seen in the writings of José de Acosta. The cognitive level of the Andean cultures did not provide a basis for Cartesian rationality, the cornerstone of Western empirical technology.

Due to their extraordinary variations in altitude and the resultant territorial imbalances, the Andes are an extremely heterogeneous region with a great many climatic zones. In the course of evolution, the genetic variety of its flora and fauna produced special preconditions. Certain ecotypes were favored by the intense solar radiation at high altitudes. Accordingly, the agrarian technology of the Andes had a sophisticated logic that resulted from observations carried out over many generations. Special emphasis was given to the region's ecological variety.

The system of irrigation, by means of canals, and the cultivation of river beds and arid valleys reveal an early sense of ecological awareness regarding the use of soil and natural resources. But this system was beholden not so much to rational logic as to a mythical injunction to live in harmony with nature. Hence, the preconditions and motivation for dealing with nature were virtually the opposite of those in the West. The emphasis fell not so much on practical utilization as on humble obeisance to a supranatural deity. Under these conditions, it was impossible to instill abstract, rationalistic methods for obtaining maximum benefits from nature without regard for its internal balance.

The basic materials for indio handicrafts were wood and stone. It was the Spaniards who, in the sixteenth century, introduced metal implements for the first time. This was yet another practical attainment of Western culture that decisively enriched the culture of the Andes. Large-scale metallurgy of a pragmatic bent was unknown in Andean culture, where gold and silver were not minted into coins or otherwise put to practical use, but were used instead for ceremonies and religious purposes. From a technological standpoint, the precious metals had no special purpose; they were not used to attain specific ends, as in Western empirical technology. This achievement had to wait for the conquistadors, who had tools and technologies at their disposal. Basic sciences, such as biology, physics or chemistry, were locked into irrational premises that had yet to attain scientific status.

There is an inherent contradiction between native Andean wisdom and the logic of Western technology. Unlike Western science, over the centuries there emerged in Andean culture a special interaction between thought and concrete forms of action. The result was not what could be called a scientific discipline, but rather a specific technology. Pre-Columbian technology was a response to questions of nutrition, with collective labor forming one of the pillars of Andean culture. This technology was found in the highlands and coastal regions alike, and was striking in its ecological soundness. The Andes region currently lacks the security of a balanced ecology. Andean wisdom acknowledged various techniques for cultivating and preserving soil conditions for purposes of self-sufficiency. Today, however, the technology policy of the Andes Pact states tends to peter out in bureaucratic actions with little impact on reality. There is a grievous shortage of native technology. This is apparent most of all in agriculture, where there is still much to be learned from existing traditions.

By technology, we mean primarily the element of technique, the material product, the implement. When we speak of imported technology, we usually think of expensive machinery and equipment. We seldom think of technology in its actual comprehensive sense as a unity between theory and practice. The central problem of the Andes Pact states is that they introduce machinery and technologies without having control over the material and intellectual processes needed to reproduce them. *The transformation of nature by means of technological processes is not simply a matter of theory; it must also be evaluated in light of the history and culture of the region involved.* Consequently, it is necessary to integrate theoretical planning with a practical technology policy in the Andes nations, as this integration has been lacking in their efforts to produce their own technology.

*Special Rationales of Thought and Action
in Andean Culture*

In summation, the problem facing the Andes Pact states is that the transition to a modern technological civilization requires abstract thought, whereas Andean rationality is based essentially on concrete examples and individual instances. This discrepancy explains the relative backwardness of the Andes region by world standards.

Even experimentation in the Andean countries was not abstract in the Western sense, but drew on concrete examples. This attitude was based on the largely mythic and magical structure of the traditional Andean world, which has persisted to the present day. However, to advance to a Western brand of scientific rationalism, Andean culture needed to distinguish between the level of conceptualization and intellect and the level of reality, a distinction without which it proved impossible to establish the body of concepts required for Western technology. Herein lay the seeds of cultural, economic and political contradiction and the roots of instability. Andean culture was unable to make this distinction take hold, for in many cases scientific rationalism implied a brusque and irreconcilable break with magic and myth.

Native Andean culture continues to recognize rationales of action and thought different than the formal or even the Aristotelian logic of the West, the basis of Western science and technology. The indios construe their cognitive categories on the pre-Columbian foundations of a mirror symmetry existing between two parts. Each of these parts is in turn further subdivided into two parts. One of the parts dominates the other, a process which is repeated on the next level of subdivision. For example, the sun and the moon are parts of the upper world and have counterparts in the lower world. The sun dominates the upper world as a masculine element, while the earth, being primarily feminine, predominates in the world below. The main issue for a comparison with Western rationalism is that, in Andean logic, intellectual conceptions and symbols do not have final meanings, although changes are governed by particular laws. The moon, for example, is feminine, but it may also have a masculine side, since it belongs to the upper world. Its assignment to one or the other world depends on the context, and particularly on whether it is in opposition to the sun or to the earth. Andean logic does not recognize horizontal and vertical levels of thought of a sort comparable to Western logic.

The foregoing examples of variant forms of rationality clearly imply that only an appropriate and suitable technology stands a chance of success in the Andes region and can ward off the disruption and disintegration of society and culture (see Chapter 7).

At first glance, the static character of traditional Andean culture poses an obstacle to modern technology, which is inherently dynamic. The goal should be to mediate between these two variants of logic and rationality for the purpose of attaining indigenous growth.

Any scientific and technological strategy for the Andes region must be in accord with an overarching view of the social, cultural and economic changes that will prevail during the next few decades. One prerequisite is that the Andean societies live in harmony with their own cultural and religious traditions. This harmony is being placed in ever greater jeopardy. Seen in this light, an indigenous capacity for science and technology is called for in order to ensure successful acculturation, i.e., the technological solutions being offered must be culturally acceptable—in short, compatible.

Every culture makes use of its own interpretation of reality. This interpretation follows a superordinate system of meaning that is largely the outgrowth of the traditions of its people. It is precisely the wide variety of these interpretations of reality that makes it so difficult to view ordering principles and work ethics outside the context of a particular cultural and religious tradition.

Suggestions for Further Reading

Adams, Richard N. *A Community in the Andes. Problems and Progress in Muquiyauyo.* Washington, DC, 1959.

Andrade Reimers, Luis. "Hacia la verdadera historia de Atahualpa." Casa de la Cultura Ecuatoria, Quito, 1980.

Ansion, J. *Essais sur la pensée andine et ses réinterprétations actuelles dans la région d'Ayacucho (Pérou).* Dissertation. Université Catholique de Louvain, Louvain-la-Neuve, 1984.

Arguedas, José María. *Canciones y cuentos del pueblo quechua.* Ed. Huascarán. Lima, 1949.

_____. *Las comunidades de España y del Perú.* Universidad de San Marcos, Lima, 1968.

_____. "Cuentos mágico-ralistas y canciones de fiestas tradicionales del valle del Mantaro, provincias de Jauja y Concepción. Archivo del Instituto de Estudios Etnológicas." *Folklore Americano* 1 (1953, Lima): 101–293.

_____. "Cuentos religioso-mágicos quechuas de Lucanamarca." *Folklore Americano* 8–9 (1961, Lima): 142–126.

____. "Evolución de las comunidades indígenas. El valle del Mantaro y la ciudad de Huancayo." *Revista del Museo Nacional* 26 (1957, Lima): 78–151.

____. "Mitos quechuas prehispánicos." *Amaru* 3 (1967, Lima): 14–18.

____. "Notas elementales sobre el arte popular religioso y la cultura mestiza en Huamanga." *Revista del Museo Nacional* 27, Lima, 1958.

____. "Puquio, una cultura en proceso de cambio." *Revista del Museo Nacional* 25 (1956, Lima): 185–232.

Arguedas, José María, and Francisco Izquierdo Rios. *Mitos, leyendas y cuentos peruanos*. Casa de la Cultura del Perú, Lima, 1970.

Arriaga, José de. *La extirpación de la idolatría en el Perú*. Colección de libros y documentos relativos a la historia del Perú, Imp. Sanmarti, Lima, 1920.

Bagu, Sergio. *La economía de la sociedad colonial*. Buenos Aires: Sin Editorial, 1949.

Basto Girón, Luis. *Salud y enfermedad en el campesino peruano*. Universidad de San Marcos, Lima, 1957.

Baudin, Luis. *El imperio socialista de los Incas*. Santiago de Chile: Zig-Zag, 1943.

Berlin, Brent, and Blois Ann Berlin. "Etnobiología, subsistencia y nutrición en una sociedad de la selva tropical: los Aguaruna (Jíbaro)." *Salud y nutrición en sociedades nativas*. Ed. Alverto Chirif. Centro de Investigación y promoción amazónica, n.p., 1978. pp. 13–47.

Blanco, Hugo. *Tierra o muerte*. Siglo XXI. Mexico, 1972.

Buehler, Anton. *La estructura y la conciencia de las clases sociales*. (Publicación Previa) Departamento de Ciencias Sociales, PUCP, Lima, 1978.

Buntinx, Gustavo. "Mirar desde el otro lado. El mito de Inkarrí, de la tradición oral a la plástica erudita." Unpublished. Postgrado de Ciencias Sociales, Universidad Católica del Perú, Lima, n.d.

____. "Los profétos de la rebelión." *Estados y regiones en los Andes*. Instituto Francés de Estudios Andinos, Lima, 1986.

Caballero, J.M. "Diez años de investigación agraria en el Perú." Revista de la Universidad del Pacífico, *Apuntes*, Lima, 1984.

Cajías, F. "Los objectivos de la revolución indígena de 1781: el caso de Oruro." *Revista Andina* 2, Cuzco, n.d.

Cardoso, Ciro F. *Historia económica de América Latina*. 2 vol. Barcelona, 1979.

____. "Sobre los modos de producción coloniales en América." *Modos de producción en América Latina, cuadernos del pasado y presente* 40 (1973, Córdoba): 135–159.

Carrillo, Alfredo. *La trayectoria del pensamiento filosófico en Latinoamérica*. Casa de la Cultura Ecuatoriana, Quito, 1959.

Cassirer, Ernest. *Antropología filosófica*. Fondo de Cultura Económica, Mexico, 1971.

Castelli, Amalia, Marcia Koth de Paredes and Mariana Mould de Pease, eds. *Etnohistoria y antropología andina*. Segunda jornada del Museo Nacional de Historia, 1979, Lima, 1981.

Castro Pozo, Hildebrando. *Nuestra comunidad indígena*. Lima, 1924.

Cencillo, Luis. *Mitos: semántica y realidad*. Bibliotheca de Autores Cristianos, Madrid, 1970.

CENCIRA-COTESU. *Capacitación campesina. Una experiencia en Huancavelica. Proyecto CENCIRA-COTESU 1979–1981*. Editado por el proyecto "Capacitación especializada y básica para campesinos." CENCIRA-COTESU, Lima, 1982.

____. *Comunidades campesinas. Proceso histórico de diferenciación*. CENCIRA-COTESU, Lima, 1977.

Cerutti Guldberg, Horacio Victorio. "Ubicación política de los orígenes y el desarrollo de la filosofía de la liberación latinoamericana." *Cuadernos Salmantinos de Filosofía* 3 (1976): 351–360.

Chaves, Milcíades. "La Guajira: una región y una cultura de Colombia." *Revista Colombiana de antropología* 1, No. 1, Bogotá, June 1953.

____. "Mitos, leyendas y cuentos de la Guajira." Boletín de Arqueología II , No. 4, Bogotá, 1946.

Chonati, Irma, et al. *Tradición oral peruana. I. Hemerografía (1896–1976)*. Instituto Nacional de Cultura, Lima, 1978.

Cobo, Bernabé. *Historia del nuevo mundo*. Madrid: Atlas, 1956.

Colombres, Adolfo. *La colonización cultural de la América indígena*. Quito: El Sol, 1977.

Cook, Noble David. *Demographic Collapse: Indian Peru, 1520–1620*. Cambridge: Cambridge University Press, 1981.

Costales, Alfredo, and Piedad Peñaherrera de C. "El indio de Chimborazo: hombre desconocido." *Boletin de Informaciones Científicas Nacionales* 5 (1953, Quito): 541–565.

____. *Historia social del Ecuador*. Vol. 4. Casa de la Cultura Ecuatoriana, Quito, 1971.

Curátola, Marco. "Mito y milenarismo en los Andes; del Taqui Onkoy a Inkarrú, la visión de un pueblo invicto." Instituto de Pastoral Andino, *Allpanchis* 10, Cuzco, 1977.

Diez Astete, Alvaro, Rodolfo Sánchez Garrafa and Jorge Perez Mundaca. "Que es el mito?" *Anthropologica* 1 (1983, PUCP, Lima): 5–36.

Dobyns, Henry F. *Comunidades campesinas del Perú*. Lima, 1970.

Dobyns, Henry F., and Mario Vásquez. *Migración e integración en el Perú*. Monografía Andina No. 2, Ed. Estudios Andinos, Lima, 1970.

Duviols, Pierre. *Cultura andina y represión*. Centro de Estudios Rurales Andinos Bartolomé de las Casas, Cuzco, 1986.

_____. *La lutte contre les religions autochtones dans le Pérou colonial. "L'extirpation de l'idolâtrie" entre 1532 et 1660.* Instituto Francés de Estudios Andinos, Lima, 1971.

_____. "Huari y Llacuaz. Agricultores y pastores. Un dualismo prehispánico de oposición y complementaridad." *Revista del Museo Nacional* 39 (1973, Lima): 153–198.

Earls, John. "La organización del poder en la mitología quechua." *OSSIO*, 1973. pp. 393-414.

_____. "Astronomía y ecología: la sincronización alimenticia del maíz." *Allpanchis* 14 (1979, Cuzco): 117–135.

Eliade, Mircea. *La búsqueda.* Buenos Aires: Ediciones Megápolis, 1971.

_____. *El chamanismo.* Ed. Fondo de Cultura Económica, Mexico, 1960.

_____. *Dioses, diosas y mitos de la creación.* Buenos Aires: Ediciones Megápolis, 1977.

_____. *Imágines y simbolos.* Madrid: Guadarrama, 1974.

_____. *El mito del eterno retorno.* Buenos Aires: Emece, 1958.

_____. *Mito y realidad.* Madrid: Guadarrama, 1973.

_____. *Mitos, sueños y misterios.* Buenos Aires: Compañía General Editora, 1961.

_____. *Tratado de historia de las religiones.* Instituto de Estudios Políticos, Madrid, 1954.

Espinoza Soriano, Waldemar, ed. *Los modos de producción en el imperio de los Incas.* Lima: Montaño, 1978.

_____. "El curaca de los cayambes y su sometimiento al imperio español." Siglo XV and XVI. *Boletín de Instituto Francés de Estudios Andinos.* Vol. 9, No. 1–2 (1980, Lima): 89–119.

Estrella, Eduardo. *Medicina aborígen.* Quito: Epoca, 1978.

Fischer, John R. "La formación del estado peruano (1808–1824) y Simon Bolívar." In *Problemas de la formación del estado y la nación en Hispanoamérica.* Bonn: Inter Nationes, n.d.

_____. *Gobierno y sociedad en el Perú colonial: el régimen de las intendencias.* Pontificia Universidad Católica del Perú, Lima, 1981.

Fuenzalida, Fernando. "El mundo de los gentiles y las tres eras de la creación." *Revista de la Universidad Católica*—nueva serie—2 (1977, PUCP, Lima): 59–84.

_____. "El Cristo pagano de los Andes: una cuestión de identidad y otra sobre las eras solares." *Debates en Antropología* 4 (1979, PUCP, Lima): 1–10.

_____. "Santiago y el Wamani: aspectos de un culto pagano en Moya." *Debates en Antropología* 5, PUCP, Lima, 1980.

Fuenzalida, Fernando, José Luis Villaran, Jürgen Golte and Teresa Valiente. *Estructuras tradicionales y economía de mercado, la comunidad de indígenas de Huayopampa.* Lima: IEP, 1968.

Galdo Pagaza, Raúl. *El indígena y el mestizo en Volquechico*. Plan Nacional de Integración de la Población Aborigen, Série Monográfica No. 3, Publicaciones del Ministerio de Trabajo y Asuntos Indígenas, Lima, 1962.

Geertz, Clifford. "Religion as a Cultural System." *Readings in Comparative Religion*. Ed. Lessa and Vogt. New York: Harper and Row, 1965.

Girard, Raphael. "Consideraciones sobre mitología indoamericana." Instituto de Antropología, *Runa* 10, Buenos Aires, 1967.

Golte, J. *La racionalidad de la organización andina*. Instituto de Estudios Peruanos, Lima, 1980.

Gómez, Antonio. "El cosmos, religión y creecias de los indios Cuna." Universidad de Antioquía, Medellin, *Boletín de Antropología* 3, No. 11, September 1969.

Gonzalez Alvarez, Luis. "El sentido de nuestra cultura." In *El hombre latinoamérícano y su mundo*. Bogotá: Nueva América, 1980. pp. 161–247.

Gonzalez Carre, Enrique. *Historia prehispánica de Ayacucho*. Universidad Nacional de San Cristóbal de Huamanga, Ayacucho, 1982.

Gow, Rosalinda, and Bernabé Condori. *Kay Pacha. Tradición oral andina*. Centro de Estudios Rurales Andinos "Bartolomé de las Casas," Cuzco, 1976.

Guaman Poma de Ayala, Felipe. *Nueva crónica y buen gobierno*. Travaux et Mémoires de l'Institut d'Ethnologie XXIII, Université de Paris, Paris, 1936.

Guevara, Darío. *Un mundo mítico-mágico en la mitad del mundo*. Imprenta del I.C. Municipal de Quito, Quito, 1972.

Harnecker, Marta. *Los conceptos elementales del materialismo histórico*. Siglo XXI. Mexico, 1971.

Hawley, Florence. "The Role of Pueblo Social Organization in the Dissemination of Catholicism." *American Anthropologist* 48 (1946): 407–415.

Hegenberg, Leonidas. *Introducción a la filosofía de las ciencias*. Barcelona: Herder, 1969.

Horkheimer, Hans. *Nahrung und Nahrungsgewinnung im vorspanischen Peru*. Berlin, 1960.

Huertas Vallejos, Lorenzo. *La religión en una sociedad rural andina*. Siglo XVII. Universidad Nacional de San Cristóbal de Huamanga, Ayacucho, 1981.

Hurtado de Mendoza, S. W. *Wiraqocha—Mitos*. Lima: Nueva Epoca, 1980.

Ibarra, Grasso, and Edgar Dick. *La representación de América en mapos romanos de tiempos de Cristo*. Ed. Grasso Ibarra and Dick Edgar. Buenos Aires, 1970.

_____. *La verdadera historia de los Incas*. Editorial. "Los Amigos del Libro," La Paz-Cochabamba, 1969.

Imbelloni, José. *Religiosidad indígena Americana*. Buenos Aires: Castañeda, 1979.

_____. "La 'Weltanschauung' de los amautas reconstruida: formas peruanas del pensamiento templario." In *Congreso Internacional de Americanistas*. Vol. 2. *Actas y trabajos científicos* 27, Lima, 1942.

Izquierdo Gallo, Mariano R.P. *Mitología americana*. Madrid: Ediciones Guadarrama, 1957.

Jijon y Camaño, Jacinto. *La religión del imperio de los Incas*. Vol. 1. Quito: Escuela Tipográfica Salesiana, 1931.

Jimenez Núñez, A. *Mitos de creación en Sudamérica*. Publicaciones del Seminario de Antropología. Vol. 3. Sevilla, 1962.

Katz, Friedrich. *The Ancient American Civilization*. London: Weidenfeld and Nicholson, 1969.

Köpcke, Hans-Wilhelm. *Synökologische Studien an der Westseite der peruanischen Anden*. Bonn, 1961.

Kusch, Rodolfo. *El pensamiento indígena y popular en América*. Buenos Aires: Hachette S.A., 1977.

Larrea, Carlos Manuel. *Prehistoria de la región andina del Ecuador*. Quito: Corporación de Estudios y Publicaciones, 1971.

Las Casas, Bartolomé de. "Denuncia profética de la destrucción de Indias." In *Ideología y praxis de la coquista. Denuncia de Montesinos y Las Casas*. Bogotá: Nueva América, 1978.

Levinas, Emmanuel. *Humanismo del otro hombre*. Siglo XXI. Mexico, 1974.

Lumbreras, L.G., et al. *Arqueología de la América andina*. Lima: Milla Batres, 1981.

_____. *Nueva historia general del Perú*. Lima: Mosca Azul Editores, 1979.

Macera, Pablo. *Visión histórica del Perú (del paleolítico al proceso de 1968)*. Lima: Milla Batres, 1978.

Malinowski, Bronislav. *Magia, ciencia y religión*. Barcelona: Ariel, 1974.

Mariátegui, José Carlos. "El indigenismo en la literatura nacional." *Mundial* 345, Lima, 21 January 1927.

_____. *Siete ensayos de interpretación de la realidad peruana*. Lima: Amauta, 1928.

Mariscotti de Goerlitz, Ana María. *Pachamama. Santa Tierra. Contribución al estudio de la religión autóctona de los Andes centro-meridionales*. Indiana Suplemento 8, Gebr. Mann, Berlin, 1978.

_____. "Los posición del señor de los fenómenos metereológicos en los panteones regionales de los Andes centrales." Instituto Nacional de Cultura. *Historia y Cultura* (Organo del Museo Nacional de Historia) 6 (1972, Lima): 207–215.

Marzai, Manuel Ma. "La religiosidad de la cultura de la pobreza." *Catequesis latinoamericana*, Asunción, 1970. pp. 7–8.

Mauss, Marcel. *Lo sagrado y lo profano*. Barcelona: Barral Editores, 1970.

Mendizábal, Emilio. "La difusión, acculturación y reinterpretación a través de las cajas de imaginero ayacuchanas." *Folklore Americano* 11, Nos. 11-12, Lima, 1963.

Métraux, Alfred. "El dios supremo, los creadores y héroes culturales en la mitología sudamericana." *América Indígena* 6, No. 1, Mexico, 1946.

____. "Ensayos de mitología comparada sudamericana." *América Indígena* 8, No. 1, Mexico, 1948.

____. *Religión y magias indígenas en América del Sur*. Madrid: Aguilar, 1967.

Milones, Luis. "Medicina y magia: propuesta para un análisis de los materiales andinos." *Boletín del Instituto Francés de Estudios Andinos* 12, Lima, 1983.

____. "Shamanismo y política en el Perú colonial: los curacas de Ayacucho." *Histórica* 8, Lima, 1984.

Molina, Cristóbal de. *Ritos y fábulos de los Incas*. Buenos Aires: Futuro, 1947.

Moreno Yánez, Segundo. *Sociedad indígena*. Manuscript. Departamento de Antropología de la PUCE, Quito, 1982. pp. 10–25.

Morote Best, Efraín. "Un nuevo mito de fundación del imperio." *Revista del Instituto Americano de Arte* 8 (1958, Cuzco): 38–58.

Moya, Ruth. *Simbolismo y ritual en el Ecuador andino*. Colección Pendoneros, Otavalo, 1981.

Murra, John. *Formaciones económicas y políticas del mundo andino*. Instututo de Estudios Peruanos, Lima, 1975.

____. *La organización económica del estado Inca*. Siglo XXI. Mexico, 1978.

Nuñez del Prado, Daysi. "La reciprocidad como ethos de la cultura andina." Instituto de Pastoral Andina, *Allpanchis* 4 (1971, Cuzco): 10–15.

Nuñez del Prado, Oscar. *El hombre, la familia, su matrimonio y su organización político-social en Q'ero*. Cuzco: Editorial Garcilaso, 1957.

Orlave, Benjamín S. "Ricos y pobres: la desigualdad en las comunidades campesinas." *Estudios Andinos* 8, No. 15, Lima, 1979.

Ortiz Rescaniere, Alejandro. *De Adaneva a Inkarrí. Una visión indígena del Perú*. Retablo de Papel, Lima, 1978.

____. *Huarochirí, 400 años depués*. Pontificia Universidad Católica del Perú, Fondo Editorial, Lima, 1980.

____. "El tratamiento del tiempo en los mitos andinos." *Debates en Antropología* 8, PUCP, Lima, 1982.

Ossio, Juan. "Apuntes para una comprensión del concepto de 'Historia' entre los Incas." *PUCP*, 1969. pp. 170–177.

Pease, Franklin. *El dios creador andino*. Lima: Mosca Azul Editores, 1973.

______. *El pensamiento mítico. Antología*. Lima: Mosca Azul Editores, Biblioteca del Pensamiento Peruano, 1982.

______. "Simbolismo de centro en el inca Gracilaso." *PUCP*, 1969. pp. 205–211.

______. "Las versiones del mito de Inkarrí." *Revista de la Universidad Católica*—nueva serie—2 (1977, PUCP, Lima): 25–42.

Rama, Carlos. *Historia de América Latina*. Barcelona: Bruguera S.A., 1978.

Reyes, Oscar. *Historia general del Ecuador*. Vol. 1. Quito: Talleres Gráficos Nacionales, 1967.

Ribeiro, Darcy. "La nación latinoamericana." *Revista Nueva Sociedad* 62, Caracas, October, 1982.

______. *El proceso civilizado*. Universidad Central de Venezuela, Caracas, 1970.

Ritter, Ulrich Peter. *Dorfgemeinschaften und Genossenschaften in Peru*. Göttingen, 1966.

Riva Aguero, José de la. *Paisajes peruanos*. Universidad Católica, Lima, 1969.

Roel, Virgilio. *Historia social y económica de la colonia*. Lima: Gráfica Labor, 1970.

Rowe, John. "El movimiento nacional inca del siglo XVII." *Túpac Amaru II: 1780* (Antología), Lima, 1979.

Silverblatt, Irene. "Dioses y diablos: idolatrías y evangelización." Instituto de Pastoral Andina, *Allpanchis* 19 (1982, Cuzco): 31–48.

Stern, Steve. *Los pueblos indígenas del Perú y el desafío de la conquista española*. Alianza Universidad, Madrid, 1986.

Tamayo Herrera, José. "Algunos conceptos filosóficos de la cosmovisión del indígena quecha." Instituto de Pastoral Andino, *Allpanchis* 2 (1970, Cuzco): 245–255.

______. *Historia social del indigenismo en el eltiplano*. Ediciones Treintaitrés, Lima, 1982.

Tapia, Fernando. "Actualidad del culto a la Pacha-Mama." Instituto de Pastoral Andino, *Allpanchis* 3 (1971, Cuzco): 21.

Troll, Carl. "Die Stellung der Indianer-Hochkulturen im Landschaftsaufbau der tropischen Anden." *Zs. der Gesellschaft für Erdkunde zu Berlin*, No. 3/4, Berlin, 1943.

Urbano, Henrique. "Del sexo, incesto y los ancestros de Inkarrí. Mito, utopia e historia en las sociedades andinas." Instituto de Pastoral Andina, *Allpanchis* 17/18 (1971, Cuzco): 77–118.

______. "Discurso mítico y discurso utópico en los Andes." Instituto de Pastoral Andina, *Allpanchis* 10, Cuzco, 1971.

______. *Wiracocho y Ayar, héroes y funciones en las sociedades andinas*. Centro Bartolomé de las Casas, Cuzco, 1981.

Valcarcel, Luis E. *Cuentos y leyendas inkas*. Imprenta del Museo Nacional, Lima, 1939.

____. *Etnohistoria del Perú antiguo*. Universidad Nacional Mayor de San Marcos, Lima, 1964.

Vásquez, Mario. "La antropología cultural y nuestro problema del indio." *Perú Indígena* 2 (1952): 5–6.

Velee, Lionel. "El discurso mítico de Santa Cruz Pachacuti Yanqui." Instituto de Pastoral Andina, *Allpanchis* 20 (1982, Cuzco): 103–128.

Waall, Annemarie. *Introdución a la antropología religiosa*. Navarra: Verbo Divino, 1975.

Wachtel, Nathan. *La vision des vaincus. Les indiens du Pérou devant la conquête espagnole*. Paris: Gallimard, 1971.

____. *Sociedad e ideología. Ensayos de historia y antropología andinas*. Instituto de Estudios Peruanos, Lima, 1973.

Wood, Roberto. "El espacio sagrado y el 'centro del mundo.'" *PUCP*, 1969. pp. 197–204.

Zorrilla, Javier. "Sueño, mito y realidad en una comunidad ayacuchana." *Debates en Antropología* 2 (1978, PUCP, Lima): 119–124.

Zuidema, R.T. "El calendario Inca." *Actas Memorias XXXVI Congreso Internacional de Americanistas*, Sevilla, 1966. pp. 25–30.

____. *The Ceque System of Cuzco: The Social Organization of the Capital of the Inca*. Leiden, 1964.

Five

Aspects of Cultural Comparison

Summary

The following discussion of the work ethics in Christian, Japanese and Islamic cultures, as compared to Latin American culture, makes abundantly clear that the cultures of the Andes Pact states in particular do not have the pragmatic and empirical approach to reality that is necessary for success in the world economy. Instead, they are dominated by a transcendental, theocentric emphasis and thus lack an ideology conducive to practical action. The work ethics of their elite are prejudiced against manual and organizational labor, while their indigenous populations are largely excluded from high-level positions by the predominant culture. Thus, in the Andes Pact states there is little awareness that shortcomings in development can be overcome only in a context that embraces all levels of society and culture, nor is there a sense of community extending to society as a whole. Any policy of economic regeneration must take sociocultural factors into account when drafting new programs to overcome passivity and to initiate steady growth in the Andean economy.

A Cultural Comparison of the Work Ethics in Christian, Japanese and Islamic Societies

Human beings live not only in geographical surroundings, i.e., in their physical world, but also in a cultural context that is aptly known in English as a "world of meaning." This latter world forms a more solid framework for their actual behavior than the physical world by itself. The following examples, taken from the cultures of Christianity, Islam and the Far East, illustrate this point as a basis of comparison with Latin America.

The world of meaning and significance is the product of those ethical, social and religious traditions that directly impinge on the way we conduct our lives. Only after comparing Latin America with other cultures and religions can we arrive at a deeper understanding of the special position it occupies. This applies to work ethics no less than to organizational capabilities and all other key anthropological categories. Ethics, rites, myths and religions in innumerable cultural variants form an indispensable basis for an understanding of national economies and the technology on which these economies are based.

In the Christian tradition, the attitude toward theology was critical for the evolution of economic behavior. In the doctrines of the Reformation, a person's profession was seen as both an existential and a personal matter in which, above all, labor became one's calling in life. The early Protestant tradition differed considerably in this respect from the view of labor held by scholastic Catholicism. This difference is amply demonstrated by the verses that Martin Luther wrote for the congregation of Wittenberg: artisans, cobblers and smiths were all enjoined to submit to the humble duty of carrying out the daily tasks to which they were called by divine providence. Labor, Luther argued, lay in the "nature" of human beings, and thus meant more than doing what was necessary to maintain human life. The term *rerum novarum*, "striving for innovation," became part and parcel of Reformation doctrine.

All efforts of Judaism and Christianity to articulate a theology of labor were predicated on the proposition of an afterlife as formulated in the mass for the dead: *Requiem sempiternam dona eis, domine, et lux perpetua luceat eis.* Their view of labor also touched upon their view of paradise; a distinction was made between paradise as a "primitive" state of innocence and paradise as an eschatological realm of the elect. This distinction was linked with the injunction to work, as well as the prohibition of labor on the Sabbath. *Both the Hebrew Bible and the Christian New Testament saw in labor the key promise to eternal life.* The early Protestant traditions of the sort that later came to fruition in, for example, North American culture differed profoundly from the scholastic Catholic tradition of early Latin America, which in consequence developed a different work ethic.

Japanese culture is noted for a special form of empiricism that was to have a direct influence on its work ethic. Early Japanese culture took it as a matter of course that the world was made up entirely of the world as experienced on the Japanese archipelago. Unlike Western cultures, which held that humanity lived in a "fallen world," the early traditions of Japanese culture maintained that the natural world represented the real world; there was no need to search for higher meaning in the hereafter. This view differed radically from Latin American culture, which had taken a transcendental slant ever since the scholasticism of the sixteenth century and thus had a work ethic geared toward the afterlife. This was accompanied *a fortiori* by a relative contempt for empiricism that found expression in unfavorable preconditions for economic efficiency.

Japan's cultural history gave it a far superior basis for the acceptance of technology, a basis that inherently called out for pragmatism and empiricism. In the fifth and sixth centuries, religious influences came to Japan from Korea and China: the ethics of Confucianism, the doctrines of Buddhism, the magical and mythical thought of Taoism and the school of Ying-Yang. In sharp contrast to Korea, which likewise fell under the influence of Chinese culture, seventh-century Japan attempted to forge a synthesis of religion, society and culture, a synthesis which was of profound importance for the later integration of its economy. Even today in Latin America, the economy has not been integrated into the state in any larger sense of the term.

The Japanese synthesis embraced all aspects of Confucianism, Buddhism and Japan's own Shintoism under the supremacy of the emperor, who headed the state through hereditary rule by virtue of his sacred status. Japanese culture can be described as an intrinsic theocracy, whereas the intellectual history of colonial Latin America left behind a culture of metaphysics, transcendence and escapism. The Japanese fashioned a practical synthesis in all walks of life by ritualizing everyday culture with an eye toward national cohesion and unity, a goal that at no time existed in Latin America. Nor were the ruling classes of the Latin American states as clearly structured as in Japan, where all aspects of government were subordinated to the emperor. The emperor was seen as the living *kami*, the sacred king and, at the same time, the supreme priest of the state. The state was viewed, in a synthetic perspective, as a family structure spreading out beneath the imperial throne in the form of a pyramid: the individual was incorporated hierarchically and patriarchally into the community, and was bound to it in loyalty and piety. How different this was from Latin America, where the individual was socially atomized and devoid of moral obligation to the community.

Life in Japan took its bearings from the twin lodestars of loyalty and piety. Feudal domination *(bakufu)* embodied a synthesis of religion, society and culture that had emerged in the seventh century. To the present day, this synthesis has served as a sustaining paradigm for the historical unity of the Japanese nation. The reason for this is that it intrinsically harbors the possibility of further evolution, vouchsafing the mutual cooperation and preservation of the national hierarchy and the state.

This aspect of the preservation of the state likewise differs markedly from Latin America, where these factors have never been able to coalesce. Confucianism in Japan served to uphold the state; even Japanese Buddhism obliquely supported the principle of national protection *(chingo-kokka)* while affirming the veneration of ancestors and family, as well as burial ceremonies. Japanese culture was an amalgam *(shin-butsu shungo)* representing an intrinsic theocracy. The very fact that this theocracy was intrinsic distinguishes Japan from transcendentalist Latin America in its acceptance of empirical technology.

The evolution of Japanese culture proceeded in different stages, and it is essential to view these differences in historical perspective, if we are to understand their effects on Japanese industrialization in comparison with that of Latin America. New elements entered the Japanese "world of meaning" as early as the thirteenth century. The establishment of a feudal regime in Kamakura, near present-day Tokyo, coincided with the emergence of new schools of Buddhism, such as the Nichiren school and Zen. At the same time, there was a strengthening of nationalist sentiment motivated by the attempted invasion of Japan by the Mongols. Imperial Japan, centered on the court and aristocracy (e.g, in Kyoto), continued to exist, but new cultural ideals of militaristic origin influenced large sections of the population. Led by Zen monks, two forms of culture emerged, one celebrating martial ideals and the other naturalness. It is these two ideals that Ruth Benedict, speaking of the fifteenth and sixteenth centuries, aptly summed up in the twin images of "chrysanthemum and sword." A synthesis of traditional elements came about through the influence of Buddhism and Chinese culture. Another factor was Japan's isolation from the rest of the world, imposed by the Tokugawa government from the seventeenth to the middle of the nineteenth centuries.

Before the first Tokugawa shogun came to power in 1600, Portugal had begun to expand its influence in Asia. Roman Catholic missionaries had won about 150,000 converts in Japan. Admittedly, due to its transcendent leanings as opposed to the intrinsically empirical culture of Japan, Catholicism was difficult to assimilate. After persecuting the Japanese Catholics, the Tokugawa regime then forbade any further contact with foreign powers, apart from Holland, Korea and China. Thus isolated, Japan brought forth an imperial regime sustained by religious institutions. The mythological traditions of Shinto gave way somewhat to the Confucian principle of natural rights. Government was based on the principle of *jinsei* as an expression of the moral order. The resultant *baku-han* system combined a national administration *(bakufu)* under the shogun with local administration by military princes *(daimyo).*

The shogunate promulgated a series of administrative and legislative principles and regulations. The social hierarchy of the Tokugawa period, headed by a warrior caste, supported the shogun and the *daimyo* in their tasks. Thus, the warriors were enjoined to learn and practice moral discipline in accordance with the martial code of behavior, *bushido.* Beneath the *kun,* the masters or princes, and the *shin,* the warriors, were arrayed the other levels of society: the peasants *(no),* the artisans *(ko)* and the merchants *(sho),* known collectively as *min* and *shomin.* They were expected to obey instructions while accomplishing the tasks imposed on them by divine authority.

The reigning work ethic was a composite of several factors: the regulations of the shogunate, the morals of the family and kinship system, the professional guilds and the parish congregations of local Shinto shrines and Buddhist temples. The success of the Shogunate in maintaining internal peace by martial law served as a background for the growth of industry and trade in urban and rural areas. In turn, this growth helped to loosen the social system of the Tokugawa period, which was originally based on an agrarian economy.

This brief survey suffices to show how various facets of Japanese culture had a cumulative effect on the Japanese work ethic long before the advent of the modern age. This point is very important for a comparison with Latin America, as it enables us to point to historical roots that produced completely different results during the period of industrialization. Only by comparing pre-modern societies can we understand the divergences among their later outgrowths.

Little is known about the historical attitude of the Japanese toward labor. The eighteenth-century Shinto theorist Motoori Noringa (1730–1801) was convinced that people were equipped from birth with the capacity to do what had to be done, and to do it in a thoroughly empirical manner. He spoke in terms of the spirit of birth and becoming *(musubi no kami)*. Even today, Shintoists believe that the historical order of Japan is grounded on individuals, on their labor *(waza)* and attendant responsibilities and professional skills. The Japanese world of meaning was erected on the ethical imperatives of Confucianism just as its empirically minded metaphysics was derived from Buddhism. Confucianism and Shintoism posited a universally valid *tao* and *dharma*. Japanese culture taught, through Confucianism, that the human and cosmic orders were both grounded in one and the same *tao (michi* in Japanese) as an ethical imperative. One's labor had to be performed responsibly in accordance with this imperative. Buddhism bequeathed to Japanese culture the paradoxical truth that the many are one, and the one is many.

The individual also received recognition according to the commandment of Tendai Buddhism with its injunction to *endon-kai* (the "perfect commandment"). Here, obedience to one commandment entailed knowledge of all commandments. It was on this basis, for instance, that monks swept the monastery grounds or performed kitchen duties, always in the belief that even the humblest path leads to enlightenment. This insight also was applied to handicrafts and other trades. Human beings attained dignity by performing subservient activities.

Compared to the contempt expressed for manual labor in Latin American culture, it is obvious that the Japanese had superior prerequisites for building up an economy. Function and responsibility were clearly outlined by the straightforward, threefold division of society into warriors, peasants and burghers. Japan's work ethic constituted an indispensable precondition for its rise to the world's leading industrial nation. There was nothing comparable to it in Latin American culture.

In the Meiji era, Japan underwent the concluding phases in preparation for its advent into the modern age. Once again, as in the seventh century and the Tokugawa period, the country witnessed a period of synthesis. The goal of the Meiji government was not merely the renewal of society *(ishin)* along Western lines. There was also an intention to reconstruct *(fukko)* or even to return to the ideal of the seventh century, to a national identity of religion and politics subservient to the emperor.

Seen in this light, the ethos of modern Japan before the Second World War was a fusion of two elements: values inspired by Confucianism, and principles embodied in the thought of the Tokugawa period. These were joined by the seventh-century ideals of a sacred monarchy, a chosen people and a unity of religion and state. Once again, we note that at no time in the history of Latin America did religion and state enter such an economically creative relation with each other. The goal of the Meiji Restoration was to erect a modern state with economic prosperity and strong defense *(fukoku-kyohei)* under the aegis of the divine emperor. The architects of modern Japan had a clear sense of priorities.

Japan began by sending explorers to the industrial centers of Europe and North America to obtain the latest knowledge in medicine, jurisprudence and, above all, technology. *The difference between Japan and Latin America is that the bearers of information were integrated in a program of strict military training and a nationally controlled system of education.* Similarly, the cult of the emperor was heightened by a phenomenon that was to become known as state Shinto. At the beginning of the Meiji Restoration, there were only four hundred soldiers under the control of the chrysanthemum throne. Before long, however, a general military conscription had registered all male citizens over the age of twenty and transformed them into servants of the military for the defense of state and throne.

The system of education transformed Japan into a literate culture. Instruction was given in ethics *(shushin)*, a combination of bourgeois morality, a system of values and a mythical history. At this stage, the notion was implanted that human beings are dissimilar by nature, that some are born to rule and others to be ruled. Everyone was attributed an ability to display industry, productivity, piety and loyalty along with a willingness to sacrifice oneself for the higher good of state, family, profession and society.

Here again, we note a fundamental difference with Latin America, where there was no historical basis for the willingness of individuals to sacrifice themselves for the good of the state. The dual strategy of the Meiji regime—economic prosperity and strong defense *(fukoku-kyohei)*—led to the rise of two familiar hubs of power: the *zai-batsu,* an association of economic conglomerates, and the *gun-batsu,* an association of the military. Both of these factors began increasingly to coalesce during the Sino Japanese War of 1894–1895, the Russo-Japanese War of 1904–1905, the annexation of Korea and the First World War. The result was both a modernization of tradition and *mutatis mutandis,* a traditionalization of modernism.

The sustaining features of the Japanese work ethic, as opposed to that of Latin America, may be summarized as follows. First came the ancient Japanese injunction to perform one's labor properly *(waza)* for the good of the social community. To this was added the notion, inspired by Confucianism, that people should immerse themselves totally in every activity, no matter how humble. The significance of the faithful execution of one's duty *(yaku* or *shokubun)* is an upshot of a neo-Confucian viewpoint. The history of Japan reveals a dialectic unknown in Latin America: on the one hand, a transformation of tradition by new influences; on the other, an accompanying tendency to traditionalize these new factors, especially in the late nineteenth century. This composite of tradition and modernity is foreign to Latin America.

Thus, what we might call a cumulative work ethic in premodern Japan was of seminal importance for the consolidation of the centralized, hierarchical makeup of Japanese culture, a synthesis of culture, religion, society, politics and the economy. Seen in historical perspective, the Japanese did not develop a system of "ethics" in the strict sense of the term, e.g., one comparable to what we understand by the Greek word *ethos* or the Latin word *mores.* Instead, Japanese ethics are eclectic. In Japanese culture, the relation between ethics and the world of meaning was maintained in poetry, whether by the Buddhist clergy, Confucian sages or feudal warrior-bureaucrats. Once it had become evident that Japan would have to strike a *modus vivendi* with the Western powers, Sakuma Shozan (1811–1864), an enlightened Confucian, formulated a new conception: Eastern ethics in their essence and Western science. These two dialectically related principles were formative for the Meiji period and constituted the basis of Japan's process of modernization. Japan witnessed its own emergence, under a strong monarchy, as a nation-state with the latest science and technology that continue to elude Latin America. Imperial regulations regarding education, for example, were designed to inculcate not only integrity of character, but also—and especially, as H. Nakamura has pointed out—a conviction that good is not limited to the individual, but is extended to include the social community, the state and the nation. This "supra-individual" nexus between family and the apparatus of state and economy is yet another fundamental difference between Japan and Latin America, whose states are set up on the basis of atomized individual interests with no responsibility to the common weal.

To obtain another revealing point of comparison with Latin America, we shall now turn to the Islamic work ethic. In order to understand the Islamic work ethic more fully, we should recall that the term "labor" is one of the most important concepts of Islamic culture and is not basically distinguished from the term "action" which appears under the same category in divine law (*al shari'ah*). If we look up the word "labor" in a bilingual dictionary, we find two equivalent translations: *amal* and *sun*. The first means action in a general sense as opposed to knowledge; the second has to do with the creation of a product in the sense of handicrafts. People embody two functions in their relation to the world: either they act within the world, or they act outside it.

The unitarian view of Islam, which makes no distinction between the sacred and the profane, reaches its culmination in a refusal to distinguish between religious actions and secular actions, i.e., between prayer and labor. Among traditional Moslems, one's fear of God and one's responsibility to God encompass not only veneration and prayer, but also labor in the common sense of the term. As we can easily see, the Islamic work ethic is profoundly influenced by cultural and religious factors, not merely by economic motives. In keeping with the words of the Prophet, or *hadith*, God forgives a person's trespasses against Himself but not those against His other creatures (*tawbah*).

Traditional Moslems maintain a sense of responsibility to fulfill this "contract" between God and humanity in order to perform their labor and to satisfy the person for whom a particular task is carried out.

Many verses in the Koran and a great many *hadiths* that have entered Islamic literature as poems and parables are meant to remind Moslems of the deep-seated religious roots of their work ethic, which must be enacted in concord with *shari'ah.* This entails a moral responsibility in all aspects of labor—economic, social and aesthetic. The Islamic work ethic is inseparable from the moral character of that which Moslems create during their earthly journey, in keeping with the strictures of divine law. Labor is intimately linked with prayer. The daily call to prayer *(al-adhan)* repeats this basic connection five times a day by proclaiming *hayy ala'l-salah* and, especially, *hayy ala khayr al-amal.* And it is prayer that gives rise to bliss of the spirit.

The work ethic of Islam applies to both meanings of the term—*amal* and *sun*—since divine law embraces the full panoply of human actions. It must therefore be seen against this universal background rather than in purely economic terms. The Koran teaches that the word *uqud* ranges from daily prayer to dealings at the bazaar. The moral responsibility placed on the shoulders of the faithful refers both to labor and to the veneration of God, and covers the whole of human existence within the confines of *shari'ah.* The basis of the entire Islamic work ethic resides in the moral responsibility that Moslems show for their deeds, a responsibility not only to their superiors and employers, but also to the labor itself, which must be carried out with the utmost possible perfection. Responsibility toward labor also resides in a respect for God, who witnesses all human actions. One's responsibility to God for all deeds, including one's labor, extends beyond death and touches upon Moslems in their ultimate entelechy as immortal beings.

As in the Judaeo-Christian tradition, Moslems are responsible for the moral and ethical consequences of their deeds on the Day of Judgement, the significance of which is stressed in the final chapters of the Koran.

Only under these conditions can the fruits of one's labor be linked with one's religion and, at the same time, be considered legitimate *(halal).* A strong element of morality pervades traditional Islam: income must actually be earned in proportion to the difficulty of attaining it, otherwise employer and employee are mutually deceiving themselves in a manner undeserving of the term *halal.*

In Islamic culture, the dispensation of permission has given rise to a highly developed system designed to confer the label *halal* on a person's income. The dialectic between *halal* and *haram* ("forbidden") marks the boundaries of labor which a Moslem can perform.

Labor and ethical perception merge; a personal, humane connection bears witness to the supremacy of God. Still, one cannot understand the aspect of quality in the Islamic notion of labor, unless the role of women in traditional Islamic culture is included. For it is the labor of women that predominates in agriculture, grazing, handicrafts, nomadic gathering and work in the bazaar.

Another crucial point is that the cosmology of enlightenment codified in the Koran—and with it the repertoire of symbols in the Islamic faith—likewise represents a paradigm for labor. Deeds take place in a sacred universe in which labor is not purely secular but invariably has religious significance.

The success of Islam in attaining its own civilization, sustained by the idea and omnipresence of the sacred as an axiom for its work ethic, should not be considered apart from the economy. Islamic culture developed different ways and means of imparting a sacred dimension to widely varying forms of labor and of anchoring the fruits of labor in an overriding complex of the community. This is an essential point of difference with Latin American culture, which never developed a sense of responsibility to the community or to the concert of nations.

Traditional Islam had many different guilds and fraternities, called *asnaf*, as well as the *akhi* movement that spread over the entire Islamic world. Labor was brought to bear on the *sufi* commandments and was seen as an extension of spiritual discipline. A particular spirit reigned in the guilds (called *futuwwah* in Arabic and *javanmardi* in Persian), a spirit likewise not encountered in Latin America.

In sum, the traditional Islamic work ethic was noted for its code of honor, its strict adherence to ethical standards, its responsibility toward and dedication to others and the assistance granted to fellow guild members. Hence, its differences from the Latin American work ethic. Even the connection between the work ethic and the emerging handicrafts made sense in traditional Islam. Every form of labor dealing with the production of objects (*sun*) was infused with religious and spiritual significance. The ethical dimension of humankind also included the aesthetic dimension, since the quality and beauty of an object were dependent on the love of its creator, and labor went hand in hand with the virtue of the good life. This view of labor, being grounded in religion, imparted spiritual depth to the laborer.

It hardly need be mentioned that the ethical quality of labor was more strongly rooted in traditional Islamic circles than in the emerging Middle Eastern technological civilizations, where ties to the Koran are weaker than in the *shari'ite* institutions, *sufi* precepts, bonds of kinship and the general culture of Islam, all of which were many centuries in the making.

Cultural Features of the Work Ethic in the Andes Region

Before we can understand the situation in Latin America, we must first study its intellectual history in order to see how its various populations and ethnic groups view themselves. In other words, we must consider America not just as a geographical unit, but also as an historical entity.

Latin America was colonized under the aegis of a universal Catholic monarchy. Its culture was contemplative in outlook; its sense of time seemed to suggest that eternity might begin at any moment. At its root lay an all-embracing pantheistic sensibility. We must assume that Latin American culture was predicated on a sense of time as flowing, but without a particular destination. Individuality, universality and a holistic view of society converged in a series of concentric circles. Without these assumptions, there is no way we can elaborate an individual ontology for Latin America that captures its telluric character.

Carlos Fuentes once aptly remarked that Latin American culture hovers between the poles of nostalgia for the "noble savage" and an eschatalogical longing for revolt, i.e., between extreme individualism and a form of apocalyptic collectivism. Its underdeveloped economy is linked to the work ethic of large parts of its population—especially that of its elites—which might be described as "conspicuous indolence." Aristocratic ideals adopted from traditional Iberian culture led to a prejudice not only against manual labor, but against administrative labor as well. Those who claimed aristocratic status in colonial and post-colonial society sought to set themselves apart by adopting life styles deliberately opposed to those of the lower classes. To avoid being brought into contact with the lower levels of society, the elites made certain that they performed no sort of labor that might conceivably be carried out by the lower orders, mestizos or indio population. In consequence, the aristocratic elite had difficulty in finding any productive work which was not beneath their dignity.

One outstanding feature of the personal structure of the Latin American entrepreneurial classes was the high percentage of foreign investors, or at least of immigrants. Rarely did entrepreneurs rise from the lower or middle classes. The Latin American elites posed insurmountable obstacles to widespread social mobility. Thus, the rational economic behavior which distinguishes, for example, North American culture, and which can give rise in special cases to entrepreneurial initiative, did not exist in the countries of Latin America. The value system of traditional Latin American culture worked against the achievement of maximum efficiency per unit of time, making it unlikely that an active managerial class would arise in large sections of the population. Similarly, the quality of management was a product of the relation between cultural values and economic leadership.

One prerequisite for a managerial class is an ability and readiness to take calculated risks. This ability is dependent on cultural values that can either further or hinder innovation. In Latin American society, with its exaggerated awareness of social status, entrepreneurs feared bankruptcy less for reasons of financial loss than for the loss of social status and prestige. Consequently, long-term, high-risk investments were few and far between. Similarly, the social status accorded to those engaged in business was considerably lower in Latin American societies than in North America. This is an essential point, for social prestige was considered more important in Latin American culture than material success. Gilberto Freyre has impressively shown how even colonial Latin America had a prevailing social prejudice against the purportedly nonaristocratic world of business. The widespread low productivity can be explained by administrative mismanagement in the state and private economy. This mismanagement ensured that considerably more time and effort had to be expended in Latin America, as compared to North America or Europe, in order to attain the same unit of labor. The state administrations in particular had an extremely low level of productivity. The consumer behavior of Latin American elites—their "conspicuous consumption," the obverse of "conspicuous indolence"—extravagantly flaunted not only their affluence, but also, and especially, their freedom. And this behavior was imitated by the lower classes.

A large proportion of indios, particularly in the populations of the Andes region, slowed down the process of modernization. These cultures, at first self-sufficient, thrived on subsistence farming and were content with the economic status quo. But most of all, they were not integrated into the national economy, a problem which the Andes states have yet to solve. These cultures are excluded from the work ethic of the dominant culture; their spiritual and religious universe hinges on meanings which stand at odds with modernism. The Andes Pact states lack a realization that backlogs in development can be overcome only in an overriding context embracing the whole of culture and society. There is a lack of cooperative spirit on all levels of society, combined with *individualismo,* a cultural feature that stands beyond social control. Yet, the evolution of a sense of community on the level of state and society is a precondition for economic growth. How different this is from Japanese culture, which also has a rigid state hierarchy, but is grounded on a principle of social consensus and characterized by an emphasis on groups, rather than on anarchic individualism.

In addition to the problem of chronic administrative and economic inefficiency, Latin America also has a world view in which life is seen as unstructured and, above all, as unpredictable, uncertain and hence threatening. This is entirely unlike the Calvinist culture in North America, which is predicated on human powers of self-fulfillment. People and institutions in Latin American culture are treated largely with distrust, making it difficult to proceed from a *cultura de la dependencia* to an independent state based on a productive economy. The contradiction between highly productive foreign businesses and local economic inertia is still too great.

Latin America's lack of trust in its own productive potential can easily give rise to a negative national identity. Octavio Paz has described Latin America's quest for self-awareness as a series of crises extending from the Spanish conquest to the revolutions to the upheavals of the present day. This process of self-discovery is still incomplete.

The question remains whether Latin America can establish a positive national identity to offset the negative image which finds widespread expression in nationalist patterns of behavior. This negative image diverts attention from the fact that, in the final analysis, Latin America has no identity at all. Moreover, its excessive dependence on European and North American culture when trying to enter the modern age posed a threat which was seen as a form of alienation. The Latin American work ethic, with its hallmarks of apathy and passivity, must be considered a critical obstruction to the long-term, dynamic development of the economy. The inertia of Andean culture—the obsolete values held by large segments of its population—is a further hindrance.

The inhabitants of the Andes region often see themselves as solitary and waiting: *el hombre que esta solo y espera.* Thus, the creole of traditional Latin American cultures lives in a state of constant hope, for the Spanish word *esperar* means at once "to wait" and "to hope."

Ortega y Gasset recognized long ago that the traditional inhabitant of Latin America lives in a state of promises and permanent detachment. What is faced is not a concrete future for oneself so much as the divided future of a common ideal, a collective utopia. This utopia has become a personal illusion of such massive proportions that it already seems to be true. Accordingly, the traditional Latin American individual is devoted not so much to reality, but rather to an image fashioned from this reality.

If this sociocultural region is to avoid slipping into an economically treacherous fatalism, it is essential to surmount the passivity, melancholy and disillusionment pervading the traditional cultures which have not been successfully acculturated. A policy of regeneration must overcome the sense of personalism that has become a fixed characteristic of traditional Latin American culture. Latin America is governed by the principle that the individual, not the community, is of paramount importance for human existence and the integrity of the state. Accordingly, the forces that motivate actual events and processes appear impalpable or inoperative. Thoughts tend to center on fate, a perennial waiting for divine intervention, a never-ending hope that things will eventually turn out well. Instead of economic initiative, there is a deference to sacred authorities that undermines Latin America's entrepreneurial potential and the ability of its individuals to form social organizations.

Any culture which holds that future events are the ineluctable product of divine intervention (in the Christian sense) or of fate (in the syncretic sense) will tend to suppress a spirit of enterprise within the larger community. Neither the individual nor the social or governmental community is the architect of its own destiny. *Traditional Latin American society had an orientation toward being rather than doing and a retrospective attitude toward time that stood in the way of any attempts to plan long-term economic, social and political projects.* Whenever future planning managed to take place, it seemed divorced from empirical reality, at times even utopian. The passage of time from the past to the present and toward the future often conveyed little impression of increasing maturity.

This sense of the ephemeral nature of earthly existence, of one's powerlessness and inability to determine one's own destiny, is combined with a work ethic that attributes no value to labor in its own right, but sees it only as a necessary burden, one of many aspects of life that must be endured. The stigma of manual labor is avoided, as it is associated with the lower rungs of society. Among the higher-placed members of the landed gentry, this contempt for manual labor, combined with an emphasis on being rather than doing, forms the bedrock of aristocratic bearing and deportment. And for large sections of the population, of various ethnic provenance, the orientation on being is intimately linked with the development of the economy.

The preceding discussion of the work ethics of the Christian, Islamic and Japanese traditions was intended to underscore precisely those factors that are lacking in Latin America, and to explain why these traditions developed preconditions for a vital synthesis of culture, politics, religion and the economy that differ fundamentally from the preconditions of Latin American culture. It also explains why Japanese culture, for instance, had a far superior starting position for industrialization in modern technological civilization than did Latin American culture, which has had a fractured relation to modernity up to the present day and has been unable to assimilate technology in a manner supportive of the state. Ever since the scholasticism of the sixteenth century, the cultural and religious traditions that predominate in Latin America have been notably metaphysical and transcendent. Small wonder, then, that they were considerably less capable than the inherently empirical Japanese culture of adapting to the equally empirical and analytical culture of modern technology.

Transcendency and Empiricism in North and Latin America

A comparison and contrasting analysis of Latin American and North American cultures proves highly revealing. The traditional culture of Latin America proceeds from a theocentric premise that stands, in essence, outside the empirical world. This premise hinges on the idea of the supranatural, from which human beings derive their *raison d'être*. Albert Hirschmann observed the extent to which North American culture is, by comparison, basically empirical, analytical, rational, logical and, especially, anthropocentric in its outlook, and thereby draws on humanity itself as the final justification for existence.

Theocentric value systems are oriented toward transcendental goals. They view relations among human beings as a question of overriding principle and ethical obligation by stressing values, such as unbending loyalty. Anthropocentric value systems view relations among humans as a question of adaptation to surroundings. Between North and South America, there is a distinction in kind between anthropocentric and theocentric values. The latter are based on the acceptance of an absolute, the former on the attainment of practical success and a functional world view. The theocentric world view asks not what one has attained or represents, but rather what one feels and what one "is." This orientation toward being results from a lack of practicality that characterizes Latin American culture as a whole, to the detriment of its economy.

Two different ideas of human dignity are involved. The Latin American emphasis on being does not necessarily presuppose that human dignity must be accompanied by material success. The very fact that a person chooses being over achievement already implies a sort of stoic dignity, recalling those paintings by Velasquez which attribute grandeur even to men trampled in the dust. Lacking a practical dimension, Latin American culture sees religious significance in sacrifice. In its economic life, particularly among the lower classes, this has resulted in a high degree of complacency without a rational and systematic effort toward gain. North American culture, on the other hand, takes its bearings from the notion that humanity is self-empowered, a notion traceable from John Locke via Jonathan Edwards to the social Darwinism of Herbert Spencer or the pragmatism of C.S. Peirce, William James and John Dewey. It proceeds from the assumption that the world and nature are dominated by humankind, that time is meant to be used rationally, that the future can be planned and serves as a guide for all human endeavor. To this is added an emphasis on action, an orientation toward activities resulting from one's attainments, which are measurable in categories that have been extracted from the purlieus of the individual and made the responsibility of the larger group and community.

In Latin America, ever since the scholasticism of the sixteenth century, responsibility for the organization and attainment of non-empirical goals has fallen to the Church. This posture involved a shift of emphasis from practical thought to a traditionalism which also proved susceptible to authoritarian government. In any event, it diverted attention from the "achievement" so typical of North American culture, even in its religious denominations. The strong influence of the Roman Catholic Church since the days of sixteenth-century scholasticism is evident; the emphasis falls on a person's soul, not only in religion but also in secular life. What is more, the religious values inherited from Spain reveal a certain affinity with the mythical values of the Andean indios. Traditional indio culture regarded labor as a religious stance to be celebrated in ritual. It lacked that secular, pragmatic and rationalist tenor which characterized attitudes in the West, especially during and after industrialization. Nor has indio culture completely assimilated the Western notion of labor even today.

This relatively weak emphasis on achievement has prevented the evolution of practical values so essential to the emergence of an indigenous modern technology and economy. The value systems of Latin American culture tended less to emphasize practical, goal-directed action than the aesthetic dimension, the world of imagination and intuition, as found in *individualismo*. The result is a stronger tendency toward being, toward expression with non-empirical goals. Failure is not explained in terms of human error, but as divine dispensation, as the work of a transcendental, supraempirical arbiter. It is not the results of an action that command respect, but the very attempt. Accordingly, error is not necessarily bound up with feelings of guilt.

The main preoccupation in Latin American culture is the quest for transcendence, for ultimate values, for the hereafter. This quest is largely incompatible with the utilitarianism and pragmatism of an emergent industrial nation. The Latin American concept of dignity reinforces this view. Pride of place is given to a person's essence and spiritual constitution, divorced from economic cost-efficiency calculations and social prestige.

In commerce between human beings, crucial importance is attached to a personal touch; an impersonal sense of trust, for example, among individuals engaged in business, is not as common as in

North American culture. The idea that humanity can be perfected is not so well established in Latin America; its cultural values derive instead from devotion and subservience to a transcendental authority, from a hope in the dispensation of grace. Success in traditional Latin American culture hinges not least of all on these factors and on the hope of being granted happiness by a transcendental providence. An exclusive concentration on labor, on the entrepreneurial achievement of self-empowered human beings, is of secondary importance. Instead, primacy attaches to being rather than to action or to pride in one's achievements.

The anthropocentric approach to the world makes it possible to act pragmatically and functionally in economic life. Feelings of guilt in case of failure cannot be passed to a transcendental authority, but must be dealt with empirically by individuals themselves. Of course, it need hardly be mentioned that all these variants of cultural expression can be found in both North American and Latin American cultures, albeit in different proportions. An unwillingness to refer the responsibility for human failure to a supranatural authority is what we mean by the term anthropocentric. By focusing on the transcendental and absolute, traditional Latin American cultures pursue what is known in scholarly circles as "supersensory absolute values." This affects their view of the ultimate meaning of life, and is hence an existential judgement. Accordingly, Latin Americans have a different way of justifying their existence to themselves.

The anthropocentric approach emphasizes that people must communicate with others in order to ensure that their interests, rather than causing conflict, will help them attain empirical results. The anthropological variant emphasizes the relativity of thoughts, which depend on the vicissitudes of the empirical world and can only be effective or comprehensive as part of that world.

The pre-industrial type of social organization in traditional Latin American culture went hand in hand with its theocentric value system, a strong influence from syncretism and Catholicism, and in the Andean region, with the legacy of pre-Columbian high cultures. Moreover, a transcendental stance is stronger in the lower rungs of society, since circumstances there diminish hope for empirical solutions. North American culture, on the other hand, is noted for its anthropocentric viewpoint, the result of increasing secularization and an upshot of ascetic Protestantism. Accordingly, its social organization is essentially industrial in character.

What is decisive at a higher level in Latin America is the interaction between philosophy, religion and the political, as well as the economic constitution. The whole of Latin American history from the end of the fifteenth century up to the present confirms our central hypothesis that a high degree of metaphysics, transcendence and spiritual life and a simultaneous lack of empiricism and emphasis on experience and logic lead to an absence of both an economic and political dynamic and an indigenous technology. The beginnings of this go back to the scholastic thought of Molina and Suarez in Spain (1548–1617).

Scholasticism was more than a philosophy in Latin America; it was a system of thought in state and society that organized all aspects of life. In Latin America, people always started from an identity of faith and government which corresponded to the Catholic notion of the state. As a reward for its struggle against the Moors, Spain and its royal house gained the right, in the sixteenth century, of nominating viceroys and other holders of high office. Subordination to the king, which was equated with subordination to God, was achieved through scholastic thought as the official philosophy of the ecclesiastical state

A comprehensive analysis of the development of Latin American philosophy, including the brief interlude of nineteenth-century positivism or the evolution of thought at the time of the great state-building movements, is beyond the scope of this study. What is pertinent, however, is that for four centuries, Latin American philosophy retained its basic physical-spiritual-transcendental outlook that also stressed aesthetic questions, but at no point included the dimensions of experience of the logical-empirical or rational and pragmatic nature that characterize North American philosophy or Japanese thought. It is thus clear that Latin American industrialization and modernization could at no point count on a history of ideas as found in North America or Japan.

Even so early an observer as Alexander von Humboldt described this brand of scholastic Catholicism, which never experienced the rupture between medieval and modern thought, faith and reasoning, theology and philosophy, to the same extent as Reformation Germany, Cromwell's England or the France of Descartes and the revolutions. Regions influenced by Spanish and Portuguese culture always preserved something of the medieval notion of unity, that identity between faith and statecraft, during the long centuries of colonialism. Even today, Latin America has not entirely rid itself of this idea in its social structure.

Mariátegui and Haye de la Torre recognized this fact as far back as the 1930s. The Spanish notion of statehood, adopted from Thomas Aquinas, proceeded from the Aristotelian idea of human imperfection when extracted from the *societas perfecta,* and called accordingly for a class hierarchy. This notion has left a mark on all the countries of Latin America. A list of works which have been extremely influential in Latin America is revealing: Bergson and the idea of intuition, the existential philosophy of Martin Heidigger, the aesthetic writings of Ortega y Gasset, or Unamuno's tragedy of life. By comparison, the doctrine of evolution, especially social Darwinism, was totally ignored in Latin America, unlike the United States, where, as propagated by Spencer, it set the tone of intellectual debate.

A few names from Latin American intellectual history should be mentioned: the Brazilian Raimondo de Farías Brito with his metaphysical mysticism; Carlos Faz Ferreira of Uruguay and Alejandro Korn and Francisco Romero of Argentina in this century, who drew on transcendental idealist traditions; and of course, the two founders of twentieth-century philosophy in Latin America, Antonio Caso and José Vasconcelos of Mexico, who, in the Ateneo de la Juventud, finally abandoned the meager residues of positivism and ensconced themselves in aestheticism and spiritualism. All of these thinkers occupied high academic positions; some were even presidents and ministers of state. This lends their philosophy a current political and economic relevance which is essential for a comparison with North America and Japan. Of course, we cannot overlook the disintegrative force of Latin America's agrarian structure, its monocultures, the absence of any sense of loyalty, its chronic political instability, the gap between constitutional law and constitutional reality. Many states, among them Bolivia and Venezuela, have had thirty or more constitutions since the wars of liberation.

The lack of a Latin American "frontier" of the sort that stimulated developments in North America; the isolated coastal settlements and the absence of a widespread settlement of the interior; the absence of a middle class to support democratic initiatives; the constant intervention of the military as purported saviors of state authority, which was never anchored in society as in North America and Japan—all of these are symptoms of decline in Latin

America, symptoms which are responsible for its present plight. What interests us, however, is a comparison of Latin America with North America and Japan as regards its philosophy, religion and intellectual history. And this comparison clearly reveals that Latin America, with its escapist, metaphysical, transcendent, spiritualist and aesthetic world view, had little of those traditions of logical empiricism, rational pragmatism and emphasis on experience that distinguished North America and Japan. Obviously, then, quite apart from the conditions of its social and economic history, Latin America at no time had the cultural prerequisites for developing a dynamism and stability comparable to those two regions.

If it is true that cultures with a pragmatic and empirical approach to humankind and reality are far more successful economically and politically than metaphysical and spiritualist cultures, then not only Western industrial cultures, but also the developing nations and countries of the Third and Fourth Worlds would seem to be threatened by a universal logico-rational imperative that sooner or later will engulf all other cultural traditions. This is of paramount importance for the future.

Suggestions for Further Reading

Galvez, M., J. Ansion and C.I. Degregori. "Lo individual y lo colectivo en la comunidad andina." *Ideología* No. 7, Instituto de Estudios Regionales "José Maria Arguedas," Ayacucho, 1981.

Gibb, H.A.R., and Harold Bowen. *Islamic Society and the West: A Study of the Impact of Western Civilization on Moslem Culture in the East.* Vol. 1, Pt. 1. London: Oxford University Press, 1950.

Jorrin, Miguel, and John D. Martz. *Latin American Political Thought and Ideology.* Chapel Hill, NC: University of North Carolina Press, 1970.

Levi-Strauss, Claude. *Anthropologie structurale.* Paris: Plon, 1958.

_____. *La pensée sauvage.* Paris: Plon, 1962.

_____. *Mythologies. Le cru et le cuit.* Paris: Plon, 1964.

Lynch, Nicolás. *El pensiamento social sobre la comunidad indígenas a principios del siglo XX.* Centro de Estudios Rurales Andinos Bartolomé de Las Casas, Debates Rurales, Cuzco, 1979.

Northrop, F.S.C. *The Meeting of East and West*. New York, London and Toronto: MacMillan Co., 1946.

Ossio, Juan. "Apuntes para una comprehensión del concepto de 'Historia' entre los Incas." *PUCP*, 1969. pp. 170–177.

Rostworowski de Diez Canesco, María. *Estructuras andinas del poder. Ideología religiosa y política*. Instituto de Estudios Peruanos, Lima, 1983.

Tawney, R. H. *Religion and the Rise of Capitalism: A Historical Study*. New York: New American Library, Mentor, 1954.

Tillich, Paul. "Critique and Justification of Utopia." *Utopias and Utopian Thought*. Ed. Frank Manuel. Boston: Beacon Press, 1967.

Todaro, M.P. "A Theoretical Note on Labor as an 'Inferior' Factor in Less Developed Countries." *Journal of Development Studies* 5, July 1969.

Trimberger, Ellen Kay. *Revolution from Above: Military Bureaucrats and Development in Japan, Turkey, Egypt and Peru*. New Brunswick, NJ: Tranasction Books, 1978.

Urbano, Henrique. "La representación andina del tiempo y del espacio en la fiesta." Instituto de Pastoral Andina, *Allpanchis* 7, Cuzco, 1974.

Weber, Max. *The Protestant Ethic and the Spirit of Capitalism*. New York: Charles Scribner's Sons, 1958.

Six

The Structural Crisis In Latin America

Summary

As far as culture is concerned, Latin America and the Andes region in particular have established a system of symbols that is decidedly non-European. The development of Latin America to date has primarily benefitted the developers, for one of the roots of Latin American intellectual history—the discovery of the Americas—played an indispensable role in the Copernican revolution. In the subsequent history of the Andes states, the governing classes were unable to align themselves sufficiently with Western modes of thought. As a result, the process of acculturation is still incomplete. In its policies, the European Community must take pains to help defuse the tensions between the mutually exclusive efforts of cultural identification and scientific/technological modernization in Latin America. It must also ensure that a proper dialogue ensues, rather than a monologue, and must acknowledge the negative political impact of the widespread mistrust of impersonal industrial organizations.

At the next stage, this mistrust must be taken into account to ensure a smooth functioning of the economy. European Community policies must aim toward constructive cultural change, conveying to large sections of the population the assurance that they can take charge of their own destinies. Private investment should be kept at levels that permit further industrialization only for tasks that will produce meaningful employment for large sections of the population, bearing in mind the given circumstances, both domestic and abroad. Nor should the native tradition of labor continue to be suppressed in multiethnic cultures; on the contrary, it should be brought increasingly to bear on science and technology. The economic task of the state should be to improve social services, to develop a viable infrastructure and to absorb laborers who are unable to find work in the private sector. The policies of the European Community should pay attention to structural reforms of the Andes Pact states with the objective of acculturizing the indio population in order to give them greater scope in the creation of indigenous technology without ultimately abandoning their own culture. It is mandatory to work toward increasing the percentage of people active in research. A new development policy must be designed to increase future scientific and technological productivity in the Andes region.

Reality and Cultural Metaphors in Latin American History

This study attempts to create a synthetic perspective that will do justice to the phenomenon of Latin America, both past and present. Thus, its viewpoint is at once diachronous and synchronous. Its aim is to avoid placing Latin America, as Darcy Ribeiro once put it, continually under the banner of a utopia, and instead to create a new order of strategic priorities that unites economic factors with political, social, technological and, especially, cultural factors.

At first glance, Latin America seems to be an intellectual construct, a creature of Europe, a product as much of human imagination as of geography and nature. From a European standpoint, Latin America was first unknown and later unrecognized. During the conquest, Europeans found themselves in a world that they were unable to judge by any known standards, criteria or experiences. Attempts to understand its history and culture were slanted lopsidedly in favor of a European and North American perspective. The reality of Latin America was not viewed phenomenologically; instead, poetic metaphors were projected onto Latin American politics, society and culture—metaphors that merely extrapolated European ideas onto the new continent with all the force of human fantasy.

Amerigo Vespucci's description of America had a formative impact on the utopian state envisioned by Sir Thomas More, partly because Vespucci lived in an intellectual environment influenced by the humanism of Marsilio Ficino and others. There is an affinity between More's utopia and the description of the Inca state left by Garcilaso (himself an Incan). A number of new voices were heard: Bartolome de las Casas, Vasco de Quiroga (who recommended to Charles V that America be kept apart from European civilization in order to implement More's utopia), Simon Rodriguez, Fray Servando Teresa de Mier. Their suggestions were brilliant and scintillating; new utopian societies were to arise, such as el Rey Miguel.

In retrospect, Miguel de Unamuno wrote of a "veiled understanding of reality" in Latin America which was later to color its politics and culture. The conceptions of European thinkers led nowhere and gave rise to historically far-fetched notions and allegations. Throughout its history, the society, politics and culture of the New World have been attributed a concept of reality misrouted from Europe, a conception that has had nothing to do with empirical reality. This discrepancy between a suprasensory reality projected from Europe and the actual history of Latin America soon led to a long-lasting fractured awareness of reality in politics, culture and the economy, an awareness that remained intact long after the colonial period had ended. Europe was able to extrapolate its millennial view of history into the future; the discovery of Latin America, however, put an end to this view of the new continent.

Ever since the days of the conquest, the European image of Latin America and the Latin Americans' view of their own history have been poles apart. The dream of erecting a New Spain in an environment with a radically different geography and culture was doomed to failure in the long run, as it stylized the new continent into an invention of the European Renaissance.

Thus, as Alejo Carpentier was later to put it, Latin America—with its archaic roots, its enclaves of modernity and its garbled industry and economy—has suffered profoundly at the hands of the modern world. Fernand Braudel realized that Latin America is still lagging behind in its material well-being in an effort to found an original civilization.

The question of Latin America's cultural identity can be posed only in the context of new notions of space and time in order to illuminate the historical basis of its cultural symbols. Our discussion hinges on an anthropology of mutual understanding and misunderstanding, on movements within culture and on the spiritual and intellectual interpenetration of processes within society and the economy—on what Roger Bastide has called "intercultural penetration." Tensions have arisen between scientific and technological modernization and the efforts to establish a cultural identity, and these tensions must be lessened by means of dialogue, not monologue. This is important for the simple reason that Latin America cannot be expected to link up effortlessly with the culture, economy and political structures of the West. Nor should we allow its forms of cultural expression to be misconstrued from a European or North American perspective.

We can see this process at work in the traditional Latin American notions of time, which rather than being linear and goal-directed are often circular, positing the eternal recurrence of a state of chaos. Latin America, particularly the Andes region, has never been a uniformly Christian continent. Archaic pre-Christian religions have survived alongside elements of the Christian faith. We even note folk-religious usages with the status of alternative faiths, e.g., the Inkarri movement in the Andes region, or the cults of Maria Leonza in Venezuela, not to mention Macumba, Candomblé and Umbanda in Brazil.

The existence of a large number of syncretic religions prevents us from speaking of a thorough-going Christianization (in the European sense) of the Latin American religious sensibility. One critical difference from European Christianity is, for instance, the cyclical concept of time, a concept which, as explained above, has also left a lasting imprint on the Latin American work ethic. Further differences are the Latin American notions of the purpose, role and constitution of political institutions and the military. Political culture in Latin America is not simply a mirror reflection of Western models. True, its political and constitutional institutions are patterned after Western examples; but Latin America's cultural awareness, like its intellectual history as a whole, differs fundamentally from its European forebears.

This situation has led to a lasting and unresolvable contradiction, especially between the historical fabric of Latin America's institutions and the overall aims of its culture. Alongside this institutional fabric, Latin America's economy evolved along European and North American lines. But it was able to do so only because vast expanses of the economy were set up in a cultural void. This is especially the case in the Andes Region.

Latin America is split by a semantic gap between its institutional and noninstitutional political cultures. We can see this most plainly in the discrepancy that exists between the standards promulgated in its constitutions and the reality of its social, cultural and economic life.

There are other historical reasons for Latin America's technological underdevelopment, particularly its lack of a genuine tradition in the natural sciences as a basis for an indigenous technology. What is more, although its educational system was set up by Europeans, this does not alter the fact that Latin America fell far behind the progress of the natural sciences in the nineteenth and twentieth centuries, with fundamental repercussions for its society and economy.

Latin America has its own brand of logic specific to its culture and geography. This logic stands opposed to that of economics, and has led Latin America to develop an economic culture of its own. Accordingly, the middle and upper classes have different attitudes toward saving money. Even in those areas where labor is performed by a modern industrial society, the fruits of this labor are routed to a different cultural sphere which usually has little in common with Western nations. Darcy Ribeiro, Octavio Paz, Alfonso Reyes, José Vasconcelos, Salazar Bondy and Leopoldo Zea have all drawn urgent attention to this state of affairs in their writings. Only by understanding the specific logics of Latin America can a dialogue ensue regarding the economy and the intellectual makeup of the continent. Latin American culture must be seen as a totality of its vehicles of meaning; it has a nexus of symbols conveying an original depiction of the human condition. Roger Bastide has referred to this symbolism as the "collective memory" of culture and society. Latin America and the Andes region in particular partake of non-European systems of symbols, even if they seem at first glance to derive from European sources.

The social and cultural order of Latin America's historical awareness has a character all its own. Concepts such as progress, nature, future, energy and efficiency have meanings in Latin America that seem at first glance to be alien to those of Europe or North America. Consequently, any acceleration on the path to the future is taken to be harmful rather than positive. Hence, development projects directed toward future progress are not necessarily regarded as beneficial; on the contrary, they are seen as moving ever closer to the threat of inevitable collapse, which had best be postponed a few generations hence. Once again, the influence of culture on the economy is unmistakable.

The Latin American concept of time, and thus the economic style associated with it, is less intent on the accumulation of capital or on future development than on the past and present. The "mundane asceticism" typical of Calvinist culture in North America since the seventeenth century was unthinkable in Latin America, whose culture, especially in its indio populations, was never intent on mastering the future. For example, unlike North America, savings and loan associations were completely unknown. It is especially revealing that the Alliance for Progress never achieved the same level of success as the Marshall Plan in Europe in the aftermath of World War II. Instead, the peoples of the Andes region sought their identity in syncretic symbols. And it was these symbols that represented the legitimacy of their economic, cultural and social order.

The Effect of European Intellectual History on Latin American Self-Awareness

The main question here is whether or not the discovery of America should be considered a creative act on the part of European culture. At the time that North and Latin America were discovered, in the fifteenth, sixteenth and even seventeenth centuries, Europe's self-awareness was so highly developed that there was little hope of overcoming a Eurocentric perspective in America. Nonetheless, over the centuries the influence of Latin America on the European cultures is in no way comparable to the European legacy in Latin America. The relation between the New World and the Old World, however, must be thoroughly reevaluated. *The discovery of America gave the European states hitherto unknown possibilities of economic exploitation and geographical territorial expansion.*

When Columbus returned from his first transatlantic expedition in the spring of 1493, the major question that faced the underwriters of his journey was how to secure sovereignty over the new territories that were constantly being discovered, and which were also claimed by the King of Portugal. Eventually, all rights of ownership were transferred to them directly by the Spanish pope, Alexander VI. The islands that had been or were about to be discovered, as well as the mainland one hundred miles from the

Cape Verde Islands and west of a north-south line of demarcation, were made the property of the kings of Castile. In 1494, the rights of title granted to Spain were reinforced by a declaration of consent from the Portuguese crown.

In Europe, Latin America was regarded largely as a fabulous source of instantaneous wealth to be obtained under the aegis of a policy of imperialism. The Casa de Contracion was founded as early as 1503; from 1524, the Consejo de Indias rose in prominence as the key institution controlling trade with America. This took place by way of Seville, where taxes were levied on all incoming precious metals from Latin America. Even so, the finances of Spain soon entered a chronic state of disarray. Between 1557 and the middle of the seventeenth century, for example, the king had to declare his state bankrupt every twenty years. Later, business relations between Spain and Latin America were mainly in the hands of private mercantile companies, most of them foreign capital societies which attempted to exercise power by virtue of their increasingly monopolistic control. By comparison, the exploitation of North America took on a completely different form. It is obvious that even in the early colonial years Spain conducted its economy and state policy with less finesse than did England with its North American colonies.

By the end of the thirteenth century at the latest, it was generally recognized in learned circles that the earth was round. This scientific insight gave additional importance to the other, still unexploited parts of the world, importance that could redound to the benefit of Latin America. Thus, it is not surprising that during the first half of the sixteenth century letters and correspondence circulated between Columbus, Vespucci, Cortez and Anghiera in many copies, and even attracted a widespread readership. To be sure, these letters reveal precious little understanding of native Latin American cultures, which were interpreted in a naive manner, ignorant of the organizing principles of the humanistic sciences. Columbus, for example, emphasized the natives' lack of clothing, their physical beauty, their unfamiliarity with iron, their lack of effective weapons and their great timidity, coupled with generosity. His words reveal the extent to which the first encounters with the indigenous cultures of pre-Columbian America were dominated by a Eurocentric world view.

There are a great many historical examples of Latin America's considerable impact on the intellectual and real-political history of

Europe. The geographical exploitation of the Americas was at the same time an intellectual exploitation which expanded and universalized the horizons of European thought and experience. As a result, European political philosophies during the age of discovery cannot be understood apart from the Americas.

German Arceniagas describes the conquest of the Americas as having transformed European political and intellectual history to a greater extent than any event since the appearance of Christianity. Before the discovery of America, the western boundaries of Europe were thought to be the Pillars of Hercules. The Age of Enlightenment would have taken on completely different forms if Columbus had never overstepped the geographical, cultural and intellectual boundaries of Europe. The naturalists of antiquity worked within narrow confines. But with Columbus's expedition of 1492, the natural philosophies of the modern period were given a new and, literally, well-rounded perspective of the world. *In other words, without the discovery of the Americas the Copernican revolution would have been unthinkable, and Galileo and Descartes would not have arrived at their basic scientific and philosophical propositions. The* imago mundi *began to take on fresh contours.*

Without the Americas as an allegedly virgin territory on which to conduct political experiments, the Renaissance would not have attained these glorious achievements. Amerigo Vespucci, in a manner of speaking, declared the Platonic world view to be empirically valid. The exploration of Latin America, which lasted a mere fifty years, was far more rapid than the opening up of Asia which took place over a period of five centuries.

Ever since the Reformation, there developed between Latin and North America a diametrical opposition in all areas of culture, society and politics. This opposition is also undergirded by differences in philosophy and intellectual history.

Especially from the seventeenth century on, the history of Latin America was part of the history of Spain, and was sustained above all by a rejection of modern civilization. The fact that the Spanish- and Portuguese-speaking cultures inherited the universal Roman Catholic monarchies and the aftermaths of the Counter Reformation was an essential factor in their failure to develop an indigenous technology in later centuries. The Reformation and Enlightenment were less well represented in the cultural history of Latin America than in that of North America.

For European civilization, the struggle for cultural self-identification and self-assertion began in the sixteenth century. Since then, Latin America has been marked by a constant admixture of cultural and ethnic traditions. Iberian, Amerindian and African elements coalesced over a period of more than five hundred years. This process of amalgamation was determined not only by the Spaniards and Portuguese, but also and especially by the native cultures, which were spread over the entire continent, rather than representing isolated ethnic minorities as in the United States.

No sooner had the conquest begun than the creole population considered itself different from the Europeans. It consolidated its own historical and cultural features in the seventeenth and eighteenth centuries. By the end of the seventeenth century, the creoles had risen to become a governing class and had produced an original culture with regard to relationships between the sexes, their attitude toward death, their work ethic and their estimation of themselves (meaning their Latin American traditions) and others (European values). However, in the long run, the creole classes were unable to derive strength from their own culture, which was formed by adapting foreign ideas. Even so, this moment represented a second birth for Latin America. The states founded in the nineteenth century attempted to pursue a line of development which had long been superseded in North America: to produce a modern nation-state with ideas of order and society adopted from Europe. Cultural pluralism was to be fused into a national project. Yet, the states were unable to achieve the uniformity they sought, despite their protestations of laicism and their formal pleas for equality and liberalism.

Due to the predominance of the creoles, who created a culture with a split consciousness, the individual states of Latin America began to reject their cultural-historical roots and to turn increasingly to Europe and North America. The result was a wave of Westernization that became an important element in the breach with the colonial legacy, especially with the dogmatism of Roman Catholic Spain. This movement, however, was not particularly conducive to cultural pluralism. In some Latin American states, this foreign-dominated consciousness gave rise to a cultural and social ambiguity that tended to paralyze the life of the nation. A genuine conflict arose between native culture, nourished on authentic indigenous traditions, and a "higher" culture that was alien to the native cultures and took on the task of drawing the nation into the rationalist civilization of the modern age.

The major historical difference between Latin America and North America is that when North American culture achieved independence, it did not break with its heritage. Latin American culture, on the other hand, denied all traditions that had governed it since the sixteenth century, though what it rejected was less a national project than a universal system of thought that was particularly hostile to the present. In North America, culture, politics and the economy function in relative harmony with each other; a productive interaction arose between democratic government, a capital-intensive market economy and Calvinism. In Latin America, however, there was a vast chasm separating republican ideas and the Roman Catholicism of the viceroys, between a mosaic of pre-Columbian traditions and institutions from baroque Spain. In a sense, Latin America had to deny its own past. The borrowed character of contemporary Latin American culture came into being; instead of developing original ideas about its future from its own traditions, Latin America appropriated points of view from European and North American models.

Latin America has been struggling with modernity ever since. The Spaniards, it is true, established institutions such as the *ayuntamiento*, a type of urban council based on a principle of self-administration comparable to "local government" in North America. However, as Alexis de Tocqueville pointed out long ago, "township" and "county" administrations were of paramount importance for popular self-determination in nineteenth-century North America, and these administrations had little in common with self-administration in Latin America, which always stood in the shadow of the twin luminaries of viceroy and archbishop, with their economic privileges. In the Latin American colonies, the Church had a strict hierarchy and a cumbersome bureaucracy that bore certain resemblances to mandarin rule in ancient China. In North America, the various religious denominations proclaimed themselves independent of the state from the moment European settlers began to arrive in the seventeenth century. Church congregations in North America embodied a free union of the faithful. From the beginning of European settlement in the seventeenth century, there reigned a wide spectrum of religious denominations expressing a basic democratic stance in state and society.

The Latin American colonies, in contrast, remained a hierarchical society devoid of representative government. One crucial difference is that when North American culture proclaimed the Declaration of Independence in the eighteenth century, it did not have to break with its own past. Thinkers such as William Penn, in his "Frame of Government," had already anticipated a democratic form of government during the colonial period. The independence of the Latin American states, however, represented a negation of everything they had been before the nineteenth century. The vision of the future that was to become obligatory for contemporary Latin America was not composed of elements from local culture. On the contrary, it was made up of props found ready-at-hand in European and North American culture.

Today, the religious basis of North American culture can no longer be traced in all walks of life. Nonetheless, it was formative for the American state because, in a certain sense, the religious revolution of the Reformation anticipated the political revolution of the eighteenth century, which led in turn to a democratic form of government. This portentous mutual interaction between religion and politics was unknown in Latin American culture. The clergy's political power enabled it to exercise a firm grip on knowledge and intellectual development. Latin American history lacks any religious revolutions that might have cleared a path for nascent political revolutions. On the contrary, its politics were governed by extreme social immobility.

Latin America's nineteenth-century political revolutions, including its wars of independence, were more indicative of the region's patrimonialism. The authoritarian state increased in power, as did centralized government under the guise of federalism and, ultimately, the political despotism of the *caudillos*. In Latin America, political independence was not the result of a triumph of liberal ideas so much as an outgrowth of the political disintegration of the Spanish empire. Unlike North America, Latin America gained independence less by political victory than by the paralysis of the mother country. The pre-Columbian legacy strengthened its determination to remain entrenched rather than to move forward, and the present was constantly made to intersect with the past. It was impossible for a bourgeois revolution of ideas or democratic government to take place.

The philosophical foundations of the absolutist Roman Catholic monarchy were provided by, among others, Francisco

Suarez and his disciples in the Society of Jesus. In Latin America, traditional Thomism resembled a philosophical bastion, a conceptual orthodoxy erected to combat Lutheran and Calvinist principles, which were seen as the spearhead of change and innovation. Neo-scholasticism defended the hierarchical principles of Latin American politics and society as late as the eighteenth century, and stood in the path of modernism in ways that can be traced even today. Accordingly, the word "revolution" in Latin America was not synonymous with a new order, for the wars of independence implied nothing but a redistribution of existing power structures. Ever since its discovery by Columbus, Latin America has been a continent of misunderstandings, especially with regard to political conceptions, such as democracy, constitution and the military, which took on special meanings divorced from and not comparable to their European counterparts.

The Latin American revolutions of the nineteenth century fell short of their critical goal: to stimulate a new political, social and economic order in preparation for the twentieth century. While the states were constitutionally separated from Spain by an act of revolution, the social order of Spanish colonial rule remained largely intact. The states were not transformed into modern nations as happened, for example, in the French Revolution, which brought about a comprehensive renewal of society. Both the French and the American revolutions were an expression and consequence of historical evolution. The Latin American revolutions tended to borrow their ideas from Europe and North America: *The Federalist* papers, the thoughts of George Washington and Thomas Jefferson, the political philosophy of Montesquieu and philosophical foundations of the French Revolution. But this did not alter the fact that at this point in time, the Latin American bourgeoisie had not progressed beyond a mercantile stage and its governing classes, unlike those of North America and France, imperfectly understood the Western world of ideas. Hence, these ideas took on the character of masks or empty facades, divorced from historical reality.

With the collapse of the Spanish colonial empire and its administration, power fell mainly into the hands of two groups: economic power devolved onto local oligarchies, and political power largely onto military elites. It became obvious that the oligarchy did not have enough power at its disposal to form a legitimate government by itself. Accordingly, the state, reinforced by the military, took a leading role in the subsequent industrialization of Latin America. The economy remained static and averse to progress; the private sector never acquired a significance comparable to that in North America. Industry, even in its first halting attempts, had exaggerated expectations *vis-à-vis* the state in the setting up of infrastructures, financial underwriting and customs legislation. The absence of an autonomous dynamism, even in the public sector, was a striking structural feature of Latin America during the nineteenth and twentieth centuries. The marginalization of local technological investment in Latin America, its imitative adoption of foreign technology, its vulnerability and external dependence (described long ago by Raul Prebisch), its halting attempts at industrialization under foreign initiative: all of these gave signs of an economic and social mutation that was anything but autonomous, and that created dependencies in the area of production.

The decline of the Spanish empire, a preliminary factor on the path to Latin American political independence, acquired special importance. Not until Spain had ended the Crusades within its own borders did it rise to the level of a world power. The unforeseen ascent of Charles V, whose attention was focused on Europe and the quest for empire, combined with the discovery of America to provide a setting against which Spain could unleash its creative political energies. In the fifteenth century, Europe witnessed a flowering of handicrafts, the demise of feudalism, the colonization of its eastern territories, the founding of universities and the intellectual culmination of the Renaissance, all of which combined to produce a dramatic upsurge of power. During this same period, however, Spain was still preoccupied with its crusades against the infidels—the Reconquista—and was thus trapped geographically in the Mediterranean area. Only thereafter could it set out on its great overseas adventure of the Conquista with its goals of uniting and consolidating a mighty worldwide Christian empire. The discovery, conquest and colonization of America were nourished by ideas that dominated Spain during the age of the Roman Catholic monarchs, Charles V and Philip II. With the Reconquista finished within its own borders and the Conquista underway abroad, Spain, the last great empire of medieval Christianity, turned its excited attention to projects spanning the continents of the world.

Spain gave a final, unified form to the ideological edifice of the Middle Ages. *Even in the midst of the High Renaissance, Spain gamely*

struggled to prolong the Middle Ages. This process was to have a forma-
tive impact on the future of Latin America. Spain's policies toward
Europe had two main thrusts: to reconstitute the Holy Roman
Empire, and to revitalize medieval thought. Even the conquest of
the New World at first meant nothing more to Spain than the
acquisition of more room for the expansion of Christianity, and
hence an enlargement of the medieval empire.

Unlike the Old World, Spanish efforts encountered little resistance in the New World. Its attack on native cultures was carried
out at a time when the other colonial powers had scant opportunity to exert their influence in Latin America. Given this situation,
the evolution of Latin America took on a distinctive construction.
In the competition among the powers of Europe, Spain became
increasingly isolated on the Iberian peninsula. In the centuries to
follow, it suffered military, political and economic setbacks and
gradually relinquished its status as a world power.

By way of comparison, we should recall that in the seventeenth
and eighteenth centuries, the rest of Europe continued to pursue
the tradition of the Renaissance. The Age of Enlightenment already
bore the seeds of later upheavals in the sciences; the Industrial
Revolution was initiated; nation-states began to appear, as did
capital-intensive market economies. At the same time that the
New World was being established, the Spanish mother country
was suffering its political demise: its urge toward world domination was sabotaged, its visions of grandeur collapsed. Spain's
obsolete political concepts could not keep pace with the changes
of history.

For a while, the Christian order remained superimposed on
Latin America's native cultures. Its religious credos maintained a
distinction (often highly ambiguous) between good and evil that
was familiar from the days of the battles against Islam and the
Huns, or the days of schisms and heresies. Latin America became
acquainted with Christianity less as a doctrine of the incarnation of
Christ than as a power-mongering political and social system of
foreign origin with a rigidly defined picture of the world. In Spain,
the Roman Catholic Church saw itself vindicated one final time in
all its medieval glory, even if the power of Spain itself was in jeopardy. In Latin America, the Spanish rulers attempted to maintain an
authority principle—*paternalismo*—in politics, society and religion.

Unlike North America and Europe, the revolutionary movements
of the nineteenth century did not leave a deep-seated ideological

imprint on large sections of the population *(reformismo)*. Relics of the previous order and hierarchy stood in the way of the liberalization of politics and a faith in scientific progress. Traditionalism was accused of prolonging feudal dependencies while movements of social and political innovation threatened to degenerate into anarchy and sectarianism. In contradistinction to North America and Europe, neither during the colonial period nor in the nineteenth century did Latin America witness the emergence of a multilayered middle class that might have been innovative and capable of government. The reasons for this lay in the agrarian nature of these societies, and also in the relationship of the feudal aristocracy to the Church—a symbiosis of the sacred and the secular. In lieu of the Spanish system of authority, there came about an increasing "herodianization" of Latin American society, as the governing classes identified themselves with urban life and turned their backs on their cultural roots.

The people of Latin America were less well acquainted than North Americans with the primacy of scientific objectivity and technological function. The application of rational thought was not readily compatible with the cultural and religious history of Latin America, as we have already seen from a number of examples. In Latin American culture, human beings were not alienated, reified or made an object; instead they remained subjects without a sense of involvement in the oligarchical institutions of power. Even if they rebelled against their social authorities, they did not abandon their conviction that they were nevertheless dealing with higher powers that commanded their respect. This is one further reason for the century-old immobility of Latin American society.

Nor did the Latin American concept of the individual and individualism resemble that of Europe and North America. In Latin America, individuals were esteemed more for what they were than for what they were able to attain. This type of individualism, though forthright and self-confident, was devoid of genuine initiative in the economic sense. Immediate impressions were considered more important that the achievement of long-term results. The focus fell on the individual rather than on objective facts, on contemplation rather than action. Notions of personal honor had high priority and gave rise to a self-complacent cult of personality. There was no direct counterpart in Latin America for the tradition, so deeply ingrained in North American culture, of competition for the purpose of attaining widespread affluence. Nor was the feeling of social solidarity, even of compassion in a Christian sense of the term, as well developed as in North America.

By the end of the nineteenth century, Latin America's economic life as well as its social hierarchy had changed little from its state in the earlier centuries of the colonial period. Until the beginning of the twentieth century, the states of Latin America mainly imported the products they consumed and paid for them in raw materials. An initial wave of industrialization began during the First World War when the traditional suppliers were unable to export their goods. A second wave was occasioned by the collapse of the export markets, which forced the countries of Latin America to manufacture those products which were no longer obtainable on the world market. Not until the Second World War did industrialization intensify in certain Latin American countries, such as Brazil, Mexico, Argentina and Chile, but not, however, in the Andes Pact states. The political revolutions of the nineteenth century did not create the necessary preconditions for radical structural change in Latin America.

Latin American Concepts of State, Nation and Society

In the history of Latin America, the state has been Janus-faced, being both an outgrowth of indigenous reality and an expression of a process of transculturation. Historically, the Latin American concept of state is linked with the concept of nation. In order to justify its integrative tasks on the basis of its internal sovereignty, the state poses as the guardian of historical values, evoking a distant image of an existing nation. This identification between state and nation has been extremely influential in the formation of political culture and institutions in Latin America. In addition, the fragile Latin American democracy arose on the foundations of a hypothetical economy. Thanks to *personalismo*, the state was not considered a social community, but rather a conglomerate, and the traditional population retained a widespread distrust of large, impersonal industrial organizations that presuppose a high degree of anonymity. These obstructive political factors must be kept in mind.

The Latin American democracies face a dual task. First, they must ensure that the traditional democratic institutions function properly. At the same time, however, they must work to create future structures in order to grant longevity to the new democratic state and to integrate all sectors of public life into the political process.

The evolution of science and technology in Latin America is linked with the rise of industrialization and its resultant imported modes of production and habits of consumption, as dictated by multinational corporations. *The Latin American economic system must be equipped with an indigenous technology capable of stimulating regional policies, above all in the areas of job creation, environmental protection, autonomous foodstuff production, the reform of regional resources, and the release of innovative forces.*

If we are to do justice to the range and variety of Latin American culture, we must take several important factors into account: the profound religious faith of the people as an underlying motivating agent, the cognitive elements of culture as expressed in the symbols of everyday life and the wide array of native and modern Latin American languages. The population of Latin America is a breeding ground for new forms of cultural expression arising both from the transplanted European and African peoples and from new contacts with ethnic groups.

Each of the many states and regions of Latin America experienced a unique unfolding of its own particular culture. After the wars of liberation, it was creole culture that gained supremacy. This fact also left its mark on the state constitutions, for example, in the exclusion of indios from the electoral franchise.

As Octavio Paz was far-sighted enough to recognize, there arose a level of time and space that was superimposed on the Latin American cultures and ultimately caused tensions between the young nation-states. Latin America did not witness religious reforms comparable to the Reformation in Europe or the Great Awakening in colonial North America. Modern Latin American culture has at times a denaturalized character: it is in essence a product of imitation. Nor did Latin America witness the emergence of that sense of community that became, in different ways, so prominent in the culture and economy of Japan and North America. On the contrary, Latin America underwent processes of fragmentation and particularization, both of which were inimical to a national economy, since they placed collective destiny at a second remove.

Latin America's long tradition of ecclesiastical and state authority eventually led to *personalismo*, an exaggerated form of autocentric individualism that borders on social anarchy. While the traditional Calvinist work ethic accorded labor a value in and of itself, in Latin American culture, labor did not have a value of its own.

Throughout Latin American history the relation between society and state has largely been one of tension. On the other hand, the economy and the state grew virtually by symbiosis. This has posed a fundamental problem to the stability of the state. For while the regulatory agencies of the national economy went some way to initiate the process of industrialization, there was never a genuine exchange between society and state that might have given rise to a "civil society" in the Anglo-American sense, in which the citizen is firmly rooted in the political process. This civil society derived from English and North American political philosophers, from Thomas Jefferson and the highly influential *Federalist* papers, and extends as far back into the colonial past as William Penn's "Frame of Government." Its objectives were to fashion a national community and to aspire to a collective identity in accord with cultural traditions. Only sporadically and in isolated instances could this same process be seen in Latin America where the result usually was an artificial hybrid of state and economy, undermined by contradictions and weakly patched together. As the oligarchical state represented the consolidation of a particular ruling class, only in a few substrata of society was the state's national project secure.

The centralized Latin American governments, then, went some way toward unifying their internal economies, but they could not integrate them into the world economy. Political power, and with it the control of resources, was founded on a combination of long-standing rural property ownership and export trade. Foreign capital was concentrated in trade, transport and finance. The state became a focal point in this development, sanctioning the alliance with foreign capital and simultaneously asserting its centralized power in a society that was still far from integrated. This was one early cause of the predominant role of the state and the poor training in the private sector when it came time to finance the growth of industry

The liberal constitutions, though based on American models (George Washington, Alexander Hamilton and Thomas Jefferson) and patterned after French forebears (Montesquieu, Rousseau and the Encyclopedists), had little effect on the actual makeup of the Latin American state during the age of the young republics. Then as now, constitutional theory and constitutional reality were worlds apart. We can clearly see why the economic crisis in Latin America is at the same time a profound crisis in hegemonical power structures and in society, and is thus a crisis of national cohesion.

The plight of Latin American society is apparent in its high level of social inequality and immobility, its creeping destitution and social disintegration and the continued march of urbanization. This combination gives modernity an extremely double-edged aspect in view of Latin America's structural inequalities. The states most affected are those with large indio populations, where internal and external poverties coincide and pose an obstacle to the stability of the state, calling into question the rule of society as a whole.

We can thus see why the project of European modernization threatens the cultural identity of the individual states, where different ethnic groups and cultural levels are lumped together and made subordinate to a modern economy. The forms of worship, traditional political movements and ideational universes, being culturally heterogenous, often find themselves in conflict with the goals of rationalized production. Consequently, the structural measures taken to date are far removed from the core of Latin American culture. In order to draw closer to the cultural autonomy of the regions of Latin America, this trend toward a peripheral economy must be reversed. Every vision of the future must harbor within it a cultural dimension that is essential to constitute the state or to democratize Latin American society.

The immediate task of the economy is to open up new markets, to diversify exports and to promote the regional and subregional integration of Latin America so as to ensure that participation in the economy and society is open to all. This will affect not only Latin America's international competitiveness, but also the utilization of its natural resources and its human potential. Latin America's economic reforms must enable it to strike a more successful balance in the structure of its society.

Private investment should no longer be autocentric. Instead, it should be kept at levels that permit further industrialization only for tasks that will produce meaningful employment for large segments of the population, given Latin America's special circumstances domestically and abroad. The task of the state in the economy should be to improve social services, to develop a viable infrastructure and to absorb laborers who are unable to find work in the private sector. Nor should the native tradition of labor continue to be suppressed in multiethnic cultures; on the contrary, science and technology should consider its potential.

There remains the question of how a new model of social organization might integrate Latin America's cultural identity. This organization must obey the strictures of equality, self-determination, sovereignty, territorial integrity and the involvement of the entire populace in the political decision-making processes. Scientific and technological development at times can make us forget that, in the final analysis, there can only be one goal: humanity itself, in deep appreciation of its cultural essence. It is the express purpose of this study to underscore this fundamental and primary connection.

Cultural Pluralism and Agrarian Structure in the Andes Region

The Andes Pact states have undergone agrarian reforms time and time again. A prime example of this phenomenon is Peru. Plans for reform had existed even before 1969, but only the agrarian reform initiated from 1968 to 1980 by the military regime brought about any deep-seated changes. Peru's agrarian reform was one or the most radical in the history of Latin America. Within the space of ten years, almost nine million hectares of land were distributed among 370,000 families. An additional 330,000 families were spread over 1,894 cooperative farmsteads, and 40,000 families were given individual plots of land. At the time of the agrarian reform, however, new irrigation laws were passed that had a limited impact on the redistribution of resources due to the low productivity in the agricultural sector. The oligarchy, intent on maintaining its power, was not disenfranchised by this process. Only a small percentage of the large rural population was given new land. Thus, there was no change from traditional to modern structures in Andean agriculture.

The Andes Pact of 1969, linking the six countries of Bolivia, Columbia, Chile, Ecuador, Peru and Venezuela, was the result of a regional agreement with the goal of economic integration. This step seemed necessary in view of the heterogeneity of Latin America's economic and social structure, especially considering the contradictions between tradition and modernity.

The forms taken by industrialization in Latin America constitute a fragile link to the agrarian sector, which gives scant encouragement to technological innovation. With the disappearance of habitual forms of tilling came an upsurge in the monetary economy, particularly in rural areas. As a result, farmers were forced to find a new relationship to agriculture. At the time, this phenomenon initiated a transformation in traditional tilling methods and also contributed to the disintegration of entire rural communities. Industrialization in urban areas brought forth novel social models quite different from their rural counterparts. The introduction of new products brought about radical changes in modes of consumption, behavior, worship and expectation. Seen from a world perspective, the transfer of technology clearly spread out from the mid-regions to the states on the economic periphery. In underdeveloped countries, a minority of the population adopted a life style that contradicted not only the overall economic development, but also the nation's cultural identity. In some cases, this has led to an unequivocal rejection of Western culture among Latin America's native cultures.

Only a meaningful and harmonious coexistence of the various cultural systems in the Andes region can allow a realistic policy to emerge in all areas of adoption, comprehension, explanation and organization of culture, as well as the reconstitution of territorial order. It is thus necessary to analyze the mechanisms of the transfer of science and technology in order to assess its effect on culture.

Whether the indios can be integrated into the national culture is uncertain. The main problem resides in defining national culture and determining how the indios should be included within it. The distinction between official and unofficial cultures must be discussed. Here the main issue is the cultural connection among the groups in a society, for Latin American cultures are *a priori* nonhomogeneous. The cultural order is apparently one of domination in all areas of social life. The culture of the dominant strata is likewise the dominant culture in society. In Latin America, this means that the creole culture dominates indio culture.

Up to now, there has been no cultural order in the Andes Pact states, and hence no underlying social order either. In order to set up an indigenous technology, culture must be successfully democratized, the cultural order must undergo a process of transformation and the contradictions between the cognitive systems of the dominant culture and the largely pre-Columbian subcultures must be resolved. These are necessary preconditions if the economy is to function soundly. The contradiction between official and unofficial cultures poses a major obstacle both to the evolution of technology and to the stability of the state.

At the same time that the pre-Columbian indio cultural universe was undermined, it proved impossible to train an intellectual elite. Today, now that the process of decolonialization is complete, what is required is a revitalization of culture. The Quechua-speaking indios, as a rural subculture, are demanding cultural syncretism. This means that the creole version of European and North American culture must be linked with indio culture to create an urban popular culture that, for all its contradictions, holds out the possibility of amalgamation.

A large percentage of the population lives in a political vacuum. Participation in the dominant creole culture must be democratized so that the cultures can begin to interact. Society in the Andes Pact states is about to enter a process of active change. For the moment, it is caught in a transition from a pre-industrial to an industrial society. However, it currently lacks the analytical tools necessary to carry out this social transformation to a successful conclusion.

A discussion of the *cholo* of Peruvian society provides an example. In colonial history, the term *cholo* referred to a half-breed who possessed the physical traits of an indio but lived in the cities under the influence of Western culture. In the wake of industrialization, the indio population was "choloized." The traditional *cholo* grew up bilingually with an indio mother tongue and a rudimentary command of Spanish. The *cholo* represented a cultural and social group which emerged from the servile mass of indios on the great plantations and moved in the direction of urbanization. The *cholo* groups play a key role in the conflict between the antagonistic and conflicting cultures in the Andes Pact states: by developing in the direction of a creole culture they could strengthen the trend toward an integration of the two cultures. The *cholo* has become the standard-bearer of innovation throughout the Andean world, and has been entrusted with the tasks of saving indio culture from complete dissolution and of granting it social mobility. Indios who become *cholos* in a process of acculturation can abandon their traditional subservience and take up a role in a changing society with new economic structures. They could overcome the disadvantages of their ethnic status and grow into the new tasks they are seeking to assume.

While the situation of the indio is hermetically sealed, the social and economic tasks of the *cholo* offer hope and promise for the future, opening up a certain amount of social mobility and boding well for a dynamic economy.

Even so, in Peru's everyday culture, it is still customary to discuss traditional Incan technology as a means of solving current difficulties. Again and again, greater emphasis is placed on the past than on the present and the future. For the cultural identity of the Andes Pact states, it is important to realize that the realm of the Incas, though defeated politically, still survives culturally for large segments of the population. Indeed, its agriculture is still frequently taken as a model for present-day Peru. No European would think of speaking in the same anachronistic terms of ancient Rome or Greece. Memories of the pre-Columbian age are much more important in the Andes states than in Aztec-influenced Mexico for establishing a cultural, political and even an economic identity. There is far less cause to speak of an Aztec utopia than a utopia of the Incas.

In the case of Mexico, the past has been preempted by the Virgin of Guadaloupe. In this sense, Mexican society is more completely integrated than Andean society: the peasantry play a more active part in official life, due primarily to the Mexican struggle for independence and the revolution of 1910.

In the Peruvian Andes, there have been frequent small-scale rebellions, but the peasants never stormed the capital and took control of the palace of government. The crucial point is that, in the Andes region, the Inca realm continues to exist spiritually, not only in folklore, but also in current political life. Large segments of the population hold the historically untenable view that the empire of the Incas was also a society governed by justice and affluence, and hence useful as a paradigm for the world of today. José Maria Arguedas, for example, maintains that for Peruvians struggle is not simply a matter of economics, but always has deepseated cultural and spiritual motives. This is a constant theme in his writings on modern culture, gradual change and the concept of progress.

This history of Andean utopia is a history of the social, political and cultural conflict between popular culture, with its traditions of oral narrative, and the culture of the elite. What is involved is not linear historiography in the Western sense, but the unfolding of different "histories" in accordance with ethnic and social strata.

Andean utopia, Arguedas argues, imparts an imaginary rationality to the course of history. Even the writings and political careers of Mariátegui and Haye de la Torre point in the same direction. In terms of political philosophy, we are dealing with messianic movements of an eschatological character that were to become crucially important for the Andes region. In the Andes Pact states, as Anibal Quijano rightly observed, there is a need to set these utopian ideas aright both culturally and politically.

Even today, the Andes Pact states are prisoners of their own history, of historical conditions which they themselves cannot resolve. They are victims of their own world of ideas, their collective imagination. Under these preconditions, it is impossible to build and master the political and economic edifices of the future. The confrontation between political reality and Andean utopia has been repeated again and again in the course of history. We must always bear this fact in mind.

A confrontation of this sort arose in the 1920s, although it had a precedent as early as the sixteenth century, and once again in the eighteenth, which like the twentieth century took on an archetypical character in the creation of Andean utopias. These utopias always resurface when Andean culture finds itself on the defensive, as it does today, being threatened by the economic hegemony of the leading industrial countries and the levelling of traditional cultural values. For years, the concept of Andean culture has no longer been synonymous with the purely indigenous and aboriginal, with highlands and rural areas. Acceptance of Andean culture has migrated from the highlands to the coastal regions as well.

As with many other structural features of Andean reality, it is the religious dimensions that tie things together. This accounts for the importance of the irrational in Andean politics and the entire constitution of the state, an importance which is so difficult for European and North American observers to comprehend. This political mysticism can also turn into fanaticism and entail a dogmatic rejection of any who do not happen to share it.

The Historical Impact of the European Legacy on Productivity in Latin America

The conquest of Latin America took place at a time when the scientific revolutions in Europe were still in their infancy. As is now well known, the indirect impact of the conquest on the sciences in Europe—and especially the natural sciences—was greater than its direct impact on the scientific-technological evolution in Latin America itself. Spain played a critical role in this process, being important in Western cultural circles for the transmission of knowledge, not least of all due to its active exchanges with the centers of humanism in Italy.

In the final third of the sixteenth century, however, there occurred a deep hiatus: the triumph in Spain of the Counter Reformation, with the resultant supremacy of scholasticism and the increasing isolation of Spain from the rest of Europe. The effects of this hiatus can be seen, for instance, in a decree by Philip II that regulated study abroad. All relatively abstract forms of knowledge were suppressed, as were all technological practices grounded in abstract thought processes. The Hispano-Jewish community, which had been the most significant social group of the Spanish Middle Ages, functioning as a vehicle for scientific activity, was extirpated, with long-lasting negative consequences. Spain witnessed a breach between the traditions of the Middle Ages and the progressive thought of the Renaissance, with its leanings toward modern science. This posed severe obstacles for the scientific and technological development of Latin America.

In other countries of the West, the Middle Ages and the Renaissance brought forth a cumulative evolution of handicrafts that gradually evolved into the industrialized labor of the seventeenth century. The evolution of thought and technology led to a scientific-technological revolution, above all in western Europe and North America. This process began to gain speed around the mid-seventeenth century, when it affected mechanics, chemistry, optics, thermodynamics and other fields of the natural sciences. This marked the beginning of the predominance of scientifically oriented technology, as became apparent in the electrical and chemical industries. From this time, the application of science in production entered a phase of acceleration. Technologies that were not grounded in a union of science and production, and were therefore less efficient, began more and more to be discarded.

Unlike Japan, western Europe and the United States, the Andes Pact states did not develop a foundation for productive technologies on the basis of their own scientific knowledge. These states, being dependent on foreign technology, consigned scientific activity to their elites, detached from their social surroundings. The colonial power decreed what kind of productive activities would be cultivated, and as these countries became independent in the nineteenth century, their national economies were incorporated into the worldwide division of labor, i.e., they functioned primarily as suppliers of raw materials.

From roughly the middle to the end of the seventeenth century, Spanish scientists paid scant attention to new thinkers, apart from a few sporadic attempts at assimilation. Spain remained largely isolated from the leading new developments in science. As a result, it was far removed from European currents in the seventeenth century, currents that were, in turn, formative for the shape of modern science. The fractured tradition of the Middle Ages and the Renaissance blunted the explorative urge of later science and technology in Spain; not until 1682 were skilled crafts introduced that permitted an early development of industry.

This basic starting position in Spain naturally affected the developmental potential of Latin America. The rigid, centralized control exercised by Spain during the colonial period, together with the strong influence of Roman Catholic institutions, limited the horizons of scientific activity.

Despite the historical truism that many European scientists visited Latin America at this time, the fruits of their labor could not be integrated into the native Latin American intellectual and academic communities of the colonial period. Moreover, at the end of the seventeenth century, following the scientific developments during the reign of Charles III, Spanish scientists wasted their time by observing the rise of science in the rest of Europe without bothering seriously to participate in it themselves. This constellation of factors helps to explain the obstacles that have had to be overcome by Latin American science and technology ever since the time of the earliest creole settlements.

One significant difference between Latin America and North America is that, in the latter, research findings were channeled into newly created economic institutions, to the benefit of the national economy. In contrast, European scientists largely considered their visits to Latin America as field trips from which they returned to their homes in Europe, leaving no further connections to Latin America.

The absence of a scientific tradition in Latin America that might have been supportive of the state is also partly accounted for by the fact that the scientific activities carried out in Latin America by Europeans were regarded as extensions of their European heritage. In consequence, unlike North America, there was no integration between native and European science in Latin America during the colonial period. The new scientific ideas adopted from Europe were not developed further in a dynamic manner. From the days of the founding fathers, the crucial scientific impetus in Latin America always came from abroad. This was to have serious and unavoidable consequences.

In the years of independence, Latin America faced the trauma of political and constitutional insecurity, which again and again hindered the emergence of a scientific and technological elite. During the nineteenth century, science received merely formal recognition, without the support and reassurance of parallel institutions to promote independent efforts. The Andes countries constantly found themselves in a colonial relationship with the scientific centers of the West, even at the outset of the twentieth century. The majority of science instructors and engineers were either foreigners or had been raised in North America or Europe. The few researchers did their work in great isolation, despite the foundation of several schools of engineering. Scientific work in the Andes countries was merely given the task of compilation—teaching, learning and repeating what other people thought—and hence lacked not only quality but also, and especially, originality. For all the rhetorical flourishes which were likewise to have negative repercussions, this lack led ineluctably to scientific stagnation.

At the outset of the twentieth century, it became clear that the crucial stimuli of Latin American industrialization were anything but original, being instead epigonic and imitative. At no time was new scientific knowledge created that might have given rise to a cumulative development. The natural sciences suffered most of all; there was little social demand in Latin America for the natural sciences, as opposed to Europe and North America. Enthusiastic initiatives in scientific and technological enterprises were few and far between. A similar schism reigned in the dynamics of and demand for scientific and technological resources. This led in turn to further social importation of technology and science.

In the Andes region, the emphasis must now fall on furthering creative capacity in technology and the economy; on cultivating the powers of the imagination, both concrete and abstract; on the ability to construct theories, to advance concepts, to perform experiments, to make inventions, to articulate, to organize, to administer, to solve problems. These must be accompanied by improvements in governmental policies, by the opening up of national territories and by the control of market mechanisms to determine both the pace and the direction of progress. The crucial issue, however, is always the internal dynamics hidden in the potential for human creativity, and hence anchored in culture.

Scientific progress can occur in the Andes Pact states only if the creative potential of these countries finds adequate expression and is converted into the reality of economic and business management.

In doing so, development must be defined more broadly in order to go beyond the merely quantitative dimensions of human existence. The spiritual and metaphysical potential of a culture or country and, above all, its capacity for innovation must also be taken as prerequisites for the fabric and dynamism of its economy. This applies to public planning, to the entire evolutionary process of society and to the various building blocks of industry and the economy.

An emphasis on past deeds of glory and a veneration of ancestors deflect attention from the current problems of planning and organization in Latin America. Not until attention is focused toward the future will change and progress become possible. In Latin America, the Calvinist concept of the elect—a strongly future-oriented concept—was not able to take root. The entire history of ideas and philosophy in North America—together with its empiricism, which became ever better suited to modern analytical technology—gave its logic and pragmatism a pronounced slant toward the future, deriving benefit from the notion that humankind is self-empowered. By this is meant that people are able to understand the world and even to change it, since the universe functions according to intelligible laws, and hence the scientific method can go far in explaining major secrets of human existence. This body of ideas bears both an affinity to and a precondition for economic progress and change. If, on the other hand, a nation's vision of existence explains worldly phenomena by referring to supernatural events and the omnipresence of divine powers, as is the case in Latin America, there will be less leeway for the evolution of rationality along Western lines. The Calvinist work ethic of post seventeenth-century North America is considerably more closely aligned with the community and with communal ethics in politics and economics than is the Catholicism of post-sixteenth-century scholasticism in Latin America, which was always more closely centered on the individual.

Thus, a theological and philosophical tradition in a country's intellectual history will have direct consequences on its political and economic empiricism and constitution. The traditional Catholicism that predominated in Latin America's ruling classes ever since the Spanish conquest was distinguished by an emphasis on transcendence, on a vision of life after death, that eventually led to a paralysis of entrepreneurial innovation.

From the standpoint of political science, Samuel Huntington has shown how extraordinarily important a faith in culture is for political stability and the consolidation of public institutions. Political culture is directly related to a capacity to organize. Latin America, however, is characterized by autocentric individualism that also kindles distrust between the various segments of society. The members of society do not identify sufficiently with the system of ethical values that sustains the state, a system that, in its efforts to attain an integrated nation-state, also affects the exercise of law and jurisprudence as a whole. Humankind's creative capacity includes factors that up to now have been undervalued in Latin American culture: a faith in evenhanded justice, for example, or in the availability of educational opportunities; the ability to experiment; a belief that one's merits and successes will be rewarded; a potential for stability and continuity.

In all these cases, culture and economic development mutually interact. *It is culture that forms the fundamental criterion; only if the inherent roots of culture are given greater attention in the functioning of government and society can those factors be isolated that have prevented Latin America from becoming part of the multinational technological nexus.*

Latin America's Scientific and Technological Backlog:
A Statistical View

The statistics speak for themselves. Since 1981, the gross national product in Latin America has risen no more than 5.9 percent while its population has increased by 51 million. During the same period, the average per capita income sank by 7.6 percent. The figures for the Andes Pact states are even more alarming. Latin America is caught in a profound structural crisis.

According to data from UNESCO, in 1980 Latin America had 91,000 scientists and engineers occupied in research and experimentation. This amounts to about 2.4 percent of the world total. About $2.8 billion was spent on their activities, amounting to 1.8 percent of the world total. Latin America's 5,800 scientific writers represent about 1.27 percent of the total number worldwide. Yet, the region accounts for 8 percent of the world's population and 6 percent of its gross national product. These figures reveal the very small proportion of science and technology carried out in Latin America on a world scale. The expenditures and the number of persons employed for science and development in Latin America are far less than the world standard, as is the percentage of the gross national product spent on science and development. From the beginning of the 1980s to the year 1990, these figures increased, but they still remained marginal by world standards. None of these countries even approached the 1 percent of GNP recommended by the United Nations Science and Technological Assessing Committee for expenditures on research and development. The figures for Latin America vary between 0.1 and 0.5 percent.

Equally low is the amount of scientific-technological activity and productivity in Latin America, especially in the Andes Pact states. Moreover, 76 percent of the amount spent on research and development, 66 percent of the researchers, 72 percent of advanced degrees, 67 percent of scientific writers and 92 percent of technological exports fell to three countries: Brazil, Argentina and Mexico. By way of comparison, the Andes Pact states—Bolivia, Columbia, Chile, Ecuador, Peru and Venezuela—were responsible for 15 percent of expenditures for research and development, 19 percent of the researchers, 18 percent of advanced degrees and 24 percent of scientific writers. What is more, they had a mere 7.1 percent of registered patents, as compared to 90 percent for the aforementioned countries. The export of technology from the Andes states amounted to 8 percent of the Latin American total, with the main portion falling to Venezuela and Columbia. Once again, the poor showing of the Andes Pact states is plain to see.

To what extent are the natural sciences a part of the cultural transition in Latin America? Is there a specifically Latin American tradition in science, and, if so, how is it delineated and where does it reveal discontinuities and fractures?

The statistics incontrovertibly demonstrate Latin America's scientific backlog. Table 1 shows the total number of scientific publications issued between 1973 and 1984 by authors living in Latin America, as compared to authors living in the rest of the world.

Table 1: Relation of Scientific Articles Published in Latin America to Those Published Worldwide, 1973–1984

Year	Latin America	Worldwide	% Latin America
1973	2,700	279,570	0.97
1974	2,532	272,807	0.93
1975	2,521	274,707	0.92
1976	2,698	276,738	0.98
1977	2,684	282,720	0.95
1978	2,754	276,244	1.00
1979	2,919	277,106	1.05
1980	3,314	280,035	1.12
1981	3,307	287,761	1.15
1982	3,412	288,128	1.18
1983	3,369	291,262	1.16
1984	3,001	263,072	1.14

Source: Economic and Social Progress in Latin America, 1988 Report, GRADE, Lima

In 1973, a total of 2,700 papers from Latin America appeared in scientific publications with an international readership, as compared to 279,570 from other countries of the world. This yields a percentage of a mere 0.97 for the whole of Latin America. In 1984, the figure for Latin America was 3,001, as compared to 263,072 for the rest of the world, yielding a percentage of 1.14. Whereas in 1982 Latin America published 3,412 scientific papers, the United States alone produced 135,953.

The next figures are of even greater relevance as far as the Andes Pact states are concerned. Looking at the distribution of Latin American papers issued from 1973 to 1984 in scientific publications with an international readership, we discover that 30.1 percent of them came from Brazil, 14.6 percent from Mexico, 24.3 percent from Argentina, 12.7 percent from Chile, 7.3 percent from

Venezuela, and a mere 11 percent from all the other states combined. Five countries—Argentina, Brazil, Mexico, Chile and Venezuela—accounted for 89 percent of the total, a figure that remained relatively constant over time. The extremely weak position of the Andes Pact states is undeniable.

The declining figures for Peru are no less striking than the stagnation in Ecuador or the increase in Venezuela during the oil boom of the 1970s, which began to trail off in the early 1980s (see Table 2).

Table 2: Latin American Papers in International Scientific Publications, Classified by Country, 1973–1974

Country	1973	1974	1975	1976	1977	1978	1979	1980	1981	1982	1983	1984	Total
Argentina	832	709	611	612	614	590	597	706	747	870	855	770	8,511
Barbados	3	3	6	5	7	3	4	3	4	2	6	4	51
Bolivia	6	7	7	2	6	7	5	4	4	2	6	5	62
Brazil	619	645	739	835	844	869	975	1,004	1,088	981	994	953	10,545
Chile	355	313	316	332	296	326	378	374	418	476	478	386	4,448
Costa Rica	38	24	39	40	33	31	19	41	29	33	28	22	378
Dom. Repub.	2	1	1	2	3	2	4	2	5	5	1	2	30
Ecuador	6	5	6	10	3	8	4	4	6	8	13	7	81
El Salvador	3	7	12	7	9	6	2	6	5	0	2	0	59
Guatemala	18	29	38	19	21	10	20	19	24	17	9	8	232
Guyana	8	3	2	2	6	1	2	4	9	5	10	6	59
Haiti	0	1	4	1	1	1	0	1	2	1	4	2	19
Honduras	5	9	3	5	8	6	3	5	2	2	2	2	53
Jamaica	70	68	44	56	56	66	56	47	56	45	34	30	627
Columbia	46	47	51	50	65	65	51	56	53	56	46	38	625
Cuba	19	14	17	30	23	18	27	28	39	51	50	33	351
Mexico	381	370	374	362	370	392	413	476	489	541	527	435	5,131
Nicaragua	4	1	1	2	3	1	0	0	1	0	0	0	15
Panama	13	9	10	7	4	3	7	8	15	9	13	14	114
Paraguay	3	2	2	2	6	0	5	2	1	1	1	2	29
Peru	38	34	37	41	28	30	26	33	27	29	23	21	366
Surinam	0	0	1	3	4	3	4	1	2	1	2	2	24
Trinidad/Tobago	39	43	25	37	17	37	24	22	27	29	33	34	367
Uruguay	29	27	29	19	27	16	26	14	20	26	28	26	286
Venezuela	161	159	144	214	229	263	265	268	229	220	202	197	2,549

Source: same as Table 1.

The future of science and technology in Latin America will depend to a very large extent on how its society and economy develop in the first half of the twenty-first century. For example, investment in Latin American science and technology from the mid-1970s to the early 1980s increased by a factor of two-and-a-half to three. Even so, these figures in fact represent only 1 percent of total investment worldwide. During this same period, the number of scientists and technicians dedicated to research stagnated to about 2 percent. In contrast, Latin America has about 8 percent of the world's population and 6 percent of its gross national product.

These figures illustrate the importance of support for science and technology. Indeed, this support is a mandatory precondition for the countries of Latin America, and especially the Andes Pact states, if they are to emerge from their subservient position in the world economy. *It is becoming increasingly imperative to draft an independent strategy for Latin American science and technology.*

During the 1980s, the universities of the Andes Pact states granted a far greater number of degrees in the social and cultural sciences than in the natural sciences, engineering and agriculture. In 1982, for instance, 62.5 percent graduated in the cultural and social sciences, whereas 25 percent graduated in the latter fields, followed by medicine with a mere 13 percent. These figures can be further reduced if we consider how many of the graduates actually take up jobs in research and the production of scientific or technological knowledge. The sharp rise in the number of university students should not immediately be seen as a positive trend.

In fact, the Andes Pact states have never been able to develop a "scientific community" comparable to those in the English-speaking world. Only Venezuela can boast of nominal outlays for research and development, thanks mainly to the oil reserves it has exploited since the early 1980s. A closer look at the subsidization policy of these countries during the 1970s and 1980s makes this discrepancy all the more evident. Bolivia, for example, spent $6 million in 1978. Ecuador, however, had already spent $12 million in 1974, and Venezuela was to spend $317 million in 1984. Columbia and Peru spent $43 million in 1982. The difference in per capita outlays is revealing. Venezuela spent sixteen times more per capita than Bolivia, thirteen times more than Ecuador, twelve times more than Columbia and five times more than Peru (see Table 3). And since the early 1980s, the figures for Peru have taken a dramatic turn for the worse.

Table 3: Research and Development Expenses in the Andes States: Total and Percentage of Gross National Product (GNP)

Country	Year	Outlays (US $)	%GNP	per capita
Bolivia	1978	6.00 mill.	0.07	1.14 US $
Ecuador	1979	11.63 mill.	0.13	1.47 US $
Columbia	1982	42.97 mill.	0.15	1.60 US $
Peru*	1980	64.23 mill.	0.30	3.71 US $
Venezuela	1984	316.84 mill.	0.39*	18.80 US $

*estimated figures

Source: Francisco R. Sagasti and Cecilia Cook: *Tiempos Difíciles: Ciencia y Tecnología en America Latina Durante el Decenio de 1980.* GRADE, Lima, 1985.

If we compare outlays in the public and private sectors, we note another highly revealing dichotomy. Expenditures for research and development clearly demonstrate the domination of the public sector. The proportion varies from 51.7 percent in Columbia to 81 percent in Peru at the beginning of the 1980s (the figure for Peru has increased in the meantime). In Columbia, Ecuador and Peru, the private sector shrinks to insignificance. It is important that future policy grant more influence and dynamism to the private economy. It should no longer simply be taken for granted that the bulk of financial resources for research and development will perforce come from generally inefficient government authorities and public institutions. In future, even in the Andes Pact states, the private sector must be involved and promoted far more seriously than hitherto.

Still another sphere sheds light on productivity: the number of projects required to achieve a patent. Whereas Venezuela and Columbia require, respectively, 30 and 49 projects per patent, this figures climbs to 118 in Peru and 139 in Ecuador. A study of the number of researchers corroborates these figures. In Venezuela, one out of every 32 researchers is able to register a patent, whereas Peru and Columbia require 130 researchers per patent and Ecuador 192 (see Table 4).

Here, too, is a starting point for future policy to attain greater efficiency and an improved performance ratio. The figures reveal that the level of productivity in the Andes Pact states is far too low, with Venezuela an exception to a certain extent.

How did this backwardness in development in Latin America, and especially in the Andes Pact states, come about? First, there was a shortage of critical researchers, making it impossible to form an institutionalized scientific community with formal channels of information exchange, as expressed in scientific publications. Then there was the predominance of an oral culture that prefers to disseminate knowledge by personal communication or by holding seminars and congresses. Another factor is an insufficient command of English, the *lingua franca* in the world of natural sciences. Publications in Spanish reach only a small number of researchers, leading to the misconception that local subjects of research are of little interest to the international scientific community. Another serious point is that neither social prestige nor academic advancement is dependent on the productivity of the researcher to the same extent as in North America. Researchers at Latin American universities are generally promoted in recognition of their years of service to the institution, not due to the quality of their research. Another obstacle is that, in Latin America, researchers do not generally live on their university salaries alone, but must augment their incomes with work outside the university, thereby undermining and limiting their research activities.

Table 4: Indicators for Scientific and Technological Productivity in the Andes Pact States (in millions of US dollars; only patents registered for nationals are included)

Country	Year	Projects/Researchers/ R&D Costs per author			Projects/Researchers/ R&D Costs per patent		
Ecuador	1979	39.71	54.71	0.83	139.00	191.50	2.91 (1979)
Columbia	1982	15.81	42.58	0.38	49.19	132.47	1.19 (1978)
Peru	1980	48.52	53.98	0.71	118.03	131.30	1.74 (1979)
Venezuela	1980	7.94	8.58	0.59	29.82	32.22	2.22 (1978)

Source: same as Table 3.

To further demonstrate the underdevelopment of science, especially the natural sciences in Latin America, we can consult the Science Citation Index, a list of worldwide publications in science and technology issued by the Institute of Scientific Information in Philadelphia. The Science Citation Index covers ten areas of science: clinical medicine, biomedical research, biology, chemistry, physics, engineering sciences, technology, space research, psychology and mathematics. These major categories are subdivided into 106 fields of specialization.

Table 5: Projects and Technology Programs in the Andes Pact States: Funds Received 1975–1983

	Source of Budgeted Funds (in US $)				
	Andes Pact	JUNAC	Foreign	Total	
PADT copper	1,691,000	220,000	1,100,000	3,011,000	completed 1982
"PADT refort"	3,310,000	421,000	4,473,200	8,204,200	levels 1–2 completed 1983
PADT nutrition	2,840,724	132,000	4,029,815	7,002,539	completed 1983
Inventory of tech. capacities	100,000	84,000	158,782	342,782	level 1 completed 1984
Technology info. system	3,126,750	396,980	1,452,410	4,976,140	since 1982
Advancement project for industrial plant	—	30,000	100,000	130,000	since 1982
PADT land	3,896,650	381,400	4,090,200	8,368,250	since Mar. 1983
Project planning	—	150,000	467,900	617,900	since Jan. 1984
Advancement project for the timber industry	2,000,000	150,000	5,000,000	7,150,000	since Jan. 1984
Dissemination of nutrition project results	10,000	10,000	50,000	70,000	since July 1984
Planning and implementation project	50,000	150,000	700,000	900,000	since Oct. 1984
Coal project	—	50,000	700,000	750,000	since Jan. 1985
Mines/metallurgy project	400,000	150,000	1,450,000	2,000,000	since 1985
Total (US $):	17,425,120	2,325,380	23,772,307	43,522,811	

PADT = *Programas Andinos de Desarrollo Tecnológico*

Table 6: Scientific-Technological Expenses Related to Population and Gross National Product

Country		Researchers and Engineers		Total Costs US $			Projects	Author
	Year	Total	Per 100,000 pop.	Total (Mill.)	per cap.	% GNP		
Chile	1982	4,530	39.46	98.45	8.57	0.41*	3,111	1,083
Ecuador	1979	766	9.70	11.63	1.47	0.13	556	14
Columbia	1982	4,769	17.71	42.97	1.60	0.15	1,771	112
Peru	1980	4,858	28.09	64.23*	3.71	0.30*	4,367	90
Venezuela	1984	4,568 (1983)	27.86	316.84	18.80	0.39*	6,197	464 (1983)

*In relation to *produto brutto interno*

Table 7: Payments in 1982, Calculated from Various Technology Import Channels in Latin American Countries (in millions of US $)

Country	Direct investment from abroad		Capital goods imported		License payments		Overall total	
	Total	%	Total	%	Total	%	Total	%
Brazil	2,634.80	42.79	3,304.00	56.66	218.00	3.54	6,156.80	100
Bolivia	34.70	18.49	150.00	79.91	3.00	1.60	187.70	100
Ecuador	60.00 (1981)	8.62	624.00	89.68	11.80 (1977)	1.70	695.80	100
Columbia	336.80*	19.57	1,377.00	80.00	7.40	0.43	1,721.20	100
Peru	55.10	4.96	1,049.00	94.34	7.86	0.71	1,111.96	100
Venezuela	253.00	6.49	3,487.00	89.48	157.02	4.03	3,897.02	100

* projected figures

Source for Tables 5,6 and 7: same as Table 3

If we look at the type of research involved, we immediately notice a decline in the areas of clinical medicine and biomedical research in the years between 1973 and 1984. Similarly, there was a relative lack of growth in chemistry, mathematics and the engineering sciences and a weak growth (by no means sufficient) in physics and biology (see Table 8).

Table 8: Distribution of Latin American Scientific Publications by Field of Interest, 1973–1984 (percentages)

Year	Clin. Medic.	Biomed. Research	Biology	Chemistry	Physics	Space Technol.	Engin. Sciences	Psychol.	Math.
1973	37.47	22.07	10.23	11.03	9.26	5.00	2.72	0.68	1.53
1974	36.27	19.84	12.37	9.96	10.21	5.07	3.14	0.89	2.25
1975	34.25	20.24	11.94	10.80	12.11	4.69	2.86	0.96	2.16
1976	32.80	17.82	12.83	11.25	12.84	4.75	4.30	0.72	2.69
1977	31.12	21.50	12.34	10.25	12.75	4.71	3.52	1.18	2.63
1978	33.08	19.69	12.38	10.14	13.54	4.27	3.95	0.42	2.53
1979	30.82	18.84	12.74	11.20	14.45	4.98	4.09	0.56	2.32
1980	31.51	16.85	13.48	11.14	14.29	5.25	4.13	0.86	2.50
1981	29.71	16.60	12.88	13.62	16.02	5.05	3.71	0.47	1.94
1982	30.10	14.33	13.57	13.86	16.21	5.46	3.70	0.50	2.26
1983	30.11	15.64	12.62	12.82	16.26	5.02	5.10	0.54	1.88
1984	25.10	17.03	14.04	11.94	19.58	4.70	4.57	0.61	2.42

Source: see Table 1.

A strong focus on sciences that deal basically with human health is typical of research in underdeveloped countries, as is an emphasis on chemistry, physics and the engineering sciences. This strong emphasis on health sciences is often referred to as the "periphery complex" of Latin American science, but it also expresses a weak connection between the goals of technology and science and the needs of society. Even in those cases where research is conducted in physics, there is no connection with technology, but rather with the health sciences. This can be explained at least partly by the frightening recent developments in demography and social hygiene in these countries.

Another combination of figures is likewise revealing. In 1980, there were 1,398,507 references made worldwide to publications in the natural sciences. Of these, only 8,409 were to articles by Latin American authors. Similarly, only 15,720 of the 2,607,894 references made in 1973 were to Latin American authors. Compared with the number of references worldwide, the years 1973 and 1980 reveal the same tiny percentage—0.60 percent—implying that practically no progress was made in this sector (see Table 9).

Table 9: References to Scientific Papers in Latin America and Worldwide, 1973 and 1980

Science	Worldwide		Latin America	
	1973	1980	1973	1980
Clinical medicine	816,887	429,690	5,759	2,409
Biomedicine	666,687	361,897	4,673	1,845
Biology	154,118	79,024	999	714
Chemistry	364,365	189,529	1,382	915
Physics	332,125	200,151	1,411	1,382
Space research	128,228	74,558	911	834
Engin. sciences	79,590	44,138	227	165
Psychology	40,055	9,174	241	81
Mathematics	25,838	10,345	116	63
Total:	2,607,894	1,398,507	15,720	8,409

Source: same as Table 1.

In short, Latin American science does not supply enough material to develop an indigenous technology policy. This can also be seen in the granting of patents, always a reliable indicator of the innovative character of research and science. Nearly all countries have laws governing intellectual property to encourage inventions and stimulate the economy. In the years between 1981 and 1984, the number of patents requested in Latin America amounted to 2.4 percent of the world total, and the number of patents actually granted amounted to 4 percent. A glance at North America reveals the exact opposite figures: here 14.9 percent of patents granted worldwide were registered. The total number of patents requested in Latin American countries was less than one-fifth of the figure for the United States, whereas the patents granted made up a third of those granted in the United States (see Table 10).

Table 10: Patents Requested and Granted for Inventions in Latin America, the United States and Worldwide, 1981–1984

Country or region	1981 req./granted		1982 req./granted		1983 req./granted		1984 req./granted	
Latin America	18,745,	18,633	21,559	20,281	19,895	14,611	19,664	12,128
USA	106,413	65,770	109,625	57,889	103,703	56,862	111,284	67,201
Worldwide	800,885	417,469	809,741	413,764	824,428	406,939	859,980	422,496
Percentages								
Latin America/ USA	17.62	28.33	19.67	35.03	19.18	25.70	17.67	18.05
Latin America/ World	2.34	4.46	2.66	4.90	2.41	3.59	2.29	2.87
USA/World	13.29	15.75	13.54	13.99	12.58	13.97	12.94	15.91

Source: same as Table 1.

As already noted in the case of scientific publications, the distribution of patents in Latin America is likewise concentrated in a few countries. The five countries with the greatest number of patents are once again Brazil, Argentina, Mexico, Venezuela and Chile. Figure 1 shows the relative percentages for patents requested and patents granted in the major Latin American countries from 1978 to 1984. These figures were compiled by the World Intellectual Property Organization. Another consideration is that a high percentage of the number of patents granted was given to nonresidents, i.e., to people who do not actually live in Latin America. In 1978–84, for example, this figure amounted to 80 percent of the total. Admittedly, the same phenomenon can be observed in other nations of the world in similar circumstances. But the percentage is particularly high in Latin America, and especially so in the Andes Pact states.

Another factor is the low efficiency in the conversion of patents once they have been granted. This can be seen in the case of Peru: of the 4,872 patents granted in the principal industrial sectors of Peru from 1960 to 1970, only 54—a mere 1.1 percent—were actually put into practice. While the percentage of foreigners who obtain patents in the countries of Latin America is very high, the technological and patent-related performance of the Andes Pact states is extremely low, even when compared to other Latin American countries. And it is especially worrying to note that in recent years all figures relating to economic efficiency have shown a downward trend.

The distribution of Nobel Prizes gives further evidence that Latin America is poorly represented in the natural sciences. In physics, for example, no Nobel Prize has been granted to a Latin American since 1901. Only in chemistry and medicine have three Nobel Prizes been awarded to Latin Americans, as compared to 80 for the United States, which traditionally takes the lion's share of these prizes (e.g., almost 50 percent in medicine). In literature, however, Latin Americans are much more likely to receive a Nobel Prize. This is yet another indication that in Latin American culture, intuitive and associative thought is far superior to empirical-pragmatic or abstract scientific thought. Five Nobel Prizes for literature give evidence to the power of intuition and imagination of Latin American authors: Gabriela Mistral (1945), Miguel Angel Asturias (1967), Pablo Neruda (1971), Gabriel García Marquez (1982) and Octavio Paz (1990).

It is precisely the indigenous and archaic culture of Latin America—especially in the Andes Pact states, with their strong slant on metaphysics and transcendence, magic and myth—that explains its poor performance in these statistics and raises the question of the incompatibility of its cultural heritage with modern technology. The only Andes Pact state that has made some headway in scientific research is Venezuela, as can also be seen in its number of patents.

Argentina, Brazil, Chile, Mexico and Venezuela account for 70 percent of the population of Latin America and 80 percent of its gross national product, but 90 percent of its scientific publications, above all in the natural sciences. We should recall that during these years Latin American authors were only able to contribute, on average, a mere 0.6 percent of the world's scientific literature. As is evident, the countries with the greatest number of references are also those with the greatest number of publications, and are thus responsible for almost 90 percent of all references to Latin American scientific literature. In this regard, the statistical contribution of the Andes Pact states is almost negligible.

A study of the statistics reveals that Latin America's contribution to the dissemination of knowledge in the natural sciences has been minuscule. These figures clearly support the view that, at the moment, Latin America is doing little for the development of science and technology in the world, and further emphasize the paramount importance of an indigenous technology for the future of the region.

Figure 1: Latin America: Distribution by Country of Total Number of Patents Requested and Patents Granted, 1978–1984

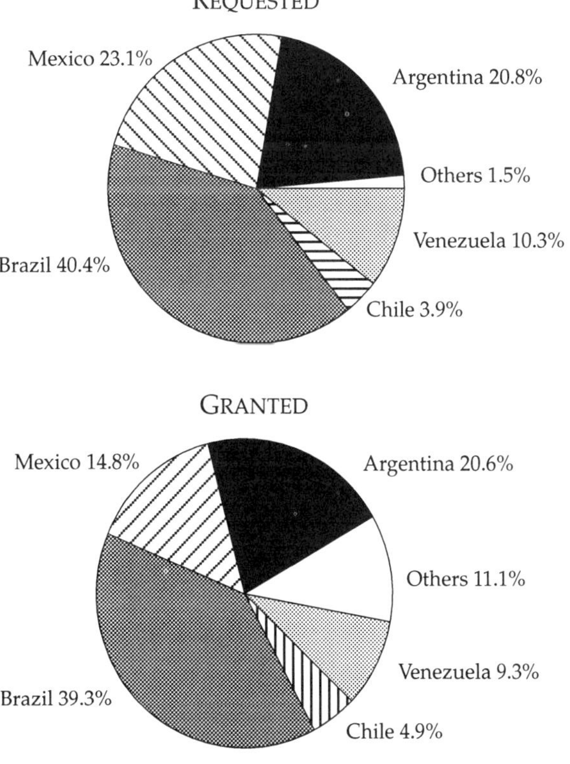

Suggestions for Further Reading

Ademan, I., and C.T. Morris. *Economic Growth and Social Equity in Developing Countries*. Stanford: Stanford University Press, 1973.

Amat y Leon, C., et al. *Realidad del campo peruano después de la reforma agraria. 10 ensayos críticos*. Centro de Investigación y Capacitación (CIC), Editora Ital Perú S.A., Lima, 1980.

Arguedas, José María. *Formación de una cultura nacional indoamericana*. Siglo XXI. Mexico, 1977.

Arrow, K.J. *Social Choice and Individual Values*. New York, 1951.

Baczko, Bronislaw. *Lumières de l'utopie*. Paris: Payot, 1978.

Burckhardt, Jacob. *The Civilization of the Renaissance in Italy*. Oxford and London: Phaidon Press, 1945.

Burga, Manuel, and Alberto Flores Galindo. "La utopia andina." Instituto de Pastoral Andina, *Allpanchis* 20 (1982, Cuzco): 85–102.

Casas, Rosalba. *Algunos lineamientos de política de ciencia y tecnología para al sector agropecuario*. Instituto de Investigaciones Sociales, UNAM, Mexico, 1986.

Clough, Shepard B. *The Economic Development of Western Civilization*. New York: McGraw Hill, 1959.

Comisión Económica para América Latina (CEPAL). Anuario estadístico de América latina, Naciones Unidas, Santiago de Chile, 1977.

Cooper, S. "Science Policy and Technological Change in Underdeveloped Economies." *World Development* 2, March 1974.

De La Cruz Gomez Rodriguez, Juan. "Comunidades de pastores y reforma agraria en la sierra sur peruana." *Pastores de Puna. Uywamichiq punarunakuna*. Ed. Jorge A. Flores Ochoa. Instituto de Estudios Peruanos, Lima, 1977.

Emmanuel, A. *Unequal Exchange: A Study of the Imperialism of Trade*. Monthly Review Press, London, 1972.

Ernst, Dieter. "Industrial Redeployment and Control over Technology—Consequences for the Third World." *Vierteljahresberichte* 83, 1981.

Farvar, M.T. "Is There an Environmental Crisis in the Third World?" *Universities Quarterly* 27 (Spring 1973): 292–303.

Flores Ochoa, Jorge, and Abraham Valencia. *Rebeliones indígenas quechuas y amaras*. Centro de Estudios Andinos, Cuzco, n.d.

Furtado, Celso. *Economic Development of Latin America*. Cambridge: Cambridge University Press, 1970.

Gerschenkron, A. *Economic Backwardness in Historical Perspective*. Cambridge, MA: Harvard University Press, 1962.

Golte, J. *La racionalidad de la organización andina*. Instituto de Estudios Peruanos, Lima, 1980.

Henriquez, Narda, José Blanes and Sandra Callenas. *Migraciones internas, estructura urbana y estructura productiva*. PUCP, Departamento de Ciencias Sociales, Lima, 1979.

Horowitz, Irving Louis. *Three Worlds of Development: The Theory and Practice of International Stratification*. New York, London, Toronto: Oxford University Press, 1972.

Hünefeld, Christine. *Sociedad y rebeliones campesinas entre 1780 y 1783*. Doctoral dissertation in anthropology. Universidad Nacional Mayor de San Marcos, Lima, 1977.

Instituto Nacional de Estadistica. *Produto bruto interno por departamento 1971–1981*. Dirección General de Cuentas Nacionales, Lima, 1983.

de Janvry, Alain. *The Agrarian Question and Reformism in Latin America*. Baltimore and London: John Hopkins University Press, 1981.

Junta del Acuerdo de Cartagena (JUNAC). *La deuda externa del Grupo Andino*, 1984.

Klaiber, Jeffrey. "'Los Cholos' y 'los rotos': actitudes raciales durante la guerra del Pacífico, *Histórica* 2, July 1978.

Maletta, Héctor. "Cambios en el Perú desde 1950." *Realidad del campo peruano después de la reforma agraria*. Centro de Investigación y Capacitación, Lima, 1980.

Mariátegui, José Carlos. *Siete ensayos de interpretación de la realidad peruana*. Biblioteca Amauta, Lima, 1928.

Marquinez, Germán. *Ideología y praxis de la conquista*. Bogota: Nueva América, 1978.

____. "Hacia una teoría antifetichista y social de los valores." *El hombre latinoamericano y sus valores*. Bogota: Nueva América, 1979. pp. 67.

Matos Mar, José and José Manuel Mejia, eds. *La reforma agraria en el Perú*. Instituto de Estudios Peruanos, Perú Problema 3, Lima, 1980.

____. *Reforma agraria: logros y contradiciones 1969–1979*. Instituto de Estudios Peruanos, Lima, 1980.

Olson, Theodore. *Millenialism, Utopianism and Progress*. Toronto: University of Toronto Press, 1982.

Prebisch, Raúl. *Crisis del capitalismo periférico*. Fondo de Cultura, Mexico, 1981.

Prescott, William H. *Historia de la conquista del Perú*. Edit. Universo, Lima, 1972.

Quijano, Aníbal. *Problema agrario y movimientos campesinos*. Lima: Mosca Azul, 1979.

Ribeiro, Darcy. "La nación latinoamericana." *Revista Nueva Sociedad* 62, Caracas, October, 1982.

____. *El proceso civilizado*. Universidad Central de Venezuela, Caracas, 1970.

Sagasti, Francisco, and Cecilia Cook. *Tiempos difíciles: ciencia y tecnología en América Latina durante el decenio de 1980*. GRADE, Lima, December 1985.

Sagasti, Francisco, and Javier Escobal. *Proyecciones del gasto en investigación y desarrollo en América Latina hasta el año 2000*. GRADE, Lima, February 1984.

Sánchez Albavera, Fernando, et al. *Problema nacional. Cultura y clases sociales*. DESCO, Lima, 1981.

Santos, T. Dos. "The Crisis of Development Theory and the Problem of Dependence in Latin America." *Underdevelopment and Development*. Ed. H. Bernstein. Harmondsworth: Penguin Readings, 1973.

Schaff, Adam. *Qué futuro nos aguarda?: las consecuencias sociales de la segunda revolución industrial*. Barcelona: Editorial Crítica, 1985.

Schumacher, E.F. *Small Is Beautiful: A Study of Economics As if People Mattered*. London: Blond & Briggs, 1973.

Sen, A.K. *Choice of Techniques: An Aspect of the Theory of Planned Economic Development*. Oxford: Basil Blackwell, 1972.

_____. *Collective Choice and Social Welfare*. San Francisco, 1970.

Servier, Jean. *La Utopia*. Fondo de Cultura Económica, Mexico, 1970.

Simmons, Ozzie G. "The Criollo Outlook in the Mestizo Culture of Coastal Peru." *American Anthropologist* 57 (1955): 107–117.

Spalding, Karen. *De indio a campesino. Cambios en la structura social del Perú colonial*. Instituto de Estudios Peruanos, Lima, 1974.

Streeten, P.P. "Technology Gaps Between Rich and Poor Countries." *The Scottish Journal of Political Economy* 19, November 1972.

Sunkel, Osvaldo. *América Latina y la crisis económica internacional: ocho tesis y una propuesta*. Buenos Aires: Grupo Editor Latinoamericano, 1985.

Tawney, R.H. *Religion and the Rise of Capitalism: A Historical Study*. New York: New American Library, Mentor, 1954.

Todaro, M.P. "A Theoretical Note on Labor as an 'Inferior' Factor in Less Developed Countries." *Journal of Development Studies* 5, July 1969.

Turnham, D. *The Employment Problem in Less Developed Countries. A Review of the Evidence*. OCDE, 1971.

United Nations Industrial Development Organization (UNIDO). *Small Scale Industry in Latin America*. Vienna, 1969.

Varallanos, José. *El cholo en el Perú*. Lima, 1962.

Young, O.R. *The Politics of Force: Bargaining During International Crises*. Princeton: Princeton University Press, Princeton, 1968.

Zea, Leopoldo. "Dependencia y liberación en la filosofía latinoamericana, Dianoia. UNAM-FCE, Mexico. *Anuario de Filosofía* 20, No. 20 (1974): 172–188.

_____. *The Latin American Mind*. Norman, OK: University of Oklahoma Press, 1963.Aceves, Joseph. *Social Change in Spanish Village*. Cambridge, MA: Schenkman, 1971.

SEVEN

INDIGENOUS TECHNOLOGY

Summary

One basic prerequisite for developing an indigenous capacity for science and technology is the existence of an institutional infrastructure to give full expression to the many different types of scientific activity. It is thus essential that each country throughout the world be given the freedom to make its own decisions when choosing its technologies. Equally essential are channels of information that enable a country to obtain technology at fair prices. Furthermore, each country must be allowed to set up effective rules that satisfy its demand for technology and facilitate technology transfer within its institutional framework. Rather than introducing high technology that is difficult to integrate into the economy, the emphasis should fall on selective acquisition of strategic technologies that can function as critical multipliers. Selective technological training must be offered in keeping with the century-old cultural backgrounds of the Andes Pact states.

In addition, indigenous technology must be supported by various preconditions. First, it must be in harmony with the cultural and social surroundings, the moral values and the customs and usages of the given culture. Second, it must be adapted economically to create jobs in both light and heavy industry. Products created by indigenous technology must meet the basic needs of the entire population. A balance must also be maintained in the ecology. To prevent highly productive modern technologies from destroying traditional technologies during the process of integration, wage and price controls must be set up on an institutional level. To enhance innovation, it must be the policy of the European Community to demand more privatization in order to increase the amount of research in the production system and above all to allow research to be carried out by private industry. The European Community must seek better training for researchers, technicians and government officials, perhaps by means of postgraduate study programs, to give indigenous technology an educational foundation. Methodologically, the European Community must find starting points for internalizing the scientific and technological evolution of the Andes Pact states by selecting aspects of traditional technology for further development. Not until careful steps have been taken in the field of education to reconcile modern science and traditional culture will it be possible to create a climate favorable to the social, economic and political transformation of the Andes states. The end of this section presents a sixteen-point plan for this purpose.

Scientific and Technological Capacity and the Crisis of Development Theories

For the purposes of this study, there are basically two kinds of countries today: those that have witnessed and continue to witness the evolution of science and technology within their own borders; and those that have undergone a quantitative, but not qualitative, increase in production, failing to develop dynamic processes for the acquisition of knowledge. The former can be referred to as countries with indigenous technology, the latter as countries with an exogenous, or borrowed, foundation for science and technology. It is the interaction of these two currents—the evolution of thought and the evolution of technology—that makes up the scientific-technological revolution.

For centuries, in the wake of the Industrial Revolution, science and technology were aligned with the world capitals and their monopoly of knowledge. The productive activities of other countries focused primarily on the colonial powers, which were mainly interested in exploiting natural resources and transferring profits to the mother country. In consequence, most Latin American technologies were introduced by European states and have remained alien to their local environment.

Scientific work, technological capability, traditional technological potential: in the Andes Pact states these three levels had little opportunity to interact. The obliteration of traditional technology left the nations and cultures of the Andes region with a sense of trauma that furthered the dissolution of its governing institutions. Nor has it proved practicable merely to retrace the experiences gained by Western states in indigenous technology. Instead, emphasis should be shifted to the selective acquisition of strategic technologies which can function as critical multipliers. In order to internalize technology in these countries, special sectors should be chosen that reveal points of contact with traditional technologies. Only in this way can the growing lethargy be held in check. This does not mean, of course, a return to technologies of the past.

Merging the technological capacities of modern production with a systematic utilization of traditional technology will make possible an independent course in which borrowed technology is replaced by indigenous creations. Yet, these efforts to develop indigenous techniques of production should not be equated with a desire for isolationism. The evolution of productive techniques merely reveals that we are faced with a long-term process of maturation.

This process affects three levels of technology in particular: its creation, its dissemination and its application to human and material resources. A national policy of science and technology can be seen as the sum total of principles and methods, of legislative and executive measures for organization and rationalization that are required to bring a nation's scientific-technological potential into line with its overriding social and cultural history. Seen from the standpoint of science and technology in the industrializing countries and the nations of the Third and Fourth Worlds, development theory has been less than satisfactory. Growth on the basis of inequality will never lead to a lasting and natural evolution. Clearly, science and technology are both at the root of the inequality between the advanced and the underdeveloped countries.

A command of science and technology means a control of political power and economic dynamism. Structural changes must be made within the underdeveloped countries before a state of balance can be struck in the worldwide race for scientific and technological benefits. The underdeveloped countries do not form a homogeneous unit as far as their economies, societies and cultures are concerned. There is too little exchange and mobility between these levels. Moreover, the technological dependence of the Andes Pact states considerably reduces their latitude to make autonomous decisions. Due to their low technological standards, they must choose between growing capital-intensive technologies and the nonexistence of efficient technological alternatives while faced with the problems of unemployment and an expanding population.

Development is always a dynamic process of structural change sustained by many different factors. First and foremost among these is economic growth, the capacity for science and technology that allows a country to turn its surplus money into capital goods with appropriate technological characteristics, as well as to utilize the effects of economic growth and technological progress in all sectors of its society. Here the key concept is self-sufficiency as opposed to dependence, and the secret is to develop modes of production adapted to local circumstances.

Due to the passive nature of Latin American economies, the demand for technology has largely been satisfied by importing tools, industrial goods and the skilled assistance of foreign technicians. Since foreign technology is readily available, little pressure has been put on the local scientific community to develop sound technological alternatives. Although the universities of the colonial period did undergo a certain development, it was not until after 1800 that the engineering sciences were taught to any extent. Even in our own century, the importance of the natural and engineering sciences has been underplayed at these universities.

Little value was placed in retaining traditional agriculture, which was based on local techniques but contributed little to economic growth. In the Andes Pact states, expenses for foreign technology, licensing fees and payments for technical assistance and knowledge far exceed the amounts spent on research and development of indigenous technology.

During the 1970s, a number of programs were started to promote local technology. The most important of these were initiated by the Instituto de Investigación Tecnológia Industrial y de Normas Tecnicas. With the sole exception of Venezuela, none of the Andes states has given precedence to preparing its own creative technological potential in research and development. The other countries of the Andes Pact entirely lack a suitable institutional infrastructure for this purpose. Consequently, the future internalization of technology in these countries can be carried out only one step at a time. One basic prerequisite for developing an indigenous capacity for science and technology is the existence of an institutional infrastructure to give full expression to the many different types of scientific activity.

The goal of any policy for indigenous technology should be to secure an autonomous potential for producing goods and services so that a country can attain the freedom necessary to make its own decisions. As Celso Furtado recognized, due to the rapid growth of production methods throughout the world, only a small core of technological innovations has received attention. Thus, he argues, underdevelopment is a result of the impact of the technological process on the worldwide distribution of labor, in which a small number of countries reached a position of economic hegemony following the Industrial Revolution. Fresh guidelines (i.e., not derived from the United States or Japan) can serve as the basis for increasing self-confidence. As paradoxical as it may seem, a country can achieve far more effective results domestically by detaching itself from worldwide competition and learning to go without state-of-the-art technology. Countries on the technological periphery must first insist on a greater degree of independence in order to be in a position to avail themselves of borrowed technology once they have created a receptiveness and a capacity for making autonomous decisions.

This study is intended to bridge the gap between diagnosis and specific practical proposals. Indicators must be found to devise a set of political tools with which to undergird technological skills in the Andes Pact states. Friction between science policy and technology policy must be avoided, as only a combination of the two can lead to an indigenous technology. Nonetheless, science policy and technology policy must be carefully kept apart in their respective tasks so that their separate results can be combined into practical action. The technological decisions of business enterprises are determined by the amount of technology a country can absorb and by the size of its demand for technology, a demand jointly created by research institutes, engineering companies, multinational businesses and suppliers, licensing agencies and consultants. The question of whether a particular technology is appropriate to the circumstances of the Andes Pact states is too often overlooked, for representatives of the industrial nations rarely are familiar with Latin American culture. The regional suitability of technology is ignored.

Today, our system of education, to no small degree, focuses on the utilization of the natural sciences and on coming to grips with them intellectually. Obviously, this concept of education will seem meaningless in the context of Latin America, where technology and the natural sciences are still a long way from supplanting the original role of natural phenomena. Even so, an increasing number of institutions and concepts which are meaningful only in a Western view of the world are being applied to Latin America to modernize its system of technical and scientific education along Western lines. This can only lead to insoluble conflicts within Latin American culture. No attempt to provoke social change artificially by transferring production methods based on the natural sciences is automatically destined to succeed. It is crucial to look first at the view of nature lying at the root of Latin American technology.

Any effort to replicate modern thought in the Andes Pact states *ex post facto* by directly transferring natural science and technology to their modes of production and institutions is doomed to failure. The reason is simple: these countries still lack the preconditions for the success of artificial scientific-technological modes of production. Moreover, it is wrong to suppose that the only production processes that can be derived from the exact sciences are those of heavy industry. On the contrary, structural history teaches us that it takes the whole of a culture to produce mathematics as a universal science. This remains a problem for the Andes Pact states because their pre-Columbian and colonial cultures did not sufficiently recognize the universality of mathematics

By itself, the transfer of technology can bear fruit only when it is supported by an appropriate cognitive structure. One example of such a cognitive structure is provided by Japanese culture, with its obedience to authority, its recognition of the sacred status of the emperor, its principle of consensus in the decision-making process and its underlying empirical outlook. The relation of Andean culture to the natural sciences and technology, however, is fractured and problematic, giving rise to a fundamental dichotomy. Scientific culture has not been sufficiently disseminated in the Andes Pact states: their cultures still do not possess what might be called a rationalistic transcendence capable of creating an intellectual climate conducive to the application of science and technology. Its educational system and universities must take on the task of initiating a process of awareness that has been described by Paulo Freyre.

Even today, the basic goals of its educational policy are undefined. There is a lack of consultation and well-considered planning. It is short-sighted to think that Latin American society can simply be reeducated and retrained. Instead, its educational system must be adapted to the development strategies of a specific country in a way that helps to sustain the state and serves as a starting point for the development of an independent technology.

The cardinal problem is that Latin American businesses are dependent on foreign sources of technology, as they have been unable to develop a sufficient level of indigenous technology. The poor competitiveness of Latin American industries on the world market has contributed to this process of disintegration. On a global scale, Latin American businesses are at a disadvantage, since their own capacities for research and development have not been given sufficient support and the state lacks means for financial investment. Accordingly, the technology gap is an educational gap as well.

Innovation and invention are intimately related. Invention is the conception of an idea, a discovery arising from the work of a single individual or group of researchers. Innovation, on the other hand, deals with diffusion, with the application of an invention in the larger realms of society and the economy. To claim that technology is a necessary factor in this line of development is not to say that it is sufficient in and of itself.

The Andes Pact states were and still are countries on the technological periphery. Since the colonial period, they have never experienced a cumulative indigenous process, resulting in a static immobility. However, we must assume that every country has areas in which it has produced its own technology, as well as a minimal scientific-technological infrastructure to develop indigenous capabilities. It is thus essential that each country throughout the world be given the freedom to make its own decisions when choosing its technologies. Equally essential are channels of information that enable a country to obtain technology at fair prices. Furthermore, each country must be allowed to set up effective rules that satisfy its demand for technology and facilitate technology transfer within the framework of its own infrastructure, which must be sufficiently developed for this purpose. A technology is appropriate only within a particular physical, economic and, especially, cultural context, and it is often unsuitable for transplantation elsewhere. Under these circumstances, it is crucial for purposes of national planning that technologies be modified when transferred.

Science must be seen as part of a larger cultural effort, both as tinder for the economy and as a basis for goal-directed industrial research. Technology can be selected in such a way that it not only advances the industrial sector quantitatively, but also impinges on human evolution, thereby affecting the quality of life as well.

Rather than the introduction of high technology that is difficult to absorb into the economy, the selective acquisition of strategic technologies, which can function as critical multipliers and enhance self-confidence, should be emphasized. Selective technological training must be offered in keeping with the century-old cultural backgrounds of the Andes Pact states.

Indigenous technology must be supported by various preconditions. First, it must be in harmony with the cultural and social surroundings, the moral values and the customs and usages of a given culture. In addition, it must be adapted economically, i.e., it must generate profits within a reasonable time span and with a small amount of capital and hard currency investment so as to generate jobs in both light and heavy industry. Products created by indigenous technology must meet the basic needs of the entire population and not merely duplicate Western lifestyles. A balance must also be maintained in the ecology; this applies to the emission of pollutants (a major problem for industrial plants in the Andes Pact states), as well as soil erosion and deforestation. Finally, alternative technologies should not only alter the nature of a product, but also lower its price.

Mobilizing alternative technologies also means taking advantage of the developmental potential of local and regional resources, which necessarily involves a learning process in society and culture. This internal transformation of culture is imperative for a country's independence. The goal must be to obtain effective control of key sectors and to make sure that needs are in harmony with the actual demands of the population.

It is important to identify the most pressing social, economic and cultural needs of large segments of the population, especially among the underprivileged classes. Technocratic nods in this direction must be replaced by social and cultural learning processes. Only in this sense can the key to economic development—

industrialization—be advocated in order to ensure that efforts are channeled in other directions, such as agriculture, energy, communication, public health and social services. Ultimately, the main issue is to inculcate new forms of national and collective independence in nations on the technological periphery. Every country should be in a position to satisfy such basic needs as nutrition, education, employment and the staples of human existence.

When traditional technology is combined with a selective and systematic application of modern science, it is important that it be upgraded and taken more seriously. For traditional modes of production can do more than provide special aspects of technology: they can also contribute to a country's cultural and national identity.

Besides meeting a country's needs in both a material and non-material sense, alternative development must place greater emphasis on factors that impart a local cultural identity to science in order to secure an indigenous foundation for science and technology. Taking recourse in its own strength and involving its entire population in the decision-making process enable a country to recover economically. The central issue is an ecumenical view of progress and development that acknowledges the plurality of cultures and thus finds ways to practice a form of science that is adapted to the actual needs and circumstances of the Andes region.

Technological Innovation and the Primacy of Culture

The theories of technological dependence have many proponents. The leading lights of the 1950s and 1960s were Furtado, Cardoso and Sunkel. In the 1970s, writers such as Constantine Vaitsos, Fernando Fajnzylber and Miguel Wionsek deliberated over the problem of technology transfer. Natalio Botana, Jorge Sabato, Maximo Halty and Francisco Sagasti studied the nature of local scientific and technological traditions.

The dependence theory posits a hybrid economy and sets out by analyzing the influence of borrowed technology on Latin America. In contrast, the autonomy approach seeks to discover and expand local capacities. The planning, organizing and cultivating of local scientific-technological efforts take precedence over the past, with its excessive import of technology. Hence, this approach, as formulated in 1968 by Forge Sabato and Natalio Botana, among others, is a normative one—Latin America must abandon its passive and imitative role and turn away from its past history in which Latin American research grossly overlooked the natural sciences until well into the 1950s and in which metaphysics, law and medicine were taught instead of the engineering sciences.

It was obvious that Latin America could only have a minor part in worldwide technological innovation. After all, science—and the natural sciences in particular—have been marginalized ever since the colonial period. The small number of pioneering technological achievements in Latin America was restricted to elite circles, and this was especially the case in the Andes Pact states.

The question of Latin America's potential for local innovation, including raw materials, the availability of labor and the size of the market, has been pursued by Jorge Katz. Improved use of available resources presupposes a certain dynamism that is largely governed by three imperatives: the transmission of knowledge from past generations to the present one; the acquisition of new knowledge; and, finally, the modification of organizational and institutional forms that are capable of consolidating scientific findings. This dynamism reveals a process that a society must undergo if it wishes to seek efficiency and at the same time maintain, reproduce and defend its inner strengths. Until recently, too little attention has been paid to the fact that the overall development of a country cannot be limited to its economic growth. If this "development" is to be worthy of the name, it must instead focus on human beings: it must be integrated into the vast panoply of human life forms, where each and every culture is characterized by its own particular style of development.

For this reason, it is advisable to make an important distinction: no development aimed solely at production and the economy is indigenous in and of itself. Before it can become so, education must be added as a vital function to this multifarious process. *We must abandon the notion of the uniform cultural supremacy of the Western industrial states. Far from representing an ultimate good, this cultural uniformity obscures a major part of the potential of human culture.*

Any attempt to make cultures and societies more uniform becomes an attack on their independence. This is why the cultural integration of the economy is so necessary in the Andes Pact states. Culture is the social matrix which imparts value to individual existence in the first place.

More awareness must be given to the various ethnic groups, cultural peculiarities and religions that abound in the Andes region. Every ethnic group should be granted an opportunity to lead a life that is not fundamentally removed from its cultural roots. Only on this basis can those new cultural identities be created that are to be captured in the legislation of the countries involved so that the existence of a multicultural society can also find expression in its legislative branch. This approach, which applies to education, professional training and to social and political organization, will increase the likelihood of success in interpreting the past, organizing the present and planning the future.

Science and technology harbor the genetic code of the societies that brought them forth. While culture expresses a people's adaptation to their natural surroundings, technology supplies the means by which they change those surroundings. Here, too, we can see an elementary point of contact between technology and culture, for they are in a state of mutual interaction. Science and technology, as they exist today, have a tendency to jeopardize cultural plurality and to supplant it with Western industrial culture. The technologies of the Western industrial states have taken hold of Latin America with no awareness of their enervating effect. The transfer of Western technology has helped to exclude a large portion of the world's population from technological evolution.

A view of technology based on the idea that science and technology are neutral falls far short of the truth. Even in the Andes Pact states, modernity can be understood only when this concept is brought into relation with traditional cultures. Hence, the demand that these cultures seek a form of modernity that accords with their own historic traditions. But the only way this can be accomplished is with indigenous technology.

Allegedly political and economic conflicts in the Third and Fourth Worlds and the industrializing countries are in fact nothing more than hidden conflicts of religion and culture. Rather than adapting education to the economy, we should bring economic evolution into line with the opportunities and needs of education. Human beings must be placed at the center of this evolution, for only in this way can the identity of cultures and nations and the authenticity of their evolution be vouchsafed. Education must emphasize not so much the transmission and reproduction, or even imitation, of imported technology as the creative and constructive power of the groups that make up a culture. Only this conglomeration of forces will lead to the emergence of an indigenous technology.

Attention must also be paid to local evolution, together with its cultural values. These local developments must be made to stand apart from the leveling influence of global culture, otherwise it will be impossible for technology to cultivate indigenous roots or for technological innovations to be tailored to specific localities. For reasons of security, we must avoid endangering the cultural personality of a country and instead try to bring it into harmony with national and economic evolution.

The active involvement of large segments of the population leads to a diversification of the forms of human existence. This truth also applies to the Andes region. Cultures, nations and societies must recall their intrinsic values in order to ward off internal instability, to make full use of their capacities and to believe in their own progress, whether this progress is material and quantitative, or human and qualitative. In this way, the potential inherent in any culture, in one form or another, can be stimulated and made manifest.

The example of the Andes Pact states makes it abundantly clear that political independence by itself is not enough to solve the problems of development. This is why the struggle for cultural identity, combined with an increase in technology, is so important. Technology is always intimately connected with the economic goals of the producers, with that realm of "surplus value" which forms the bedrock of any economy.

Giving scientific knowledge a social purpose allows basic criteria to be determined for the future importation of technology. Productive powers always define a new social order. This applies in particular to the urgently needed restitution of present-day technology to the traditional cultures of the Andes region. Technology is called upon to reestablish a natural bridge between science and production. In mutual interaction, a new cultural form of adaptation must arise to enrich the national scientific policies of the individual countries in the Andes region.

The national policy of science and technology has its center of gravity in the improvement of human resources, whether they be scientific researchers or technological innovators. A development strategy for science and technology can be valid only if it takes into account mid-range and long-term consequences beyond the confines of five-year plans. This is especially the case if we are intent on incorporating science and technology within the state using the three stages of evaluation, assimilation and integration.

Scientific activity must be conducted as part of a learning process that leads to concrete results in the industrial sector. Any reorientation of science and technology must give its results a social significance by means of specific training programs in the school system or in adult education. In this way, scientific activities that generate new knowledge will be linked to production techniques, with the emphasis falling on the reconciliation of modernity with a traditional technological basis of production.

Technological innovation depends on various economic factors, e.g., the type of market involved and the availability and price of productive forces. Industrial enterprises can be the basic marketing factor for technological development, provided that the company, rather than being just the recipient of these technologies, is an active force and can itself contribute to the increase of knowledge.

A new governmental policy must be devised that fosters the growth of an economic environment conducive to technological innovation in business enterprises. The center of focus should be shifted from the laboratory to the needs of these business enterprises.

Technological changes are the mandatory prerequisite of productivity, which is made up of three factors: technological progress, business management and the institutionalization of economic activity. But the concept of productivity also includes such factors as worker efficiency, the availability of capital, natural resources and especially the country's history, religion and culture. To upgrade these factors within a country is to increase the innovative potential of its productive sector, and thus its competitiveness in the world market.

Science and Technology in the Andes Region: Relations and Idiosyncracies

The human view of the world has changed in the course of evolution. Starting with the magic-mythical tradition in pre- and paleohistoric cultures, it has passed through various interim religions to a scientific view that, at the present time, pervades technological civilization. In the Andes Pact states, however, rudiments of magic-mythical thought still exist alongside the scientific world view, with both levels seeming to be mutually exclusive. Herein lies the essence of the problem. The major contribution of the West has been, and still is, the application of scientific methods, and thus of a world view made up of abstractions and empirical observations.

A distinction must be made between countries in which the evolution of scientific activity has led directly to progress in production technology, and those in which knowledge building has not been similarly transformed into technology. The Andes Pact states are of the latter category.

Countries with a history of indigenous technology underwent an internal process of accumulation (as in western Europe) or of integration (as in the United States and Japan). The result in these cases was the systematic creation of knowledge in a process linked to organic production and grounded in production technologies that, in turn, derived from scientific thought and technological discoveries. The fusion of technology with evolutionary thought is known as the scientific-technological revolution. This revolution, spread over long expanses of human history, was a complex and multifaceted affair during which science and technology mutually conditioned each other. In western Europe, this line of development, over the last three hundred years, remarkably increased the human awareness of industry.

The evolution of Western thought differs profoundly from that of the Andes culture. Looking at its origin in the Hellenic period, we can see how the potential for abstract thought slowly emerged in pre-Socratic philosophy. Aristotle elaborated early systems of logic and methodology. The Greeks were aware of humankind's ability to grasp the world in concepts. This same awareness pervaded the Roman Empire and, later, the European Middle Ages. A preexistent divine order formed the cornerstone of the world order. Islamic culture, which influenced Europe toward the end of the Middle Ages, helped develop symbolic expression and furthered the use of abstract concepts, e.g., algebra. The investigation of natural phenomena during this period was practiced by alchemists. The Renaissance strengthened the human capacity for exact observation. This benefitted the natural sciences, mediated between abstract concepts and natural phenomena and opened up the path to modern science.

Western philosophers mused on the possibility of inanimate machines and made systematic astronomical observations as an aid to navigation. The contributions of Copernicus and Galileo eventually led to the triumph of rationality over dogma and ushered in a transition from religion to science. Newton continued along this same path by introducing the idea that the universe was predictable and followed discrete laws which could be discovered and tested. Since then, science's contribution to the development of production technologies has expanded enormously.

Countries with indigenous histories of science and technology, unlike those with traditional values sustained by magic and myth, were nourished by the belief that humankind is in principle capable of comprehending, predicting and controlling events in government and politics, in society and the economy, and—not least of all—in nature. In the world of the Andes region, still immersed in magic and myth, this belief was unthinkable.

Being largely reliant on borrowed technology, the Andes Pact states did not develop production technologies on their own that were grounded in science and capable of generating knowledge.

To a certain extent, Venezuela constitutes an exception. Until the Second World War, it was primarily an agricultural country relying on animal husbandry, with limited economic success. Its political evolution was stunted by dictatorships. All of this changed radically during the oil boom. The spectacular rise of the oil industry during the Second World War made the country one of the most affluent in Latin America, although it had to wait until 1958 for political stability. Compared to the other countries of the Andes Pact, Venezuela's agrarian reforms took on a shape of their own, as they were not part of a revolutionary process and were limited in scope.

The process of democratization in Venezuela was aided and abetted by its agrarian reforms. In consequence, the agrarian sector was accorded a political role of a sort unknown elsewhere. Between 1960 and 1980 the number of job offerings rose to become 60 percent greater than in any other Latin American economy; capital accumulation rose accordingly. During the same period, the Latin American economies used 19 percent of their resources for investment; in Venezuela, this figure was 33.2 percent. On the other hand, Venezuela faced a problem that was to become typical of Latin America as a whole: capital flight and an inability to integrate productive resources in the manufacturing of goods and services.

Today, even Venezuela—for all its many pronouncements to the contrary—has failed to produce an explicit technology policy to deal with the creation, evaluation, selection, utilization, adaptation, improvement and diffusion of technologies involved in the industrial process. Venezuela is still dependent on completely secular matter, developing a separate form of colonization following the conversion to Christianity. Even if we regard modern science and technology as European traditions, there is no reason why they cannot be assimilated homogeneously into other cultures. A step-by-step process of recovering and upgrading the traditional basis of technology in the Andes Pact states must not be mistaken for a regression to a putative Golden Age or an uncritical assessment of past achievements.

In Latin America, the disappearance of indigenous technologies was more radical than in late-medieval Europe. As the colonial powers were interested solely in exploiting natural resources, most of the technologies they introduced were alien to Andean culture. To develop indigenous technology in a country, however, it is important to cultivate its traditional technological foundations.

The pre-Columbian cultures painstakingly subdivided their ecology in order to make appropriate use of their resources as the basis of traditional culture. A number of rudiments remained after colonization to serve as a basis for the further development of traditional technology today. This is important in light of the increasing need for local scientific and technological activities. In post-colonial Andean culture, these traditions have remained in a state of limbo. All the same, they are extremely important for the Andes Pact states. They are an integral component of their cultural heritage and will continue to be important in the future.

The contribution of traditional production goes beyond the aspect of technology, thereby helping to affirm the cultural and political identity of a country. The pre-Hispanic Andean cultures, for example, had a tradition of dividing territory into different economic and ecological areas to attain a vertical control and a high degree of ecological balance. This traditional link to the environment, calling for a wide spectrum of viable technologies, was in effect severed by the Spanish conquest.

It is important to identify which traditional technologies can now be brought to bear on modern technology. The selective improvement of traditional technology opportunities, particularly in agriculture and the agrarian industry, might embrace a wide array of social and economic activities.

Indigenous technology presupposes a new order of scientific activity. The objective is to adapt the traditional agrarian economy in order to improve traditional technological agrarian techniques with the aid of scientific research. In this way, the productive system can be redesigned to meet the actual needs of the population.

Both factors—the evolution of new forms of science with an expressly local bias, and the rediscovery of traditional knowledge and technology—illustrate the many ways of building up indigenous science and technology. Care must be taken to ensure that the magic-mythical impetus of pre-Columbian culture is transmuted to a simplicity and objectivity that offers real starting points for modern science. To do this, it is imperative that the educational system of the Andes Pact states be changed both in its structure and its contents.

The Priority of Indigenous Technology and the Precedence of Education

In order to make science and technology indigenous, a number of factors must come into play. Among these are educative technology, with a simultaneous emphasis on traditional cultural heritage for integration purposes, and the creation of favorable preconditions for economic, social and political transformation.

Education has a two-fold task: to inculcate an awareness of modern science and technology, and to preserve the cultural heritage. This should be sufficient to supply the conceptual tools necessary to create an indigenous foundation for technology. Science and tradition must coexist organically; this is possible only if they are allowed to interact, both materially and spiritually. *Science and technology can never become indigenous as long as the social, economic and political fabric of these countries remains the same.*

The process of indigenization must be selective, and it must take place gradually so that the technological revolution can be carefully adjusted with a view to cultural compatibility. Nor should this process be allowed to destroy indigenous technology; on the contrary, the tools and equipment of production technology must be made indigenous on the basis of scientific discoveries.

At the center of any strategy for autonomous development is the way that scientific knowledge building is combined with the evolution of modern production techniques and the systematic revitalization and assessment of indigenous technology. This triumvirate of factors can lead to a progressive substitution of borrowed technology in the Andes region, but only if we accept that this process will be a slow one with only middle- and long-term gains. Key concepts, such as efficiency, success and obsolescence, must be given new meanings so that the borrowed technological foundations can first be replaced in the educative and professional training sectors while the country's scientific-technological potential is being made indigenous. In order to set up these structures, it is important that compensatory institutional arrangements be made to govern wages and prices. This will prevent highly productive modern technologies from destroying traditional technologies with a lower productivity, thereby allowing the latter to be upgraded one step at a time.

Political and economic decision making calls for special organizational prerequisites that are still lacking in the Andes Pact states. The institutional history of this region illustrates the slow pace of its research and service institutions, deriving from poor financial backing ever since the colonial period and the nineteenth-century wars of liberation. Latin America never had a large-scale demand for knowledge and services. Even the nuclei of these institutions lacked structural backing.

The more rigorously a state develops its science and technology to integrate them organically into a system of production, the less need there is to distinguish between scientific and technological policy, and the greater the possibility of triggering a chain reaction of innovation.

To be indigenous invariably means to be on one's own, and thus to be ecologically responsible. Only on this basis is it possible to make structural changes in order to progress from borrowed technology to indigenous technology, and thereby to anchor an independent citizenry in the decision-making process.

The future world civilization must consist of a dialogue among national cultures, as befits the plurality of human culture.

To change technology policy, four points are essential: (1) the creation of local demand for technology, (2) an increase in the capacity to absorb technology, (3) the regulation of technological imports, and (4) an indigenous production of technology.

In the future, the Andes Pact states should examine the complementariness of these factors. Since one of the principal problems is the low demand for local technology, the first step must be to make indigenous technology attractive at the national, regional and subregional levels. This can be done by inverting the demand for foreign technology and aligning it with scientific and technological activity that meets the actual socioeconomic needs of the population.

Bilateral and multilateral agreements could be used by the Andes Pact states to regulate application at the regional and subregional levels. Venture capital is still required for the development of indigenous technologies, for dispensing low-term credits so that research centers in private businesses can apply these technologies, for the services of technology research institutes and for direct financial support of the scientific technological infrastructure.

By applying these tools in combination at the legal and organizational level, it should be possible to generate substantial growth in the demand for indigenous technology, thereby ensuring that the Andes Pact states have an efficient and autonomous science and technology of their own.

The goal is to equip businesses with an improved capacity to understand technological principles in order to consolidate the specific conditions for indigenous technology. The quality of technology and services would then rise on the regional and national levels. Step by step, the capacity of a country to absorb and master imported technology—and thereby to halt the disintegration of its own technological cohesion—will gradually give way to the emergence of indigenous technology. Imported technology must interact profitably with indigenous technology in order to offset the domination of borrowed technology and to ensure a smooth transfer of technological knowledge. Research and development projects must appear alongside a supportive institutional infrastructure with the ultimate goal of producing an indigenous technology in keeping with the primacy of culture and the needs of the population.

Imported technology, then, should not simply be adapted, but also modified and combined with indigenous technology in underdeveloped countries as part of a quest for imaginative solutions. Technological independence and, ultimately, greater political leverage would be the result. The process of attaining technological independence must come about in the context of alternative development strategies.

In recent decades, and especially since the 1960s, Latin America has witnessed an increasing awareness of the importance of science and technology. The Science and Technology Conference in La Castala, organized by UNESCO in 1965, marked a milestone, as did the efforts of the OAS in 1960 to create a unit for technological development and the report on science policy issued by the American Health Organization in 1966. Even at this time, structural features appeared that later influenced the 1970s, 1980s and 1990s: a shortage of highly skilled workers, a lack of financial resources, an absence of an institutional infrastructure for science and technology and a lopsided relation between indigenous and imported technology.

In the years between 1960 and 1970, the number of students registered at universities of the Andes Pact states tripled. However, unlike in North America and Europe, most of them were enrolled in the humanities and social sciences, not in the natural sciences. Moreover, after completing their studies the graduates seldom took up professions that had a bearing on scientific and technological development.

A glance at Europe suffices to illustrate the deficiency of the Andes Pact states on this point. At the end of the 1960s, approximately 48 percent of university students in Belgium, for example, were enrolled in fields related to science and technology; in Norway the figure was 31 percent, in the Netherlands, 43 percent; in Switzerland, 52 percent; and in Sweden, 31 percent. In France, 30 percent of the students began around 1965–66 to take up careers in the natural sciences at the beginning of their university studies. Similar figures are revealed in England (28 percent) and Germany (25 percent).

At Latin American universities, however, the natural sciences continued to remain far back in rank of importance. At the end of the 1960s, for example, and at the beginning of the 1970s, expenses for the natural sciences amounted only to 5.5 percent of the budget allotted to higher education. Positions for post-graduate researchers were so rare that a majority of students emigrated to the United States. Statistics compiled by the OAS reveal that in the early 1960s in Latin America, there was an average of 0.5 natural scientists per 10,000 population. This is one-tenth of the figure for the United States. In recent decades, about 2 percent of the gross national product was spent worldwide on research and development; in the Andes Pact states this figure was never higher than 0.3 percent.

Considering that in the mid-1970s the countries of Latin America could boast of about 10 percent of the world's population, it is clear just how deep the gulf was and is that separates them from the industrialized countries. Even the shift from the humanities to the natural sciences during this period was extremely slow. In 1970, only 5 percent of university graduates took degrees in the natural sciences, 14 percent in engineering, 14 percent in medicine, and 4 percent in the agricultural sciences. In 1978, these figures had hardly changed, being respectively 3, 14, 14 and 4 percent.

Since the mid-1970s, there has been a noticeable increase of investment in science and technology. Nevertheless, the amounts are still insufficient, since the Andes Pact states have not placed priority on overall scientific-technological development, without which there can be no economic growth or productive innovation. Even in the mid-1970s, the number of researchers in the Andes Pact states was a mere one-twentieth of that in the United States. The relative upsurge of financial resources for science and technology in the mid-1970s was limited to Mexico, Venezuela and Brazil. In contrast, these outlays hardly increased at all in the Andes countries. The national committees for science and technology, together with their planning staffs, were extraordinarily inefficient. As a result, research became more and more fragmentary, as is evident even today. Institutional fragility followed upon political and economic instability. To reduce this problem, it is necessary to press forward with training programs for researchers, technicians and governmental officials, for example, by means of post-graduate programs of study. In this way, indigenous technology could be given a firm basis in the system of education.

The commercialization of technology is hampered by the excessive influence of governmental bureaucracy evident throughout managerial circles. This affects the registration of licensing agreements, legislative and administration measures governing technological imports and the importation of capital goods, which is one of the major means of technology transfer.

In short, initiatives in the Andes region fell short of what was needed, despite the efforts of the OAS and its Regional Programme for Scientific and Technological Development in the 1970s, the attempts by UNESCO to establish a regional network of scientists and research projects in physics, biology, chemistry and the social sciences, or the efforts of the United Nations to set up regional and subregional projects to facilitate technological cooperation in the iron and steel industries, as well as in agriculture and education. The hopes raised at the end of the 1970s proved to be deceptive.

The lopsided relation between local and imported technology also led to characteristic shortfalls on internal markets in the Andes Pact states, to limitations in the availability of capital and to a further reduction in the qualifications of unskilled laborers. This reduced the demand for local technology even further. Political programs must see to it that scientific activity is not kept separate from society as a whole, but is integrated into a national policy. This also explains the stultifying effect of having scientific and technological research carried out not so much by private companies as by state institutions—by governmental agencies and the organs of higher education—as is the case in the Andes region. This situation cries out for fundamental changes, particularly in the area of professional training, which can serve as a springboard for the indigenization process.

The Andes Pact states must ratify guidelines for technology transfer within the Andes region in order to strengthen their position against the technology-exporting countries. The amount of direct foreign investment in local technological development must be monitored.

The nations of the Andes Pact must work toward reconstructing their ethnic groups, not only for a mercantile phase, but also for an industrial phase. The goal should be to incorporate these groups into the economic life of the country, since they make up a large percentage of the population. Native culture must partake of the national economy in relation to its importance.

In the Andes region, the replacement of traditional forms of production caused many age-old indio technologies to vanish. This process must be rectified and directed to new ways of revitalizing the traditional heritage. The starting points for a gradual indigenization of scientific and technological evolution in the Andes Pact states must be systematically defined. And one eminently practical way of doing this is by including traditional technology.

Modern science must be integrated into the Latin American cultural heritage, rather than standing apart from it as it has until now, thereby preventing a process of creation from emerging. What is required is a basic anthropological perspective that does justice to native versions of such key concepts as success and progress. Beyond mere material improvements, a change in attitudes and postures is required, one that is related to the changes of thought, values, creeds and mental behavior that human beings undergo as part of their culture. Nonmaterial changes are essentially no less profound and significant than material changes. Cultural values and intellectual history influence the ways and means by which we conceptualize problems, and especially the way we adapt and execute scientific activities in order to integrate them into our local world. Even the formation of hypotheses and theories is subject in a deeper sense to culture.

Not until careful steps have been taken in the field of education to reconcile modern science and traditional culture will it be possible to create a favorable climate for the transformation of social, economic and political structures in the Andes Pact states. In this way, a truly need-oriented policy (whether material or nonmaterial) can be implemented that outlines a vision of the nation's own future and is indigenous in the full sense of the term, coming from the heart of the culture. There must be an inextricable and mutual bond between the growth of indigenous science and technology and alternative development strategies. One level cannot exist without the other, and both are necessary to overcome the *dependencia* that has relegated the Andes Pact states to a lower rung of development.

Technological pragmatism and functionality must be "Andicized" in order to render them compatible. This is also a prerequisite for a new investment behavior, whether economic or real-political. The magical-mythical tradition of the Andes region, with its metaphysics and transcendence, should be reconciled with the empirical and objective methodology of modern science and technology. This is the crux of the entire matter. And it can come about only by a process of gradual change and active (rather than merely passive) acculturation on the various levels of culture and society.

Political strategies aimed at this goal should follow the principle of step-by-step change in order ultimately to attain a fundamentally new order of the state and the economy. Care must be taken to establish a basis for scientific research in the Andes Pact states that is fully in accord with these countries and their multifarious historical backgrounds.

The following strategic guidelines should be observed by the international economic community:

1) A basic structural transformation should be carried out in a way that allows the economy of Latin America to reorient exports on a world level, to open up substitution markets and to pursue

selective import policies that will permit greater independence in the long run.

2) A new formative policy must be devised for those sectors of the economy with greater potential for development.

3) Natural resources must be controlled with the same attention as their rational utilization and local exploitation.

4) High priority should be given to internal Latin American trade, including a system of payment based on floating-value units of account rather than the United States dollar.

5) Cooperation with other "southern" countries should be pursued, including those of Asia, Africa and the Pacific basin.

6) New forms of industrialization should favor production methods that ensure internal demand not only in each country, but also regionally, subregionally and interregionally.

7) A Latin American policy of nutrition should be created that guarantees a basic nutritional minimum for the region.

8) Similarly, an improved internal Latin American system of transportation should be established.

9) A system of financing should be set up to secure efforts to exchange money within Latin America.

10) Economic trade mechanisms must be created to stand up to the world economy and to institute new guidelines on this basis.

11) For the future process of change, it is important that Latin America continues to attain greater autonomy so as to emphasize its political and cultural identity.

12) A line of development aimed at the continuity of the state, society and economy, and embracing the whole of Latin America should be set in motion.

13) The utilization of Latin America's natural resources must be ensured by means of a dynamic market.

14) The participation of large segments of the population in the private economy and in public decision-making bodies is desirable, as is a dramatic improvement in the system of education.

15) Income must be redistributed over a larger social spectrum to strike a greater balance within society as a whole.

16) An end must be put to technological dependence on the First World states. A more active and balanced exchange is essential if Latin America is to develop an indigenous technology policy with corresponding managerial and executive capacities.

Up to now, most of these points have been ignored in practical policy making. In the future, they should be given special attention in order to form a more realistic assessment of development opportunities in the Andes Pact states and to ensure that these countries, too, will contribute to modern civilization.

Suggestions for Further Reading

Adelman, I., and C. Taft Morris. *Economic Growth and Social Equity in Developing Countries*. Stanford: Stanford University Press, 1973.

Altimir, Oscar. *Las búsquedas de nuevas alternativas para el desarrollo de América latina*. Junte del Acuerdo Cartagena. Seminario sobre el Grupo Andino: Nuevos enfoques para el desarrollo y la integración subregional, 17–19, Lima, September 1985.

Antonorsi-Blanco, Marcel. "Estilo tecnológico y proceso de creación y evaluación de tecnologías." *Ecología y planificación del desarrollo: la alternativa des ecodesarollo*. Eds. R. Gonzalez Almeida and Raizabel Andrade. I. Congreso Nacional de Ciencia y Tecnología, Caracas, July 1975.

Avalos, I., and M. Antonorsi. *La planificación ilusoria*. Caracas: Editorial Ateneo, 1981.

Baarck, Erick, and Andrew Jamison. *The Technology and the Culture Problematique*. Lund, 1985.

Benassy, J.P. *The Economics of Market Disequilibrium*. New York: Basic Books, 1982.

Bhalla, A.S. *Blending New Technologies in Traditional Sectors*. Oficina Internacional de Trabajao (OIT), Geneva, November 1985.

Bifani, Paolo. *Deasfíos de la biotecnología para la política científica y tecnológico*. Documento de Trabajo, Oficina Internacional del Trabajo (OIT), Geneva, 1986.

Bravo Bresani, Jorge. " Anotaciones sobre el desarrollo tecnológico en el Perú." *Aproximación crítica a la tecnología en el Perú*. Lima: Mosca Azul, 1982.

Carr, M. *Economically Appropriate Technologies for Developing Countries: An Annotated Bibliography*. Grupo de Desarrollo de Tecnología Intermedia, n.p., 1976.

Coleman, J.S., et al. *Equality of Educational Opportunity*.Washington, DC: Government Printing Office, 1966.

Comisión de las Comunidades Europeas. *Europe 1995—nuevas tecnologías y cambio social*. Informe FAST, FUNDESCO, Madrid, 1986.

Comisión Económica para América Latina y el Caribe (CEPAL). *Crisis y desarrollo: presente y futuro de América latina y el Caribe*. Reunión de expertos sobre crisis y desarrollo de América latina y el Caribe, Naciones Unidas, Santiago de Chile, 29 April–3 May 1983.

____. *América latina y el programa de acción de Viena: ciencia y tecnología para el desarrollo de los años ochenta*. Noveno período de sesiones del comté de expertos gubernamentales de alto nivel (CEGAN), Naciones Unidas, Montevideo, 23–24 January 1984.

Concejo Nacional de Ciencia y Tecnología (CONCYTEC). *Situación estado de la tecnología en el Perú*. Lima: CONCYTEC, 1983.

_____. *Tecnología y desarrollo del medio rural*. Lima: CONCYTEC, 1983.

Contreras, H., et al. *Conservación de los recursos naturales y equilibrio ecológico en Venezuela*. Universidad Central de Venezuela/Universidad de los Andes, Caracas, 1978.

Cordova, A. "La estructura económica tradicional y el impacto petrolero en Venezuela." *Aspectos teóricos del subdesarrollo*. Eds. A. Cordova and H. Silva. Caracas: Universidad Central de Venezuela, 1973. pp. 129–154.

Cotlear, Daniel. *Technological and Institutional Change among the Peruvian Peasantry: A Comparison of Three Regions at Different Levels of Agricultural Development*. London: University of Oxford, 1986.

Dagnino, Renato P. *Novo desinvolvimento e novas tecnologías: una equação a resolver*. Mimeographed. XIII, February 1986.

Davilar, Guillermo. "Acerca de políticas tecnologías alternativas." *Aproximación crítica a la tecnología en el Perú*. Lima: Mosca Azul, 1982.

Ernst, Dieter. "Industrial Redeployment and Control over Technology—Consequences for the Third World." *Vierteljahresberichte* 83, 1981.

Flit, Isaías. *Tecnologías apropiadas o manejo apropiado de tecnologías*. Mexico, 1979.

Freeman, C. *The Economics of Industrial Innovation*. Francis Pinter, n.p., 1982.

Gallegos, H. "Administración pública versus administración privada: aspectos de eficiencia." *Revista venezolana de desarrollo administrativo*, No. 1 (1982): 107–116.

Galvez, Modesto. *Problemas y perspectivas de la investigación sobre tecnología campesina*. Primer seminario sobre tecnologías adecuadas, CCTA, Ayacucho, 1978.

García, Norberto, and Víctor Tokman. "Transformación, ocupación y crisis." *Revista de la CEPAL* 24, Naciones Unidas, Santiago de Chile, December 1984.

Green, Raúl H. *Amérique latine: tendances et changements des échanges agro-alimentaires*. Institut National de la Recherche Agronomique, Paris, March 1985.

Herfindahl, O. *Los recursos naturales en el desarrollo económico*. Siglo XXI. Mexico, 1970.

Hofstede, G. "The Cultural Relativity of Organizational Practices and Theories." *Journal of International Business Studies*, No. 3 (1983): 74–89.

Jencks, C. *Inequality*. New York: Harper Colophon Books, 1972.

Jenkins, G. *Non-agricultural Choice of Technique: An Annotated Bibliography of Empirical Studies*. Institute of Commonwealth Studies, Oxford, 1975.

Katz, Jorge. *Importación de tecnología, aprendizaje e industrialización dependiente*. Fondo de Cultura Económica, Mexico, 1976.

____. *Reflexiones acerca de la relación entre la capacidad tecnologíca interna, acumulación y productividad industrial*. FENAC, Forno de la empresa nacional sobre inter-relación entre "ciencia—tecnología—empresa" (Cuaderno No. 10), Buenos Aires, 1986.

Lancaster, K.J. *Consumer Demand: A New Approach*. New York: Columbia University Press, 1971.

Lehman, David. *Ecology and Exchange in the Andes*. Cambridge: Cambridge University Press, 1982.

Leon, J.B. *Ecología y ambiente en Venezuela*. Vol. 2. Colección Geografía de Venezuela Nueva, Ariel Seix Barral Venezolana, Caracas, 1981.

Mariátegui, José Carlos. *Ideología y política*. Lima: Biblioteca Amauta, 1969.

____. "El indigenismo en la literatura nacional." *Mundial* 345, Lima, 21 January 1927.

____. *Siete ensayos de interpretación de la realidad peruana*. Lima: Amauta, 1971.

Ominani, Carlos, ed. *La tercera revolución industrial*. Buenos Aires: Grupo Editor Latinoamericano, 1986.

Pérez, C. *Cambio estructural y asimilación de nuevas tecnologías en el sistema económico social: contribución al debate sobre los ciclos de Kondratiev*. Ministerio de Fomento, Caracas, 1983.

____. "Structural Change and Assimilation of New Technologies in the Economic and Social Systems." *Futures* 15, No. 5, October 1981.

Plaza, Orlando, and Marfil Francke. *Formas de dominio, economía y comunidades campesinas*. DESCO, Lima, 1985.

Prebisch, Raúl. "Renovar el pensamiento económico latinoamericano, un imperativo." *Comercio Exterior* 36, No. 6, June 1986.

Reynolds, Lloyd G. *Economic Growth in the Third World, 1850–1980*. New Haven: Yale University Press, New Haven, 1985.

Riggs, F.W. *Administration in Developing Countries: The Theory of Prismatic Society*. Boston: Houghton Mifflin Co., 1964.

Rosenberg, N. *Perspectives on Technology*. Cambridge: Cambridge University Press, 1976.

Sabel, C., and M. Piore. *The New Industrial Divide*. New York: Basic Books, 1985.

Sagasti, Francisco. "Hacia la incorporación de la ciencia y la tecnología en la concepción del desarrollo ." *El Trimestre Económico* I, No. 3, Summer 1983.

____. *Ciencia, tecnología y desarrollo latinoamericano*. Fondo de Cultura Económica, Mexico, 1981.

Sagasti, Francisco, et al. *Un decenio de transición*. Lima: GRADE, 1983.

Samaniego, Carlos. "La tecnología y los recursos agrobiológicos." *Aproximación crítica a la tecnología en el Perú*. Lima: Mosca Azul, 1982.

Samir, Amin. *Le développement inégal. Essai sur les formations sociales du capitalisme périphérique.* Paris, Editions du Minuit, 1973.

Sánchez, A. Pablo. *El ecodesarrollo, una importante alternativa para el desarrollo del espacio andino.* Lima, 1984.

Sánchez, Vicente. *Modalidades de desarrollo, relaciones internacionales y políticas ambientales.* Programa desarrollo y medio ambiente, El Colegio de México, Mexico City, December 1985.

Schultz, T. *Transforming Traditional Agriculture.* New Haven: Yale University Press, 1964.

Schumpeter, J.A. *Theorie der wirtschaftlichen Entwicklung.* n.p., 1912.

Soldi, Ana, and H. Lechtman. *La tecnología en el mundo andino.* Vol. 1. UNAM, Mexico, 1981.

Tokman, Víctor. "El proceso de acumulación y la debilidad de los actores." *Revista de la CEPAL* 26, Naciones Unidas, August 1985.

Troll, Carl. "Die Stellung der Indianer-Hochkulturen im Landschaftsaufbau der tropischen Anden." *Zs. der Gesellschaft für Erdkunde zu Berlin*, No. 3/4, Berlin, 1943.

United Nations Industrial Development Organization (UNIDO). *Industry 2000— New Perspectives*, Vienna 1979.

_____. *Reindustrialization in the Advanced Countries and Its Effects on the Developing Countries, in Particular in Latin America.* Vienna, November, 1984.

_____. "Report of the International Forum on Technological Advances and Development." Tbilisi, 12–16 April 1983.

Urquidi, Víctor, Vicente Sánchez and Eduardo Terrazas. *Perspectivas y alternativas de América latina ante los problemas mundiales.* Centro Tepoztlán, Mexico, May 1981.

Vaitsos, C. *Comercialización de tecnología en el Pacto Andino.* Instituto de Estudio Peruanos, Lima, 1973.

_____. *Distribución del ingreso y empresas transnacionales.* Fondo de Cultura Económica, Mexico, 1974.

EIGHT

MODERNITY AND RATIONALISM

Summary

The dichotomy between tradition and modernity is the central issue of our times—and not only in the Andes region. Latin American culture can be successful in the future only if all its people participate in its economy and society within the fully integrated structure of the state. The unity of Western rational thought can be counteracted in the Andes Pact states by a multiplicity of cultures that look back upon an historical rationalism of their own. Modern rationalism has failed to take hold in these countries because it is felt to be a serious threat to their freedom and independence. An idiomatic form of modernity can arise in Latin America only through an interaction between secularization and the integration of existing political, cultural and religious orders.

Historical and Instrumental Rationalism

A new national self-image is beginning to take shape in the Andes Pact states, an image in which modernity is not only a positive force for structural change, but also one of its consequences. The Andes Pact states illustrate the fundamental lesson that modernity must result primarily from the internal dynamics of a country and its society, rather than being imposed by external forces. This explains why the Andes Pact states have had such difficulty in defining their internal modernity: it is not a product of their own histories. Modernity cannot be equated with the spread of Western values. It must take on a specifically Andean form, drawing on age-old features of culture and religion in order to have an impact on the country's internal dynamics.

A distinction must be made between modernity in consumption and modernity in production; these two forms of modernity need not coincide. Before we can speak of integrated development in the Andes region, the process of modernization must be made to involve not only local elites but also large segments of the population, including the indios.

The central issue of our times is the dichotomy between tradition and modernity—and not only in the Andes region. Modernity, when detached from the peculiarities of local culture, runs the risk of being equated with a progressive annihilation of all the defining features of culture, society and religion. We must fight against an image that pictures modern civilization as an all-enveloping uniformity beholden to Western rationalism.

When modernity is conceived as a universalist project, it threatens the cultural identity of a country, casting its different ethnic groups and levels of culture into a single heap and subordinating culture to scientific-technological modernization. Due to the heterogeneity of human culture, beliefs, traditional political movements and ideologies that are rooted in culture often come into conflict with the goals of production streamlining. As a result, modernity is far removed from the heart of Latin American culture with its peripheral economy.

Countries on the periphery cannot accept the hegemony of a universalist Western model, yet intercultural dialogue becomes impossible if we proceed exclusively on the assumption that we are dealing with different kinds of natural science and technology. The Andes Pact states must take a mediating position in this process in order to link these two levels together. We must come to understand why, and in what way, human beings are one and the same and yet so different in their past histories. The Andes Pact states must attempt to forge a unity between these two extremes, a unity that reconciles universality and particularity, tradition and modernity, rationalism and intuition, as handed down by their pre- and post-colonial history. In short, the modernity of the Andes region must be redefined, and to do so its past history must be reintegrated. Latin American culture can be successful in the future only if all of its people participate in society and the economy within the fully integrated structure of the state. This will bring the whole of Latin America a good deal farther along the road to autonomy.

For the Andes region, then, we cannot presuppose a Western notion of modernity. Nor should we equate modernization with modernity. We must examine the multiplicity of ways and means toward modernization and the unity of modernity in order to pinpoint the specific cultural connections leading to this unity.

The world today is divided by a hardened stance between the universalism of Western rationalism on the one hand and cultural identity on the other. Hidden in this stance is a potential civil war between the two hemispheres. For the Andes Pact states, then, it is essential to conduct comparative studies with the aim of initiating changes in politics, culture and society. Only in this way can they ensure that Western rationalism does not gain supremacy over the region's historical modes of cognition.

Modernity came late to Latin America and was imposed from the outside. We should recall that the very concept of modernity is a product of post-eighteenth-century European history. It then spread to all those regions of the world that were subject to European domination, and hence to Latin America. This presents us with a problem which has yet to be properly conceptualized. For Europe, Latin America was more than a geographical discovery; it also meant confronting alien and, at first glance, unintelligible histories, and involved a basic encounter with Latin American myths. Europe's vision expanded as it came into contact with the reality of the New World. And it was the native cultures of the Andes in particular that triggered a broadening of the European imagination.

The ideas of modernity would have been unthinkable without this new perspective of the future that entered the human imagination. At the same time that Europe was aspiring to achieve the promise of modernity, it was hampered by a struggle against feudal hierarchies, absolute monarchies and the primacy of mercantilism. It was at this moment that Latin America entered Europe's historical purlieus and thereby precipitated the outgrowth of modernity in the seventeenth and eighteenth centuries. In the course of history, Latin America, reinforced by post-seventeenth-century North America, became not only a recipient but also an agent of change in the historical universe.

When Alexander von Humboldt travelled to Latin America, he was at first evidently surprised at the extent to which Latin America's intellectual elite and politicians shared the ideas of their

European colleagues. Pablo de Olavide, a Peruvian, achieved fame in European Enlightenment circles; he befriended Voltaire and joined the inner circle of the French Encyclopedists and the savants who determined the course of the Enlightenment in Spain. Even during the age of Latin American revolutions, political philosophers propagated a radical liberalism of the sort that found expression in Latin America's constitutions.

Modernity in Europe went hand in hand with a consolidation of the capital-intensive market economy and its consequences for the production of goods and services and for interpersonal relations. In Latin America, however, especially in the first half of the eighteenth century, modernity took a different course. The social necessities of modernity were confronted by a fragmentary mercantile economy. This gap left its mark on Latin America's self-image until well into the nineteenth century, and determined its notions regarding modernity.

In Europe, modernity became a consolidated concept that affected the daily lives of many people. It thus became established not only as a nexus of theoretical, politico-philosophical ideas, but also in social practice. In Latin America, however, the gap between the modernist philosophies that sustained the state and their actual impact on everyday society and the economy grew wider and wider, even within the political institutions themselves. In the nineteenth and twentieth centuries in particular, Latin America permitted modernity as an intellectual construct, but not as a factor in the workings of society and culture.

Latin America, then, developed a paradoxical stance toward modernity, a fractured relation which has remained an obstacle to indigenous development to the present day. In North America and Europe, modernity evolved under the aegis of pragmatic rationalism. Here, again, Latin America was different. The history of modernity began, for all practical purposes, with the encounter between Europe and the Americas at the end of the fifteenth century. In the resultant colonial empire, native Andean rationalism was unable to find its way into government and society, and still less so following the revolutions of the nineteenth century. Originally, the concept of rationalism in Latin America meant a historical rationalism which was also related to pre-Columbian cultures, to liberation from arbitrary rule and despotism. It was a battle cry in the fight against the existing political order. This historical rationalism stood opposed to purely pragmatic rationalism, yet it rarely entered political practice, becoming instead a sort of theoretical ideal for Latin America.

Modernity of the pragmatic Western sort was in keeping with an Anglo-Saxon tradition linking British hegemonical power and the supremacy of North America. Latin America, having evolved from the tradition of sixteenth-century Catholic scholasticism, did not partake of this Anglo-Saxon tradition of pragmatic rationalism. The logic of a capital-intensive economy and the primacy of reasoning took on a different character in Latin American history. Latin America and especially the Andes Pact states developed their own indigenous rationalism that is difficult to reconcile with European modernity. It had imaginative foundations with utopian undertones of the sort known in fourteenth- and fifteenth-century Europe. Its vehicle was the oligarchic creole culture that presided over the social, economic and cultural disintegration of the Latin American countries. The conflict with pragmatic rationalism and European modernity is plain to see.

For the Andes Pact states, the native rationalism of pre-Columbian culture is a lasting and mandatory legacy. Though these traditions have mingled with European and North American rationalism, the acculturation process has been fragmentary and largely unsuccessful. To the present day, Latin America has remained a living and ancient source of an historical rationalism that at times assumes the guise of a utopian rationalism of liberation with visionary, but hardly real-political qualities. This rationalism continues to have an impact on thought and action in everyday culture, and on the relation between state and society. Given the rift between state and civilian society, there is a contradiction between the cry for freedom and the capacity for order and authority. Latin America's historical rationalism is not capable of mastering the relation between freedom and order to the same extent as pragmatic Western rationalism, which embeds the demand for freedom within its concept of modernity. In Latin America, the relation between private freedom and the claims of state and society for order has taken on a completely different form than that of Europe or North America. The relation between the private sphere and the public domain of the state is not organized and structured in the same way as in Europe and North America, nor does Latin America have a rationalism of the marketplace—to the detriment of its indigenous technology.

The point to be discussed is the emergence of a new, historical rationalism in the Andes Pact states, despite the increasingly universal scope of modernist culture. Obstacles to the development of indigenous technology must be removed.

In Latin America, especially toward the end of the eighteenth century, mercantilism underwent a metamorphosis that produced a stagnation in culture, politics and the economy, a stagnation not helped in the least by its colonial dependency. Whereas modernity in Europe was part of a gradual transmutation of state, culture and society that paved the way for the breakthrough of intensive market economy, developments in Latin America followed a different path from the end of the eighteenth century. In a retrospective sociohistorical context, modernity was linked with the economic stagnation and political disintegration that followed upon Latin American mercantilism.

In intellectual history no less than in politics, however, modernity took hold of Europe, went beyond the realm of interpersonal relations and manifested itself in the economy. This line of evolution never occurred in Latin America, where modernity largely remained a question of rhetoric, an abstract and imaginary phenomenon devoid of historical substance. The colonial nature of the Latin American state and society outlived the revolutions of the early nineteenth century, thereby preventing the state and the economy from consolidating. Rationalism could not be "Westernized" and made more pragmatic, since it did not harbor a genuine and viable promise of political and economic freedom and success. This was one of the early causes of the shortcomings of Latin America's economy and indigenous technology. Pragmatic rationalism, after all, was viewed as an outgrowth of European colonial hegemony, and later of North American economic supremacy. An overlap of pragmatic rationalism and political liberation was unknown in Latin America. *Modernity was equated with modernization, with the restructuring of the world to meet the needs of the hegemonical powers of Europe and North America.*

This helps to explain why Latin America, and especially the Andes Pact states, developed an intrinsic aversion to modernity. The triumph of pragmatic rationalism was equated with a victory of the colonial powers and was seen as a sign of bondage, even of political and cultural defeat. Latin America denied modernity for decades because it came cloaked in the mantle of modernization. For Latin America, pragmatic rationalism stood for the connection between rationalism and domination; it was placed on a par with Europe and North America and their "imperialistic" postures, as expressed in their economic hegemony, in the Monroe Doctrine of 1823, in the Alliance for Progress and in their supremacy following the Second World War. Latin America saw itself as the victim of modernization and blocked the path to a modernity rooted in its own culture by failing to assimilate modern rationalism. Even today, the Andes Pact states in particular are dominated by this dichotomy between pragmatic and historical rationalism. Then as now, pragmatic rationalism was equated with colonial dependency. Modern rationalism has yet to enter the history of the Andes Pact states.

The heterogeneity of society and culture was maintained in the indio populations of Peru and Ecuador, for example. This put Andean rationalism in even greater conflict with pragmatic rationalism: to the same extent that modern rationalism underwent a metamorphosis in the Andes Pact states, indio culture fell prey to political disintegration.

Historical Obstacles to Acculturation in the Andes Region

One reason why the Latin American identity differs from that of Europe and North America is that Latin America sees a different relation between history and time. In the Andes Pact states, the past merges into the present and there is less emphasis placed on the future. Pragmatic rationalism is contrasted with lost innocence. Even today, the Latin American view of reality is not without magical and mythical traits.

Rationalism in Latin America does not "demystify" the world, as Max Weber understood the term. The symbolic forms of art and literature underscore the original form of Latin American rationalism, giving rise to what Juan Rulfo and José Maria Arguedas have referred to as magical realism. Once again we note that Latin American rationalism and pragmatic rationalism are leagues apart.

Latin America has never ceased to be aware of its dependence on Europe and North America. This is one important reason why it is still searching for an alternative rationalism, and has continued to experiment with political and cultural utopias to the present day. Even so, Andean rationalism must eventually be brought into alignment with pragmatic rationalism. This future goal posits a Latin American identity defined ontologically by the multifarious historical factors that are now struggling to establish a new connection between, on the one hand, pragmatic rationalism with political and economic responsibility and, on the other, Latin America's own cultural and religious background.

Since the Industrial Revolution in Europe and North America, the interplay between science, technology, industry and political power has intensified. The interpretation of the universe has become more mechanistic, not least of all through the insights of physics. It is here that we encounter a major difference with the magic and myth of pre-Columbian culture. This discrepancy also accounts for the difficulty of adapting the Andean cultures to pragmatic rationalism and technology.

In the Western tradition, there arose a notion of infinite space, with all its theoretical implications. It is here that we find the principles of modern physics, with its mechanistic picture of the universe. Seen in this light, modern science is a phenomenon of the fifteenth and sixteenth centuries, causing a clean break with the medieval traditions of metaphysics and transcendence. At this time, people still relied on the muscular strength of animals until they, in turn, were replaced by machines and industrial production. The process that liberated people from physical labor called for a different concept of nature, one that had not yet arisen to the same extent in sixteenth-century Andean culture. There was nothing in Andean culture to resemble the streamlining and redistribution of labor that took place in the Judeo-Christian tradition. Medieval Europeans were influenced by two notions: that the world was created for humankind's benefit, and that labor was a form of atonement for original sin. These decisive factors were lacking in Andean culture.

Andean logic and rationalism suffered a collapse which can be seen all too clearly in its methods of agricultural production. The Andes region was noted for a lack of arable land; the soil on its steep slopes was heavily eroded. In consequence, agriculture was carried out on multilevel, ecological terraces. Andean agriculture centered on cultivation with the *takila*, a wooden plow, and the *raywana*, a wooden shovel. At the same time, we note how deeply Andean culture was rooted in mythology. Concepts such as *hanag pacha* and *urin pacha* (uphill world and downhill world) bear witness to this, as does the figure of Viracocha Pacha Yachachi, an

Andean deity. The revitalization of the ancient Andean myth known as *Taki Onyoy* is a manifestation of the colonial period which can be seen both as evidence of the incursion of the dominant Spanish culture and as a sign of resistance to the conquerors.

The traditional inhabitants of the Andes confronted time and space by means of a social organization that relied on solidarity among ethnic groups. The emphasis fell on manual labor; agricultural tools were rudimentary. Considering the later difficulties in developing an indigenous technology, it is especially significant that these tools were never improved or refined. Domination of nature by means of tools was an idea introduced to the Andean world by Europeans. The same applies to the associated forms of production, which presupposed that human beings were clearly distinct from nature. This presupposition did not exist in Andean mythology or agriculture. The alienation from nature provides an early explanation for later failures in the attempt to adapt Western technology; it also constitutes a major historical obstacle to economic development. The attempt to perfect production techniques, and thereby to improve rural production, brought with it a distribution of labor within society, and above all an abstraction from nature that conflicted with Andean mythology, logic and rationalism.

The Western tradition of reasoning proceeded from the general to the specific. It was based on analytic techniques that placed great value on abstraction and universality, a universality that was not found in the Andean experience. The Andes region was populated in widely dispersed ecological niches and crisscrossed with different climatic zones that inhibited uniform crops with large harvests. Thus, in the Inca state, sowing and harvesting by no means took place at the same time everywhere, as the positions of the stars and sun were never the same in the various parts of the empire. It should also be noted that the agricultural tool known as the *chakitakila* differed greatly in form and size, depending on the consistency of the soil, the vegetation and climatic conditions. Diversity was the order of the day. For example, more than one hundred fifty plants were cultivated in the Andes region for the production of foodstuffs. To reduce nature to the end of production was in keeping with Western thought, but not with pre-Hispanic Andean thought. This contrast is also underscored by the institution known as *mitmaq*, i.e., the simultaneous cultivation of different ecological terraces and their effects on society. Andean culture was never centered on machines whose functions determined the distribution of labor in society along the specialist lines. Specialization in the Western sense was foreign to Andean culture, which only recognized the categories of agriculture and handicrafts. Andean rationalism was a rationalism of ends, whereas Western rationalism was basically one of means. This fundamental distinction had to be assimilated during the colonial period; indeed, the distinction still persists. Besides a shortage of specialists, there was also a large degree of complacency well-suited to the basically static character of Andean culture. Both of these were and continue to be factors that obstruct the progress of technology and its subsequent economic dynamism.

We can see why the indigenous rationalism of the Andean region could not be brought into line with the ascent of Western logic. The same applied to the mechanization of private and professional life, since agrarian production in the Andes cultures was based on complementarity and multiplicity. The large number of types of crops cultivated in the Andes region decreased during the influx of Spanish colonization. The imposition of Western technology caused the soil to erode, and the highlands turned increasingly into that craggy wasteland with which the economies of the Andes Pact states, especially Peru and Ecuador, are still struggling today.

In contrast to Andean culture, European thought no longer recognized a mythical relation to nature. Instead, it was governed by the idea that nature was an object and stood apart from humanity as something separate. This separation was precisely captured in the Cartesian distinction between *res cogitans* and *res extense*. With the first signs that nature was being investigated scientifically using modern coordinates, the breach with scholastic tradition was complete. The scholastic tradition saw nature as a creative matrix *(natura naturans)* with, to a certain extent, a sacred character, since the natural order was flanked by a supernatural one. To a medieval thinker, however, nature was *victoria dei opificis*.

The central issue when drawing comparisons with Andean cultures and their systems of reasoning is the notion that nature can be dominated, a notion that arose in the aftermath of the seventeenth century. In 1620, Francis Bacon spoke of the knowledge of nature and its domination *(tantum possumus quantum scimus)*. Descartes, too, saw in scientific knowledge a subjugation of nature when he wrote in 1637 of the *maîtres et possesseurs de la nature*. To Descartes, nature was devoid of imagination. In contrast to the

Andean view, nature was not a divine authority but an empirical world. In the Andean view, nature was not quantifiable; nor was it, as in the Christian view, the servant of humankind. In the latter line of evolution, scientific progress ran parallel to the ascendence of rationalism. Condorcet spoke of the *progrès de l'esprit humain* and was celebrated in his own lifetime throughout Europe. He recognized, rightly, that the nascent scientific civilization was on its way to becoming a universal civilization.

In the emerging modern age, objects were increasingly defined by their functions. It was precisely this functional element that was lacking in Andean rationalism. The power lurking behind an object's function—a power recognized by such thinkers as Friedrich Georg Jünger, Ortega y Gasset, Erich Fromm, Ivan Illich and Raimundo Panikkar in a grand alliance for Western modernism— was unknown in Andean culture.

Problems of Modernity in Latin America

Today, as we have already seen in many instances, the Andes Pact states are still far from being scientific, industrialized and techno-logic countries. The reasons for this can be found in their relation to technology, their historical evolution and their present eco-nomic policies. No sooner had colonial rule been established than the self-contained rationalism of the indios was called into ques-tion. Europeans of the sixteenth century were so convinced of their superiority that it was impossible for them to understand the values of a seemingly alien culture in the same way as their own. Leopoldo Zea rightly remarked that the discovery of Latin America likewise cast a shroud of silence over its history.

At first, modernity was a Western concept that was not to be found in any other culture. Non-European cultures live with tem-poral images and archetypes that contradict the Western notion of time. In Buddhism, time is emptiness; in Hinduism, it is being without properties or attributes. For the Greeks and Chinese, as for the Aztecs and the Incas, time is cyclical. In each case, we are faced with different notions of time and therefore of modernity, notions which are now at the mercy of the global onslaught of modern technology.

The Western concept of modernity could only have arisen in a Christian culture which, since the Middle Ages, had viewed historical time as finite, successive and irreversible. This notion of time is an implicit critique of the Christian concept of eternity, which does not exist in the same way in other cultures such as Islam. Modernity repudiates cyclical time no less vigorously than St. Augustine had done centuries ago: all things take place once and once only, and cannot be repeated. In Latin America, with its wide array of indigenous cultures and archaic traditions, a notion of time still reigns that contradicts Western modernity. This must be taken into account when trying to explain the economic under-development of the Latin American continent.

Even the Latin American revolutions reinforce this picture: they neither changed society in any fundamental respect, nor freed Latin America from its liberators. Moreover, Spain itself was in a process of disintegration, not least of all due to the Napoleonic invasion and the efforts of Hispano-American revolutionaries to gain autonomy. Independence, when finally achieved, only accelerated the disintegration of the empire. On the other hand, the atomization of Hispano-America took place against the backdrop of oligarchies and military castes, neither of which was able to bring this movement to a halt. Sarmiento was right to recognize the masquerade character of the Latin American republics—their feudalism disguised as bourgeois liberalism, their absolutism without royalty but with tribal chieftains in the form of presidents who set up tyrannies of lies. Not even nineteenth-century positivism, whose impact and longevity were vastly overrated in Latin American philosophical circles, was able to introduce the tenor of empiricism and practicality in government and society that Herbert Spencer was able to do in North America with social Darwinism, or John Dewey with pragmatism, or Roosevelt with the New Deal.

A longing, ancient and yet new, arose for established religious verities. Never was there a faith in progress comparable to that felt in Europe or North America.

Octavio Paz, with complete justification, speaks of the borrowed image of modernity that pertains to Latin America. Latin America was supposed to adopt an image of the future that was fashioned for an entirely different culture. Moreover, modernity in Latin America was born of a fascination with Europe and North America, not of a dynamic indigenous to the continent itself.

Under these circumstances, the concept of modernity could not provide Latin America with a well-considered solution. It was founded neither in democratic traditions nor in the birth of national economies. There arose instead a fractured society that more closely resembled a caricature of modernity—a "hidden reality" whose political and cultural roots were marred by inauthenticity.

At the outset of the twentieth century, we find pseudomodern democratic constitutions on paper, Latin America's own brand of positivism in retreat, pre-Columbian *caciques,* symbolic poetry and the same massive illiteracy that pervades the continent today. Modernity failed to liberate Latin America's future from its past, whether in culture or religion, politics or the economy. Today, Latin America must strive to attain a modernity that is not ensnared in these contradictions. Modernity cannot be a project of imitation or sheer material consumption when deep-seated beliefs nestle in the collective conscious. Latin America never experienced a profound religious revolution, nor a thorough critique of religion and worship, except perhaps for a liberation theology of the sort established recently by Gustavo Gutierez or Leonardo Boff.

Secular modernity stands in conflict with the cultural and religious history of Latin America, threatening the identity of its various regions, reducing faith to an ideology and leading ultimately to a depersonalization of the individual to an extent previously unknown in Latin America. Modernity can arise only through an original synthesis of cultures which is at once hybrid and ritualistic. Secularization must be allowed to interact with the integration of Latin America's political, cultural and religious systems. Until now, Latin America has possessed only a peripheral modernity which has been at the mercy of conflicts in the ever changing constellations of its culture, politics and religion.

Latin America should be given an opportunity to achieve its own brand of modernity by integrating these three formative areas of human existence. In doing so, Latin America should meet with the success that has eluded it to date.

THE VANISHED AMERICA

by G. Bataille

T he life of the civilized peoples of the Americas before the arrival of Christopher Columbus was prodigious for us not only because of the fact that they had been discovered and then immediately disappeared, but also because there had never been so bloody an eccentricity of human insanity, i.e., the series of crimes committed in broad daylight for the sole purpose of satisfying deified nightmares, terrifying fantasies. The cannibalistic feats of the priests, the ceremonies around corpses and streams of blood were more than a mere historical adventure and recall the dazzling orgies that the illustrious marquis de Sade has described.

True, this statement applies to Mexico above all. Peru represents perhaps a unique mirage, an incandescence of sun-like gold, a brightness, a troubling *richesse*; but the reality did not correspond to this vision. Cuzco, the capital of the Inca empire, was situated on a plateau at the base of a kind of fortified acropolis. That city was characterized by an overwhelming and massive grandeur. Tall, thatched houses without decor or windows were built in a square from enormous boulders, giving the streets a somewhat sordid and sad appearance. The temples that overshadowed the houses were constructed in an equally naked style. Only the pediments were completely covered by plated gold. Materials of radiant colors were added to this gold which were worn by people of wealth and elegance; yet none of this was able to dissipate the impression of a mediocre savageness and above all a brutal uniformity.

Cuzco was in fact the seat of one of the most bureaucratic and regulated states ever created by humans. Following important military conquests, achieved with the help of the meticulous organization of a huge army, the power of the Incas extended over a large region of South America, i.e., Ecuador, Peru, Bolivia, northern Argentina, and Chile. In these regions that had been opened up by a system of roads, an entire people followed the orders of officials just as soldiers obey the orders of officers in the barracks. Work was divided up and marriages arranged by these officials. The soil and the crops belonged to the state. The religious feasts of the government were the only popular festivities. Everything was predetermined in a life that did not allow for individual breathing space. These forms of organizations must not be confused with those under modern communism. It was essentially different since it was based on the principles of heredity and class hierarchy.

Given these conditions, it is not surprising that relatively little can be said about what was brilliant in the civilization of the Inca. Even the horrors did not make much of an impression in Cuzco. The victims were choked to death with the aid of belts in the temples, for instance in the Temple of the Sun in which, despite everything, a statue of pure gold collected during the conquests preserved a magic aura. Although the arts were quite highly developed, they were nonetheless of no more than secondary interest. The textiles, the potteries in the shape of the heads of humans or animals are noteworthy. But to find creations that really deserve our interest we must look for peoples other than the Incas.

In the north of Bolivia, at Tihuanaco, the famous sun gate offers testimony of a highly developed art and architecture that must be attributed to a much earlier epoch. Various fragments of potteries can, through their style, be connected to that ancient gate. During the age of the Inca it is the peoples of the coastal regions with older civilizations that produced the most remarkable objects. At the time of the conquests, Columbia, Ecuador, Panama and the Antilles also had highly developed civilizations whose art we find striking today. It is also to the peoples of these regions that we must attribute the weird statues and the dream faces that put pre-Columbian art at the center of present-day interest.

Still we hasten to say that nothing of this vanished America can, in our view, be compared with Mexico—that region in which we must clearly differentiate between two very different civilizations: that of the Maya-Quichen, on the one hand, and that of the Mexicans in the strict sense, on the other.

The culture of the former is generally seen as the most brilliant and most interesting of all vanished American civilizations. Indeed, it is probably the creations of this culture that archaeologists usually treat as particularly noteworthy. The Maya-Quichen civilization unfolded in the eastern parts of Central America several centuries before the Spanish conquest—to be precise, to the south of present-day Mexico in the Yukatan peninsula. It was in full decline when the Spaniards arrived.

The art of the Maya is certainly more human that any other in Latin America. It is difficult not to connect this art with that of contemporary Asian art, for example that of the Khmer with which it shares the portrayal of rich and heavy vegetation, although it is certain that no such connection existed. Both civilizations developed under heavy skies in very hot and unhealthy climates. The bas-reliefs of the Mayas represent gods in the shape of humans, but they are heavy and monstrous, highly stylized and above all very uniform. We could also regard them as highly decorative. And in fact they were part of very large architectural constructions that made it possible to compare the civilizations of the Americas with the great classic ones. At Chichen-Itza, Uxmal, and Palenque we continue to discover the ruins of temples and imposing palaces with rich decorations. We are also familiar with the religious myths and social organization of these people. Their emergence no doubt was a major influence and largely determined the subsequent civilization of the high plateaus. Still, its art has something stillborn about it, something hideous despite its perfection and its rich detail.

If one looks for lightness and violence, for poetry and humor, it is not to be found among the people of central Mexico who had achieved a high degree of civilization prior to the Spanish conquest, i.e., in the course of the fifteenth century.

To be sure, the Mexicans whom Cortés encountered were no more than barbarians who had recently been civilized. They had come from the north where they had lived the nomadic life of the Indians; what they had assumed from their predecessors had not been assimilated in a particularly convincing way. Thus their writing system was analogous to that of the Maya, but nevertheless inferior. And yet among the different Indians of the Americas, the Aztec nation, whose powerful confederation conquered in the fifteenth century what is the Mexico of today, was vibrant and exerted, even through its insane brutality and its somnambulistic behavior, a most seductive attraction.

Up to a point, historians who have dealt with Mexico have generally been rather dumbfounded. If, for example, one takes account of the literally extravagant way in which gods were depicted, all explanations seem very weak. As Prescott put it: "If one casts an eye over a Mexican manuscript, one is struck by the very grotesque caricatures of the human body, with their monstrous and enormous heads stuck on small, stunted and deformed bodies whose contours are angular and stiff. But on closer inspection it becomes clear that this is less a clumsy attempt to depict nature than a symbolic convention to express images in the most straightforward and striking way—just as equivalent pieces on a chessboard have corresponding shapes although they usually do not look like the object that they are supposed to represent."

Prescott's interpretation of those horribly and grotesquely deformed figures that so disturbed him appears insufficient to us today. If we go back to the period of the Spanish conquest, we find an explanation on this point that deserves to be taken seriously. It was the monk Torquemada who attributed the horror images of Mexican art to the demons that possessed the mind of the Indians: "The figures of gods," Prescott wrote, "were similar to those of their souls due to the sin in which they lived forever." Evidently there is a link to be made between the way in which Christians represent the devils and the way the gods are represented by the Mexicans.

The Mexicans were probably just as religious as the Spaniards; but they blended their religion with a sense of horror, of terror, to which they added a black humor that was even ghastlier than the horror. The majority of their gods are ferocious and, in a bizarre way, mischievous. Tezcatlipoca seems to take an inexplicable pleasure with certain "deceptions." His adventures, which have been recorded by the Spanish chronicler Sahagun, represent a strange counterpart to the Golden Legend. The Christian honey is juxtaposed to the Aztec aloe; the healing of the sick man is contrasted with sinister jokes. Tezcatlipoca shows himself skipping and dancing with a drum among the crowds. The people dance around and push absurdly toward an abyss where the bodies are smashed to pieces and turn into rocks. Sahagun reports another "evil coup" of the necromancing God as follows: "It rained rocks, and then a boulder, called *techcalt*, fell from the skies. After this an old Indian woman wandered to a place called *Chapultepec cuitlapilco*, offering for sale little paper flags and crying: 'Little flags!' And whoever had made a resolution to die, said: 'Buy me a little flag.' And when he had received one, he went to the place where the *techcalt* lay, where he was killed without anyone attempting to say: 'What about us?' And all were seized by madness."

It seems fairly evident that the Mexicans take an uneasy pleasure in mystifying things in this way. It is also probable that such nightmarish catastrophes cause them to laugh in a certain way. In this fashion one is led to understand hallucinations that are no less delirious than the gods of the manuscripts. Body-eater or bone-man are words that are associated with those brutal personages, with evil and sinister jesters, full of mischievous humor, like the god Quetzalcoatl who, sitting on a little board, slides down from the high mountains.

The demons set in stone around European churches would be quite comparable (no doubt they were part of that same essential obsession) if they also possessed the power and the grandeur of Aztec spirits, who are the most cruel of all those that have ever lived in the terrestrial clouds.

As everyone knows, bloodthirsty in the literal sense of the word. There is not one among them whom one would not regularly on the occasion of his feast bespatter with human blood. The numbers that are being given vary. Nevertheless we may assume that the annual figure for human sacrifices in Mexico City alone reached at least several thousand. The priest had a man held up with his belly in the air with his lower back bent over a kind of boundary stone; he then cut the flesh open with a sharp stone knife. While the body was cut into pieces, the priest seized the heart with both hands and tore it so forcefully and quickly from the chest that the bloody mass continued to contract rhythmically for a few seconds over the red-hot charcoal; the corpse then fell back and heavily tumbled down to the foot of the stairs. In the evening, after all corpses had been skinned, cut up and cooked, the priests came to eat them.

The latter were not always content to soak themselves in blood as well as the walls of the temple, the idols and the bright flowers that were heaped on the altar. During certain ceremonies, in the course of which the victim was immediately skinned, the excited priest would cover his face with the bloody facial skin of a dead person and his body with the latter's skin. Dressed in this incredible way, he would deliriously pray to his god.

However, here we must stress emphatically a surprisingly happy aspect of these horrors. Mexico was not only the bloodiest of all human slaughterhouses; it was also a wealthy city, a veritable

Venice with canals and bridges, with ornate temples and above all with very beautiful flower gardens. Flowers were cultivated with passion, even on the waters. The altars were decorated with these flowers. Before the ceremonies, the victims were made to dance "wearing necklaces and garlands of flowers. They also carried shields of flowers and perfumed reeds which they smoked and smelt one by one."

It is easy to imagine the swarms of flies that were whirring around in the hall of sacrifice when the blood was flowing. Mirabeau, who was already dreaming of his *Jardin des supplices*, wrote that "in these surroundings of flowers and scents there was nothing repugnant nor terrible."

Death was nothing for the Aztecs. They implored the gods not only that they would receive death joyfully, but even that the gods would help them to find charm and sweetness in it. They wanted to regard the knives and arrows as something delicious. Still, the ferocious warriors were no more than affable and sociable men like all the others who gathered for drinks and talks. It was customary during Aztec feasts to get high on one of the drugs that they used all the time.

It looks as if these extraordinarily courageous people had an excessive taste for dying. They delivered themselves to the Spaniards in a state of hypnotic insanity. Cortés's victory was not won due to superior power, but rather through a veritable enchantment. It was as if these people who had reached this level of happy violence had a vague feeling that the only way out for them and for the victims with whom they appeased the capricious gods was a horrible and sudden death.

To the end they wanted to serve as a "spectacle" and as "theater" for those fantastic personages; they wanted to "serve their laughter," provide them with "entertainment." This is in fact also how they perceived their bizarre excitement. Bizarre and precarious, for they died as suddenly as an insect that is being squashed.

A Conversation with Octavio Paz

Conversation with Octavio Paz on December 2, 1991 in his hotel in Madrid. The discussion dealt with subjects that appear in this book, but it should be seen as an independent appendix. Its incorporation here is not necessarily to be taken as evidence that Octavio Paz agrees with the arguments to be found on these pages. Rather the author wanted to provide the reader with a further benefit; he wanted Octavio Paz, as one of the most experienced Latin American thinkers, to share his views on these issues. In its synthetic form, this dialogue offers a survey of questions that are being broached in this book, but have also belonged to the existential topics in Paz's cosmopolitan thought for many years. A conversation appeared to be the best and most concise format to give the reader a special insight into the cosmos of Paz's thought.

1. *In* Reading and Contemplation *you write about "the Other"; what does this notion in fact mean to you?*

This is a fundamental and at the same time quite multilayered concept. The phrase "the Other" has a variety of different meanings. Sometimes the Other is hidden inside us; we are the Other without being aware of it. All human beings carry another side in themselves. We are never a whole; we are bilaterally and trilaterally constructed. This is not merely a psychological, but also a metaphysical idea. It is also a metaphor for the constant transformation of being as such. We are at every moment different from what we think we are. However, the Other that you have in mind is concerned with other human beings. The Others are juxtaposed to the people of my own country, my own culture, my own age; they are people of another period or another civilization or culture. It is true that I do use the term of the Other that you mention. In an anthropological sense the Other is the foreign, what is different from one's own culture.

2. *Neither magic, nor moral, aesthetic and scientific existential meanings can easily be transferred from one culture to another, can be acculturated. In the face of a global world civilization that levels historic and religious traditions and operates under a technological imperative and the dictate of the logos, the question is raised ever more insistently of a universalism that challenges the multiplicity of cultures. Against the background of this question, are you more a cultural universalist or a relativist?*

This is one of the major questions of our age. I am afraid that I am split on this question and especially its solution. There is one voice inside me that professes adherence to cultural relativism, and another that leans toward universalism.

I support the variety of cultures and civilizations. But since we make cultural comparisons, we cannot rely on the values of a certain culture; we need comparative yardsticks, if we want to make comparisons at all. If we compare—and even the greatest relativist compares cultures since one is not a prisoner of one's own culture—it involves a certain universalism, and it is in this sense that I try to combine the two aspects. If I speak of linguistic relativism, I also take into account how, in this view, another language, culture, vision of cosmology is being dealt with. In a way, this possibility to see another side is "human" in the original sense of the word. Cultural relativism is contradicting itself at this point; but thanks to it we value divergent cultures.

3. *Would the perspective of an intercultural identity be of help here?*

Yes, certainly. However, the notion of identity in this instance is questionable. It starts from an ensemble of characteristics and qualities that do not exist in static form, since cultures are exposed to constant change. We should therefore ask ourselves whether identity is the appropriate word in this in principle correct context. The phenomena of culture and civilization cannot be understood without an insight into diversity. Western civilization, for example, must understand how much ancient Greek culture owed to Asian cultures. Civilization invariably entails the capacity to accept other values, to transform them, to change them and thus to reverse outside influences. This is how we might comprehend the interaction of cultures.

4. You like to paraphrase the American anthropologist B. Whorf, who speaks of Chinese and Turkish scientists who are being taken out of their cultural traditions and arrive, for example, at the Princeton Institute for Advanced Study, where they become acculturated to a Western logic that is different from their own cosmologies. And yet they have to grapple with this Western logic that is often not compatible with their own spiritual or metaphysical cultural traditions.

I believe that there is a scientific logic that is universal. Here I am contradicting the cultural relativists and above all B. Whorf. I think the human *ratio* is universal; science and logic are universal. However, other values are culturally very specific, for example, ethical and aesthetic values; but even they carry within themselves seeds of universality. Take the example of human sacrifice among the Mexican, pre-Columbian civilizations that the Christian tradition had such difficulty in understanding at first. But then the early missionaries found strange similarities between these human sacrifices and the sacrificial death of Jesus Christ. The abhorrence of the missionaries had the same root—the Christian sacrifice could be interpreted as another expression of the value of human sacrifice in other cultures, religions, and civilizations. This is one example. Another is the great admiration that the Romantics had for other epochs, such as the gothic and its art; or there is the great fascination of the cubist painters for archaic African art and its masks. Finally, in all cases there occurred an assimilation; this is true even of the Japanese *haiku* to the poetic traditions of the twentieth century.

5. You are dealing with the notion of time in its different perceptions, above all with that of cyclical time in Indian cultures, but also with Chinese and Asian-Indian cultures. There appear to be civilizations, for example, in Latin America, that dispose of a measure of intuitive, emphatic and associative thinking that is opposed to the analytic, empirico-logical and pragmatic thinking of North American culture from John Locke to William James and John Dewey.

This is correct and a consequence of cultural history. Traditional Latin American culture, for example, the culture of the Incas, is radically different from this pragmatic tradition. Another difference emerges with the Old World: despite many differences, there were many points of contact from Japan to Spain. In the Mediterranean, there existed a mutual interaction between the civilizations of the Middle East and those of the Mediterranean. The Hindus were exposed to Persian and Greek influences and vice versa. The Chinese sent missionaries to India to collect Buddhist manuscripts and became Buddhists in the process (Chinese civilization was very Buddhist at a certain point). Certain fragments of Buddhist art have Greco-Roman origins. This is where we have a fundamental difference with the pre-Columbian civilizations of Latin America. Up to the sixteenth century, they were completely ignorant of the existence of other civilizations. As a result, Latin America's civilizations experienced slow growth. A more rapid growth would have required foreign influences. It was this unilateral growth which resulted in the fact that the Other could not be understood. The Others—in this case the Spaniards—were classified as divine beings.

6. *If we regard the Q'ero Indians of the Peruvian Andes as the last descendants of the Incas, we can see to what extent they adhere to a mythical and magic cosmology; even their astronomy was geared to transcendence, to metaphysics. Of course, these were poor preconditions for a subsequent acculturation to Western, empirical and logical technology.*

Yes, there is no question about this. Herein lies the difficulty. Successful acculturations are often voluntary. If we think of the acculturation of Chinese culture by the Japanese, we may speak of such a voluntary development. If acculturation is imposed, it becomes a much more difficult process.

7. *How, in your view, can we bring about a compatibility between cultural identity in the traditional sense and the need to have modern technology?*

The Latin American states have a chance to do this because their cultures are not purely pre-Columbian or Indian, but can be counted as part of Western civilization. We are an eccentric and extreme case of Western civilization. Japanese culture took over Western technology by adapting Confucianism and Buddhism to it. Latin America could move from Christianity and Catholicism to technology with special features. Consider contemporary Mexico, where this movement is emerging. The important point is that this assimilation leads to a new quality of civilization. If Latin America assimilates something new in a more profound way, it will transform itself. This is the precondition.

There will be conflicts during the assimilation process of new technologies in Latin America; we cannot avoid this. Latin America has gone through the experience of acculturating to Catholic Christendom in the sixteenth, seventeenth, and eighteenth centuries. The indigenous Indian population became Christianized, and today these Indian Christians are better Christians than the Europeans and North Americans. What emerged was a new kind of Latin American Christianity that is very different from European religiosity.

8. There is a connection between America as described by Amerigo Vespucci and the utopian state à la Thomas More. Vespucci had been influenced by Marsilio Ficino and other Humanists; there is an affinity between More's Utopia *and Garcilasco's description of the Inca state. Can we speak of a special utopian quality of Latin American culture and politics?*

Yes, this is certainly true. The history of Latin America varies greatly from Mexico to Argentina. Mexico has its peculiarities, but the utopian character can be demonstrated particularly clearly there. These features appear as early as the sixteenth century. Mexico City was rebuilt in accordance with the ideas of the Renaissance; the Spaniards tried to create a city in the sense of Alberti and to apply neo-Platonic concepts. There is a genuinely utopian element that was extended; then came the baroque. During the independence movement of the nineteenth century, the utopian element became reinforced. There was above all the model of the French and American revolutions, of Thomas Jefferson's writings, of *The Federalist* papers, and of the ideas of Montesquieu. These influences were bound to take on a utopian character against the background of Latin America's own history.

For example, in the nineteenth century there was never an identity between the text of the constitutions and constitutional reality in Latin America.

Yes, that's right; this, too, demonstrates the utopian character. Marxism was the last great utopian system that we experienced in the twentieth century. At the moment, we are entering a new period of world history that may become very dangerous, though. Just think of the huge separatist movements in the former Soviet Union or in eastern Europe that will have their repercussions in Latin America as well.

9. Would you say that a linear, one-dimensional notion of progress which quantifies humankind is still applicable to Latin America today?

At the moment, Latin America is trying to apply such models, at least in the economic field, presumably in line with North America and Europe. At the same time, we live in a period of great crisis. However, we should not look at Latin America from the perspective of a secure Europe. We find ourselves in a changing situation. Change in Europe is often very dangerous, and that in itself may become the trigger of a major crisis—and we do not know how it will evolve.

10. *The notion of another world, of transcendence was very highly developed in the cosmology of pre-Columbian civilizations.*

Yes, but this transcendence was very significant also in the sixteenth, seventeenth, and eighteenth centuries as a remnant of scholasticism. Mexico's great art is rather more spiritual, religious art. Since secularization, the idea of transcendence is on the wane, but not entirely. Today, we witness the decline of those ideas that were supposed to replace transcendence—utopian ideas, for example. Everything is being called into question.

11. *Once I directed a larger research project, funded by the Thyssen Foundation, that compared the history of philosophical thought in Latin America from the scholastic epoch of Molina and Suarez to José Vasconcelos and Caso in Mexico, Romero in Argentina and Faz Brito in Brazil. These traditions were very metaphysical, transcendental and spiritual if compared with North American philosophy with its empiricism, logic and pragmatism from John Locke via William James to John Dewey or Quine at Harvard today. You have shown so admirably in your book* The Labyrinth of Loneliness *with regard to Mexican and North American culture how markedly anthropological constants—human attitudes toward death, nature and the supranatural—diverge in the two hemispheres. This can also be shown in philosophy.*

That is absolutely right and also my view.

In my view, positivism is being overrated in Latin American philosophy. It was a phenomenon of the nineteenth century that disappeared at the beginning of the twentieth century with the original contributions made to Latin American philosophy by Ateneo de la Juventud in Mexico, for example, and in José Vasconcelos' and Antonio Caso's work whose orientations were clearly spiritual and metaphysical.

The great philosophical movements indeed occurred more in North than in Latin America. We do not have a William James or Peirce. But we can also put the question the other way round. We

do not speak of great personalities, but of movements. Following
Ateneo de la Juventud, Latin America came to know the influence
of phenomenology. Husserl was important, and so was Max
Scheler later on. Bergson's philosophy of intuition and Martin
Heidegger's existentialism were transmitted by Spanish philosophers in Mexico, for example, by José Goas. Later at the time of the
Frankfurt School, German philosophy once again became significant, but to a certain degree also the British and North American
tradition of analytical philosophy.

I am not certain what the current orientation of thought in Latin
America is. I hesitate to give a clear-cut answer here. I do not see
right now a new, outstanding philosophical mind in North America and Europe following the classical philosophers of the twentieth century. But I am not myself a real philosopher in order to be
able to judge this. I favor a philosophy that rests on solid foundations, and I believe that in this respect North American and European philosophy is superior to that of Latin America.

*Latin America has produced the most important literature of the last
decades instead, don't you agree?*

Yes, perhaps; but I do not like to compare in terms of value. Lit-
eratures are different, and we should leave it at that.

12. *People of the pre-Columbian civilizations were not motivated by
the idea to conquer nature (as was characteristic, for example, of the
Calvinism of North American culture), but rather to protect it.*

Yes, nature was to be reconciled. Nature was sacral, was creation and destruction in one. Nature's cruelty stood side by side to
the desire to come to an arrangement with it. It is an originality of
pre-Columbian civilizations that they assumed a unity between
nature and the whole world, between nature and human beings.
Both lived in the same cosmic order. Humanity was not seen as
passive, but rather a participant in the cosmic order. This order 
consisted of creation and destruction, often also of creation
through destruction. It is for this reason that human sacrifices
were so important. The gods sacrificed themselves in order to create the world—not in the Christian sense to save humanity, but to
create humanity in the first place.

This was the significance of human sacrifices. Another was that
without such sacrifices, nature was assumed to come to a stand-
still. Human activity was conceived fundamentally as being religious; it was not secular, but sacral. This was true of politics and

economics. The highest goal was to participate in the perpetuation and creation of the cosmic order. This is a notion that is fundamentally different from that of the Western tradition. In light of today's ecological movements and of the rediscovery of the value of nature, we should take the pre-Columbian civilization of Latin America very seriously. It contains some extremely topical concepts for a modern understanding of nature.

Of course, we cannot simply take over the old traditions today; but we should try to learn and draw lessons from them.

13. *If we look at the endeavors to develop an endogenous technology, does this not offer a chance, unlike exogenous technology, to reconcile cultural identity with technology?*

I am not as pessimistic in this respect as Heidegger, who was the precursor of the view that technology is the enemy of the cultural. The same can be found in Spengler. What is correct about this view is that modern technology can be very dangerous if we apply it in a unilateral sense; at this point the foundations of human civilization can be called into question. We should oppose these tendencies, but not in the sense of total negation, like Heidegger—although he was not entirely clear in his expositions on the subject. Thus, we cannot do away with electricity, here at this moment, as we would be without light in this room; this would be an absurdity. Still, we might come to the insight that this electric light is not the only reality in this room. We must change our angle of vision, our perception. Humanity is very slow to learn to be more critical of technology. It seems that the bad experiences with technology do not suffice yet. Two world wars, the atomic bomb, the ecological problems of today, perhaps further disasters in eastern Europe—all this may well help us to shift our basic position.

Are you therefore for moderate technology?

We must change our attitudes. I had a friend, André Breton, who was opposed to technology on principle, much more than Heidegger. But all he took refuge in was occultism or the discovery of foreign philosophies. That's not enough. The decline of human values, the excess in advertisement and the threatening offerings of television on an international scale, the misuse of the media—all this makes life increasingly shallow, turns it into a banality, an empty space. The culture of success also contributes to this, the sheer materialism. All this is, in a certain sense, a result of technology, of a utilitarian morality. Bentham, if he returned to earth today, would be just as horrified as Marx would be entering the former Soviet Union.

We must revive what are traditional values of the past and must give them a new meaning. I learn from history that civilizations were capable of renovation and reconstruction. It is thus my hope—and here I do not speak just of Latin America, but of the whole of Western civilization—that we can make a fresh start on some essential points.

If we do not succeed in this, humankind will be doomed. For the first time the question is not whether a civilization dies—be it pre-Columbian or Roman—but whether this is going to be the end of human existence. Technology is certainly one of the causes, but even more so our attitude.

You once said technology produces uniformity without being a unifying influence.

The potential of hatred and rivalry between divergent strata, groups, societies and states is not being reduced by technology, but on the contrary is being multiplied.

14. *Asturias spoke of magic realism, Alejo Carpentier spoke of wondrous reality. There emerges a certain irrational element in Latin American reality as compared with the pragmatic reality of North America.*

Reality is somehow always wondrous. This does not necessarily imply a violation of natural rights in a religious understanding of things. Magic is also irrational. There is always an element of surprise in reality. Through it we recognize another dimension of our existence which opens up reality. Great art is always close to reality; it unlocks reality, and through it we can have new experiences of reality. This is as true of human existence as it is of the cosmic one.

15. *Pre-Columbian culture had a different notion of theory and reality. Theory invariably also appeared in the light of mythology. This is very different from the contemporary Western tradition of logic.*

The pre-Columbian civilizations found it difficult to make a distinction. For them, astronomy equalled astrology; the element of religion, of the other world was very powerful. At the beginning, we talked about the notion of the Other. Here I remind you of Rudolf Otto and his notion of the sacred. For me, the sacred is always the Other.

16. *Japanese culture had an intrinsic theocracy with empirical and pragmatic traits when Confucianism, coming from China via Korea, moved into Japan in the sixth century A.D. A sense of loyalty and obedience already existed within the feudal structures. This sense was very helpful during the state-building phase. There exists a fundamental difference with Latin America here where these traditions did not exist.*

Prior to the conquest, Latin America did not have a neighbor like China. The arrival of the Spanish came as a great surprise to the pre-Columbian civilizations. Japanese culture was used to living with a neighbor that had a more advanced civilization; they sent missionaries and an ambassador to Korea and China. The encounter between the pre-Columbian and the Spanish civilizations was bloody, violent and also had religious undertones. The population was Christianized, but only after the leading strata had assimilated. The other part of the population was obliterated.

17. *Consider the paintings of Velazques that reveal a basically stoic note and elucidate a different understanding of human dignity. According to this view even a man who lies in the dust is a great man. It is my sense that Latin America has a different notion of human dignity than the pragmatic and utilitarian idea of North America.*

In North America, we can speak of human dignity in the constitutional sense of modern democracy, for example, during the emergence of new religious denominations in the Protestant regions. The Church was not hierarchically organized like Catholicism in Latin America. North America certainly was the first modern society in a literal sense. Latin America was the last one in the nineteenth century. The struggles for independence were directed not merely against the Spanish, but also against our own past.

18. *To this day, Latin America appears to have a fractured relationship toward modernity.*

Yes, this is right—in a polemic-religious sense.

Modernism and modernization were confused with one another.

We Latin Americans are the descendants of the Counter Reformation. We have a polemical relationship with modernism; this is of the greatest importance. These are the features of Latin America's modern history since the eighteenth century.

19. *Do you think that the First World can still learn from the innocence of archaic civilizations in Latin America, Africa or Asia?*

Consider in the eighteenth century Rousseau and European thought as a whole. Perhaps. Certainly we can learn through our attitude toward technology. We can exploit and use nature only up to a certain extent. The civilizations of Central America had a different attitude toward nature. They admired it; they lived in a sacral communion with nature. Above all, we can collaborate with nature. To my mind, this is the greatest achievement of the pre-Columbian civilizations. I would like to write a text relating to what we can learn from the pre-Columbian civilizations, especially with regard to cooperation with nature.

20. Max Weber rightly spoke of the "demystification of the world." How can we survive today in a desacralized world of Western modernism that, wedded to the primacy of logos and a utilitarian rationality, has developed increasingly since the Renaissance; what could be the basis of new values at a secular level?

That is the biggest question. The only possibility seems to be that our will power is fractured through a major disappointment. If we do not succeed in this, I anticipate a catastrophe. We need to rediscover traditional values as well, for instance, those of transcendence, of a certain religiosity and of the sacral. We cannot go back from fundamental technological development. However, we can change our attitudes—not toward technology, but toward nature. This is where the key lies for a better understanding of things.

BIBLIOGRAPHY

Anderson, Perry. *In the Tracks of Historical Materialism*. Chicago: University of Chicago Press, 1984.

Asad, Talad, ed. *Anthropology and the Colonial Encounter*. New York, 1973.

Asad, Talal. "Are There Histories of People Without Europe? A Review Article." *Comparative Studies in Society and History* 29, No. 3 (1987): 594–607.

Bennassar, Bartolome, and Pierre Chaunu, eds. *L'ouverture du monde, XIVe–XVIe siè-cles*. Paris: Armand Colin, 1977.

Bernstein, Richard. *The Restructuring of Social and Political Theory*. Philadelphia: University of Pennsylvania Press, 1983.

Bolter, J. David. *Thuring's Man: Western Culture in the Computer Age*. London, 1984.

Bourdieu, Pierre. *Outline of a Theory of Practice*. Cambridge: Cambridge University Press, 1977.

Braudel, Fernand. *Grammaire des civilisations*. Paris: Flammarion, 1987.

Clifford, James. *The Predicament of Culture*. Cambridge, MA: Harvard University Press, 1988.

Comaroff, Jean. *Body of Power, Spirit and Resistance*. Chicago: University of Chicago Press, 1985.

Curtin, Philip D. *Cross Cultural Trade in World History*. Cambridge: Cambridge University Press, 1984.

Czitron, Daniel. *Media and the America Mind*. Chapel Hill: University of North Carolina Press, 1982.

Fabian, Johannes. *Time and the Other: How Anthropology Makes Its Object*. New York: Columbia University Press, 1983.

Fischer, Michael M.J. "From Interpretative to Critical Anthropologies." *Trabalhos de Ciencias, Serie Anthropologia Social*, No. 34, Fundacao Universidade de Brasilia, 1982.

Giddens, Anthony. *Central Problems in Social Theory: Action, Structure and Contradiction in Social Analysis*. Berkeley: University of California Press, 1979.

Harris, Marvin. *America Now: The Anthropology of a Changing Culture.* New York: Simon and Schuster, 1981.

Jean, Clinton M. *Behind the Eurocentric Veils.* Amherst: University of Massachusetts Press, 1991.

Kracke, Waud. *Force and Persuasion: Leadership in an Amazonian Society.* Chicago: University of Chicago Press, 1978.

Ortner, Sherry B. "Theory in Anthropology Since the Sixties." *Comparative Studies in Society and History* 26, No. 1 (1984): 26–66.

Sahlins, Marshall. *Culture and Practical Reason.* Chicago: University of Chicago Press, 1976.

____. *Historical Metaphors and Mythical Realities: Structure in the Early History of the Sandwich Islands.* Ann Arbor: University of Michigan Press, 1981.

Shweder, Richard A. *Thinking Through Cultures: Expeditions in Cultural Psychology.* Cambridge, MA: Harvard University Press, 1991.

Solow, R. "Economics: Is Something Missing?" *Economic History and the Modern Economist.* Ed., W. Parker. Oxford: Blackwell, 1986.

Sperber, Dan. "Ethnographie interpretative et anthropologie theorique." *Le savoir des anthropologues.* Paris: Herman, 1982.

Stern, Steve. "Feudalism, Capitalism and the World System in the Perspective of Latin America and the Caribbean." *American Historical Review* 93, No. 4 (1988): 829–72.

Tambiah, Stanley J. *Magic, Science, Religion and the Scope of Rationality.* Cambridge: Cambridge University Press, 1990.

____. *World Conqueror and World Renouncer.* Cambridge: Cambridge University Press, 1976.

Todorov, Tzvetan. *The Conquest of America.* New York: Harper and Row, 1984.

Wallerstein, Immanuel. *The Modern World System: Capitalist Agriculture and the Origins of European World Economy in the 16th Century.* New York: Academic Press, 1974.

Walzer, Michael. *Spheres of Justice: A Defense of Pluralism and Equality.* New York: Basic Books, 1983.

Wolf, Eric. *Europe and the People Without History.* Berkeley: University of California Press, 1982.

Young, Crawford. *The Politics of Cultural Pluralism.* Madison: University of Wisconsin Press, 1976.